The cataclysm of the Holocaust seer ⬛⬛⬛ in the heart of that darkness, sp⬛ ⬛⬛⬛ alive. From these sparks, Rabbi Edward Feld suggests, Jews and others can renew a faith and find a language that recovers the holy even after experiencing the reign of a Kingdom of Night unimaginable to previous generations.

In a voice that is engaging, often poetic, Rabbi Edward Feld helps the modern reader understand events that span almost 4,000 years of the history of Judaism and the Jewish people. With rare clarity, insight, and gentleness, he offers a thought-provoking yet accessible study of the way tragedy has shaped Jewish history and the self-understanding of Jews.

The Spirit of Renewal explores four key events that reshaped religious expression, two ancient and two modern: the Babylonian exile; the Bar Kochba revolution; the Holocaust; and the establishment of the State of Israel.

The Spirit of Renewal shows how, even under the most traumatic of circumstances, Judaism survives, renewing itself and flourishing again.

This profound and wise meditation opens the way to a powerful new understanding of the nature of God and the spiritual life.

"Written with passion, reason, and eloquence."

—**Amy Gutmann,** director, University Center for Human Values, Princeton University

"Carefully analyzes how the Holocaust differs from previous events in Jewish history. . . . Has forged a new theology of Judaism. Highly recommended."

—*Library Journal*

"With rigorous intelligence and moral grace . . . he acknowledges what we can't say, can't believe, can't hope for anymore . . . and then he finds reasons for hope."

—**Michael Walzer,** professor of social science, Institute for Advanced Study, Princeton University

THE
SPIRIT
OF
RENEWAL

Finding Faith after the Holocaust

EDWARD FELD

JEWISH LIGHTS Publishing
Woodstock, Vermont

The Spirit of Renewal:
Finding Faith after the Holocaust

Third Printing 2004
Second Printing 1999
First Printing 1994
©1994 by Edward Feld

Library of Congress Cataloging-in-Publication Data
Feld, Edward, 1943–
The Spirit of Renewal: finding faith after the Holocaust / by Edward Feld
    (p. cm.)
Includes bibliographical references and index.
ISBN 1-879045-40-0
1. Holocaust (Jewish theology). 2. Holocaust, Jewish (1939–1945)—Influence. 3. Suffering—Religious aspects—Judaism. 4. Judaism—Doctrines. I. Title.
BM645.H6F45 1994   94-30252
296.3'11—dc20   CIP

First Paperback Edition
10 9 8 7 6 5 4

Manufactured in the United States of America
Book designed by Levavi & Levavi
Cover illustration by Henry Isaacs

Published by Jewish Lights Publishing
A Division of LongHill Partners, Inc.
Sunset Farm Offices, Route 4, P.O. Box 237
Woodstock, VT 05091
Tel: (802) 457-4000   Fax: (802) 457-4004
www.jewishlights.com

To the memory of my mother,
Rachel Rosansky Feld,
who transmitted her Jewish tradition to me,
and taught me the value of caring
and
to my teacher
Rabbi Norman Frimer
who led me into a religious life as an adult.

TABLE OF CONTENTS

ACKNOWLEDGMENTS

This book was begun more than fifteen years ago as a lecture delivered at a B'nai B'rith Hillel Summer Institute. I am grateful to Rabbi Sam Fishman for encouraging me to expand and develop that talk into a book. The support of my colleagues in Hillel, particularly annual meetings with Rabbis Jim Diamond, Danny Leifer, Alan Letofsky, and Max Ticktin as well as two sabbatical leaves provided by the B'nai B'rith Hillel Foundations enabled me to complete the work. During my sabbatical in 1977-1978, I made extensive use of the Boston Hebrew College Library, and my last sabbatical, 1989-1990, was spent at the Shalom Hartman Institute, which provided a home and a supportive atmosphere during my year in Jerusalem.

The manuscript was read by Professor Uli Knoepflmacher, of Princeton University, and incorporates many of his suggestions. My publisher Stuart Matlins has been wonderfully encouraging, and my editor Marie Cantlon has helped shape my prose. Gil Orbach's generous help in checking sources is much appreciated.

I do not believe that this work would have been accepted for publication had I not been prodded and encouraged by my wife, Merle. Her belief in me has given me the energy to complete this task.

I came to know the meaning of the religious life as an adult through the example and teaching of Rabbi Norman Frimer, who was my Hillel director during my college years. It is to him that I gratefully dedicate this work. Though I know that he would vigorously argue with many of the positions I have taken, he would also respect the honesty and the struggle with the tradition that they represent. I am forever grateful to him.

My mother died while this book was nearing completion. It is right that this work honor her memory also.

INTRODUCTION

When I was growing up, people hardly spoke about the Holocaust. Born in 1943, I was a war baby. With the end of the war, most Americans wanted to get on with their lives. Survivors who reached these shores report that when they came here no one wanted to hear their stories.

Perhaps what they had to tell was too shocking, and time had to pass before people could begin to listen. Perhaps guilt over not having stopped the mass destruction caused people to avoid speaking of these events. For whatever reason, the Holocaust was a repressed memory.

My generation needed to comprehend what had happened. We knew that the Holocaust was a centrally defining event of our time. The world had witnessed evil on such a mass scale that our sense of what humans were capable of, what the Divine would permit, and what the world was like were radically reshaped.

But we also sought spiritual nurture. It was not sufficient that the Holocaust constituted a radical critique of traditional theology; we yet sought a means to recover the sacred—for hadn't the obliteration of all that was holy been at the center of the Nazi enterprise? Was not the recovery of the sacred our most important task? Faced with the wasteland of spiritual values that formed the landscape of America in the 1950s, and the decline of belief in the secular redemptionist ideologies of communism and scientism, the search for religious meaning became an imperative.

Attempting to overcome this spiritual lack, I turned to Jewish sources to see how earlier generations had responded to crises and how they had been religiously renewed. I realized that the problem of evil was central to Jewish theology and that the gropings of previous generations provide models for how we might understand our own situation. This book, then, is the fruit of my own struggle: I was impelled to write it to work through the theological questions at the core of my being. I publish it hoping that it helps others in their quests.

I write as a Jew who experiences the Holocaust as a shattering and overwhelming event in history. But I speak not only to Jews. I believe that a Jewish perspective on the Holocaust and the question of renewal contains a basic human message, that the Jewish experience of our time is paradigmatic for all of humanity, and that locating the Holocaust within Jewish history is not a parochial enterprise but is instructive for all peoples. Having seen so much that went up in smoke, we need to find a new religious vocabulary to describe what we have experienced. The events of the Holocaust subvert humanity's most fundamental assumptions and challenge us to adopt a different set of beliefs and course of behavior.

In attempting to trace the variety of theological responses to the problem of evil and the issue of renewal after mass destruction, I first of all turned to the Bible, which offers the basic language, the initial paradigms, with which all later Jewish theologies must come to grips. The Bible represents the first and clearest statement of the problem: if God is good, if creation is a blessing, how can chaos reign in history? Should not the events of history have a discernible meaning? In what sense is the human created in the image of God when people are capable of terrible cruelty? How does the one who innocently suffers face God? The centrality of these questions is clearly demonstrated by their constituting the subject matter of the first three chapters of the first book of the Bible—Genesis, and thus forming an introduction to all of Biblical literature.

For the last three hundred years, Bible scholars have argued that the Bible was shaped after the destruction of Jerusalem in 589 B.C.E., and during the subsequent exile in Babylon. In this view, the final Biblical redaction, including that of the first five books—the Torah—took place under the impact of exile and destruction. Even without resort to historical analysis, it is obvious that the experience of tragedy is at the heart of much of the Bible, for many books explicitly say they were written in exile and deal directly with that theme. Kings and Chronicles end with the exile and their story is written from that point of view. Isaiah, Jeremiah and Ezekiel, the three major literary prophets, all say that their careers included the Babylonian conquest; Ezekiel completely so. Daniel and Esther depict tales whose settings are Babylonia and

Persia respectively, and anonymous Biblical books like Job deal with the theological problems the exiles had to face. The destruction of the Temple, the Babylonian exile, the sufferings attendant on these events, and the attempts to reestablish religious life after these massive traumas had a profound effect on Jewish theological understanding, an effect traceable in huge portions of Biblical literature.

There is no single Biblical view of suffering and the question of evil. Rather there is a community of argument, a variety of responses to the problem. Questions and answers were thought through during the hundreds of years in which the twenty-four books of the Hebrew Bible were written. One generation's solution became the next generation's problematic. To do a full-scale analysis of Biblical theology would require a book in itself. In this work I have chosen to deal with what I think are the paradigms most decisive for later Jewish history. First, I attempt to delineate a normative Biblical view regarding God's justice, the relationship of blessing and prosperity to good and evil, and then I analyze two of the most creative Biblical responses to the problem of God's goodness and the existence of evil: those found in the Book of Job and in Isaiah.

I then go on to examine aspects of this problem as it is represented in rabbinic literature, the next critical stage of Jewish theological development. The syntheses developed in this period are vital to all subsequent Jewish self-understandings. Modern Judaism is formed by the texts that constitute the Mishnaic and Talmudic periods. Here too, there is a rich literary heritage, a vast body of work written over a period of almost a thousand years. To do justice to this literature would have required a book in itself. In Part II, I trace what I think are the most significant strands for later Jewish history.

This period, too, was formed out of the critical need to address the theological doubts arising from the devastation wrought by defeat and exile. The destruction of the Second Temple in 70 C.E., with the attendant desolation of the land and the psychological dislocation caused by the annihilation of the center of Jewish life, forced a major rethinking of basic motifs and practices.

Rabban Yohanan ben Zakkai, who was instrumental in reconstructing Jewish life after the Second Temple had been destroyed, saw himself as providing only an interim solution, for he and his generation looked toward the speedy rebuilding of the Temple. Just as the First Temple had been rebuilt in seventy years, so they believed the Second would be similarly reconstructed.

Sixty years later, Bar Kochba and his pietist associates, Akiva and other scholars of his generation, saw themselves as the new Maccabees, defending the faith against pagan incursion and freeing Jerusalem from Roman violation. The failure of the Bar Kochba revolution (132-135 C.E.) constituted one of the most devastating moments in Jewish history. If we are to take the Roman accounts seriously, almost half the population of Israel was killed; Judea did not have a majority Jewish population again until the twentieth century. The failure of the revolt led to the martyrdom of the leading rabbis of the time, as well as the outlawing of the teaching and practice of Judaism. This tragedy made no sense to that generation for it could not be understood through the perspectives offered by any previous Jewish model. All hope for the immediate reconstruction of the Temple proved unrealizable.

I focus on this critical moment, the Bar Kochba revolution and its aftermath, for I believe that in response to these events a totally new theological outlook was developed, one that has had a decisive impact on Jewish self-understanding down to our own day. The theological innovation of the generation following Bar Kochba resulted in the formalization of institutions that had a permanency in Jewish life and provided the common grammar of Jewish religious language for the next two thousand years. Prayer, study, and repentance, although certainly forming part of the continuous vocabulary of Jewish religious language, took on a new depth of meaning and became prime values through this generation's innovative work.

The medievalists for the most part found Biblical and rabbinic models sufficient to explain their own tragic circumstances. For instance, the chronicles of the first crusade largely use the vocabulary of Biblical and rabbinic literature to explain their own suffering. To be sure, the medieval tradition formulated new responses to their own situation, but the Biblical and Talmudic layers always remained crucial for any understanding of the way the mass of Jewry understood their suffering.

Out of necessity, *The Spirit of Renewal* discusses only some of the ways in which Jews have dealt with suffering, the problem of evil and the reconstruction of religious life after the trauma of devastation. The reader, however, will discover that previous generations under the impact of historical events have had to radically reshape their self-conception and their understanding of the relationship with God. The destruction and devastation in their time caused these Jewish generations to arrive at profoundly different views of God, humanity and the relationship between them. These new understandings had practical and institutional consequences. The most basic Jewish attitudes regarding the meaning of life were formed out of the cycles of tragedy and destruction and the subsequent effort to reconstruct a spiritual life.

Each moment in Jewish history has had to find its own voice, and our own time also must speak. We must examine whether traditional theology in relation to the problem of evil works for us, or if we too must shape a new Jewish religious vocabulary as did those who experienced the destruction of the First Temple and the devastation of the second century.

For Jews, the events of mid-twentieth century Europe are the most tragic of the two millennia that separate us from the former events. The shock has been so great that to speak at all in its aftermath is difficult. It took two or three decades till major works were produced which attempted to describe and understand these awful events, and then a seemingly unending stream of books and films appeared that represent a collective effort to comprehend the almost incomprehensible events that constitute the Holocaust.

The more cataclysmic the event, the more difficult it is to find a language with which to describe what has happened. Yet, precisely because the effect is so overwhelming, we must try to comprehend and find a theological vocabulary that speaks to our time. Our need is not only to understand these terrible events, but to reconstruct a religious life after that horrible experience.

The Holocaust raises devastating questions for our faith and also demonstrates the depths of depravity to which human beings can descend. Our time, more than any other, may have undermined religiosity, but equally we need its saving message.

Jews are witnesses to a massiveness of destruction that previous generations could never have imagined, and we have experienced, as well, the breathtaking incarnation of many ancient hopes. Do we not need a theological matrix to begin to understand and to articulate our own history? Do we not need to recover a sense of the holy? Surely we must find the syllables of a religious language that would speak to our time even if what we say is like a child's first utterances. For the overwhelming events we have seen demand speech; our inner being clamors for it.

Edward Feld
Princeton, N.J.

June, 1991
Tammuz, 5751

PART ONE

The Biblical Period

1 GENESIS: The Biblical Heritage

Even in the very first chapters of the Bible, when talking about the origins of humanity and the world, the themes of goodness and suffering, blessing and punishment, at-homeness and exile are already addressed.

The Bible presents us with the story of the relationship of humanity, the physical universe, and God: the opening chapters of Genesis preface the tale. As in a musical overture where the central themes of the score are tantalizingly stated, the opening chapters of Genesis introduce the major theological elements that captivate the Biblical mind.

These crucial beginning chapters of Genesis are not singleminded in intent. Instead in the very first sentences of Biblical discourse, we are presented with opposing views: there is not a simple melody accompanied by its harmony, but two instruments in the orchestra struggle against each other for melodic dominance. The dissonance is as much the message as the individuated melodic themes.

Or, to use a visual metaphor: the Biblical presentation of the genesis of the world surprises us with kaleidoscopically alternating scenes. We view creation through distinctly colored filters, changing perspectives. The effect is to see the events as if we are walking back and forth past a split mirror set at an angle in its midpoint causing us to perceive the world through the shimmer of constantly changing reflections.

The first chapter of Genesis and then again the next two chapters express opposite attitudes regarding the relationship of the human and the world.[1] No single image captures God's word. The theological message is dynamic, not easily fixed on the static page, a shimmering dream not to be possessed. Presented with two opposing visions of the fate of humanity, we are left with the tension of a spring, of questions poised for response.

Chapter One of Genesis lives in the joy of God embracing the world. Here to say that the world is beneficent is almost tautological since God is its creator— "And God said, 'Let there be'…and there was…." Each day God admires his handiwork, "sees that it is good." Finally, as God forms the last being, Adam, God looks over the whole of creation: "And God saw all that had been done and found it to be very good," conveying a sense of God stepping back and enjoying creation, a metaphor completed in the image of God resting, finding fulfillment and satisfaction with creation. The seven days of creation culminate in blessed calm.

God's majestic speech makes life viable. The Divine word is coeval with and constitutive of creation, and so, by implication, history is an unfolding of a divine message that can only be good. Contemplated by the person of religious vision, the days and weeks can easily be understood as the words and sentences that disclose the beneficent divine speech that caused them to be.

Life speaks God's meaning, and history God's message. One day utters speech to the next. By implication, as more is disclosed, and further rungs attained in the ladder of time, we come closer to the exhilarating satisfaction of surveying ever-widening distances in a unified divine perspective.

The stately unfolding of creation issues from the proximity of God's presence and involvement. Each day has its function—just as creation as a totality has a purpose. The world is the locus of divine order. The hand of God can be seen through all of nature. The first week moves to its apex, the creation of man and woman, and then to its most transcendent moment, the Sabbath. The first week, the archetype of all time, ends with the Sabbath which is the key to all history, for the end of time will be salvation itself, quintessential blessing, divine restfulness. All of history is guided by this sense of order and inevitable progress.

Suddenly, someone shakes the kaleidoscope and this harmonious image is replaced by a more fearful, conflicted one. To be sure, Chapter Two begins with the pastoral radiance with which the first chapter ended, but the sabbatical restfulness and harmony have been replaced by dissatisfaction and restlessness. Adam, placed in a bounteous garden, finds himself lonely, unfulfilled, and Eve, upon her creation, also finds herself with unsatisfied fantasies and yearnings. Here God's created world is not one of blessing alone, but is also a place where boundaries limit satisfaction, where desires go beyond the given, reaching past God's explicit word into a hidden realm clouded with threatening terrible consequence. Instead of being filled with God's presence, the world can become a place of exile, distanced from God.

In this second telling of the creation story, the image of the world has changed from one of unity and order to one of falling, of separation, of exile. Adam and Eve discover how different they are from each other, from God, and from the world. Creation becomes disparate, fragmented, at war with itself.

The image of bounteousness and blessing in the first story continues in the first few sentences of this new telling of the genesis of the world. Adam, finding himself amidst the wondrous Garden, imitates and reflects God's primal act. He begins his life on earth with the word: naming all the animals. But Adam's words, enumerating and categorizing creation, serve, as well, to objectify reality and thus place him outside the ecological whole. For Adam, language leads to the discovery of otherness and thus to the knowledge of limitation and lack—he is alone, missing a partner—his life is unfulfilled, even though he is with God, abiding in the magical garden. God's word created the world, and Adam's undoes it: language has become the means by which we discover our separateness, our exile from the unity of creation. (Indeed, as history progresses, after the Tower of Babel, language itself becomes a curse—a permanent source of human isolation.) The word no longer guarantees the world's ultimate unity and order.[2]

The separateness and otherness highlighted by language becomes the reiterated message of the second genesis story. No longer is the world given to Adam as in the beginning: "to tend, to keep," and even self-confidently to "conquer," but, on the contrary, the world now will be where Adam and Eve are forced to labor and sweat without guarantee of result—work bringing forth "thorns and thistles" (3:18). Adam and Eve, and we as their descendants, are to understand our condition as that of exiles. We are to live East of Eden, outside the bounteous Garden with its blessed unity.

The generation and regeneration of life is no longer a sign of blessing, the constant iteration of divine bounty: birthing is now to be pained, and traumatic. Life is a war with the world, a war with one's self, a war between the generations. Eden is forever closed to us.

Adam, who in the first telling of Genesis is described as being in the very image of God, now must live with the constant reminder that he is not divine: he is mortal, an eternal sign of lack of divinity. Death is the ultimate reminder of exile, of separation from God; finitude is the fate of the human condition.

So Genesis views the world from two perspectives—promise and terror. The world is first of all God's creation and gift, but the world is also the place of labor, suffering, exile and death.

In these spare opening chapters central Biblical themes are already present. The end is foreshadowed in the beginning. The Bible begins with the exile of the primal family and ends with the exile of the chosen people. Sin attends man and woman from the beginning, as does God's blessing. History will unfold between the two poles, and Israel's fate will exemplify this oscillation.

But even the second telling of the genesis story holds out promise: as Adam and Eve are about to be banished from the Garden, God clothes them. Their need for clothes arises out of their discovery of shame and secrecy, a consequence of their sin in disobeying the divine command. Yet here, as it were, God acquiesces in their humanity—God's grace is to be present in the newly found world of good and evil, just as God will still be present for the people in exile.

Monotheism sets in motion its own unique theological problematic: If God is good, how can the universe, God's own creative and intimate handiwork, be the locus of evil? Why is our own experience of creation so bitter when God's promise is that life is a blessing? Why do the people of God suffer, wandering over the face of the earth, never finding rest, never being at home? God created the world, therefore it is good; the world, God's creation, is a place of promise and hope. Existence is suffused with meaning, and the road we travel on is blessed. Never has this view, implicit in the very notion of a Creator God who is good, been more elegantly enunciated than in the stately unfolding of the very first chapter of Genesis.

But our daily reality contradicts this optimistic and joyful perspective. Our lives contain too much hurt, too much loneliness, too much emptiness to accept this cheerful theology. And the historical experience of the people of Israel was totally different as well. They tasted the bitterness of exile, first of the Northern Kingdom and then of the South. They experienced a terrible disparity between the promise of blessing and the tragedy of their daily reality. Their lives contradicted the simple assertions of monotheistic faith.

For the pagan, this theological contradiction is never a struggle. In the world of mythology, gods war with one another and humans are merely incidental to those battles. In this view the world is not a dwelling place of meaning but a battlefield of opposing forces. We humans are impotent bystanders who may suffer when we happen to be in the way of the gods. We are ruled by a story beyond our control, our lives are subject to irrational forces. The best we can hope for is that the gods take no notice of us. Life's outcome is fated.

Not so in the world of the Bible. Chaos preceded God's entrance into the world, but God's creative word establishes blessing, a fecund world. The One God assures that creation is not conflicted but ordered. That is the theological manifesto of monotheism proclaimed in unfolding dignity in the first telling of Genesis. And to this credo the second telling of Genesis counterposes the reality of our existence. Our experience of the world is not that of goodness and blessing but of labor and pain, of separateness and misunderstanding. The world that is supposed to display the presence of God exhibits God's absence.

These opening chapters of the Bible not only elaborate a question, they also indicate a response: sin has separated the human from the divine. The human mishandling of desire, our own sense of lack, blinds us to God's bounty.

But the second telling of Genesis, the story of our exile, does not wipe away the first; rather, they exist alongside each other. Exile has not vitiated the promise of blessing. It is as if Chapter One is the pentimento of Chapters Two and Three. Standing back, we can see through the brushstrokes of the second telling of Genesis to the distant but ordered presence of God shimmering beneath the surface. Our own weekly experience of sabbatical rest amidst the workaday world is an assurance that this is so.

Power and equilibrium, stasis and change, joy and terror, blessing and curse, oneness and aloneness confront us in these first chapters of Genesis, and yet even as one voice may emphasize the suffering, the effect of the whole bespeaks the promise of salvation.

It is not accidental that Genesis ends with the Children of Israel in Egypt with the threat of slavery and oppression in the distance, or that the Five Books of Moses end with the forty years of wandering almost completed, with the Land of Israel in sight but not entered or conquered. Genesis portends what the Torah spells out—history swings between the poles of salvation and exile, between suffering and promise.

2

EXILE:
The Suffering
of Job

*The sufferings experienced by the people of
Israel in exile challenge their belief in a
good and just God. The author of the book
of Job proposes a radical revision
of Jewish theology.*

The Bible records that Jewish optimism and trust in salvation underwent its most extreme test in the Babylonian exile.

The Davidic Kingdom survived for hundreds of years: David established Jerusalem as his capital city sometime after the year 1000 B.C.E.; Nebuchadnezzar and his Babylonian army destroyed the city in 587 B.C.E. During the rule of the Davidic dynasty, Jerusalem withstood sieges, wars, and the splitting of the kingdom into two. Though the Northern Kingdom of the Ten Tribes was destroyed by Assyria in 722 B.C.E., Judea managed to remain unconquered for yet another 150 years. Jerusalem seemed impregnable: God's presence in the Holy Temple assured the safety of the people. This was no ordinary city, this was God's city.[3]

Now, though, the exiles sat in Babylon, a defeated people. But their perspective had changed—they could accept what they had so often denied in their homeland: God was the author of history and their fate was a result of God's judgment. They had done evil—they had worshipped pagan gods, sacrificed their children, committed sexual offenses as part of cultic practice—and now God had wreaked his vengeance. The exiles came to accept the prophetic critique that sin would be punished, that exile would be the attendant fate of Israel's constant wrongdoing. They and their fathers had sinned, and now they were refugees. They accepted their suffering as divine decree and inexorable fate, and now recognized it as inscribed law, incorporated in the Book of Leviticus:

> But if, despite this, you disobey Me and remain hostile to Me, I will act against you in wrathful hostility; I, for My part, will discipline you sevenfold for your sins. You shall eat the flesh of your sons and the flesh of your daughters. I will destroy your cult places and cut down your incense stands, and I will heap your carcasses upon your lifeless fetishes.
>
> I will spurn you. I will lay your cities in ruin and make your sanctuaries desolate, and I will not savor your pleasing odors. I will make the land desolate, so that your enemies who settle in it shall be appalled by it. And you I will scatter among the nations, and I will unsheathe the sword against you. Your land shall become a desolation and your cities a ruin. (Leviticus 26:27-33)[4]

The prophets who had been maligned and persecuted were now recognized as having transmitted a true message from God. Jeremiah, who only a few months earlier had been thrown into prison, became a talisman of salvation as exiles fleeing to Egypt demanded that he accompany them despite his protestations.

The workings of God's justice could be readily seen: sin had led to punishment. The prophets had warned that if Israel continued in its ways disaster would follow, and now, in fact, they were a defeated people, living in exile.

So strongly was this sense of God's just and inexorable law felt that while earlier interpreters had argued that sin is not necessarily paid for in one generation but that the descendants of the sinner would suffer the consequence of an evil deed, Ezekiel, prophesying in Babylonia, insisted that fathers will not be punished for their children's sakes, nor children for the deeds of their ancestors. Each person will be judged on his or her own merit. The obvious connection between the sins of Israel and the people's fate made this theology readily apparent.

The historical books of the Bible, Kings and Chronicles, which received their final editing in this period, explicitly tell their story from this perspective. Israel's behavior during the first Temple period had been a chain of acts betraying God's grace. Exile, then, was an inevitable outcome.

These theological arguments were persuasive. Unlike the exiles of other nations, Israel in Babylon did not abandon its ancestral faith; rather, exile solidified the people's monotheistic commitment—now they realized that the prophetic world view had been validated. Israel would now be faithful to God, and the people would be repaid by returning to their land, regaining their sovereignty and reestablishing themselves as God's chosen. As a symbol of their faithfulness, they hung up their harps by the waters of Babylon and refused to sing a new song to a new master.

It was God who was the author of their ill-starred fate. Instead of being their protector, God had become their enemy, for it was God who was responsible for their exile. This is the perspective of the Book of Lamentations, which was written in the immediacy of the horrible events of the destruction and exile. Jerusalem has been laid waste:

> All her inhabitants sigh
> As they search for bread;
> They have bartered
>   their treasures for food,
> To keep themselves alive.
> See, O Lord, and behold,
> How abject I have become....
> All who pass along the road!
> Look about and see:
> Is there any agony like mine,
> Which was dealt
> out to me....
>
> (Lamentations 1:11-12)

But what is most horrible for the author of the Book of Lamentations, and in this he must not be seen as an individual creative artist but as the mouthpiece of his people, is that God has become the enemy. The author of Israel's suffering is not Nebuchadnezzar, but the Lord of Hosts.[5]

> The Lord has done what He purposed,
> Has carried out the decree
> That He ordained long ago;

He has torn down without pity.
He has let the foe rejoice of you,
Has exalted the might of your enemies.

(Lamentations 2:17)

God has defeated his people; destruction could have been wrought by none but Him. But the accustomed way back to God is foreclosed, for the Temple, the direct link between God and Israel, is destroyed. Israel would now wait faithfully upon God so that it might once again return to God's favor.

One generation followed another. Still they remained faithful to an ancestral ideal. But what had been one generation's incontrovertible truth became the next generation's burdensome heritage. That first generation could accept its condition as a product of sinfulness, but how was the new generation to understand itself? A pious community, the offspring of parents who had taught them to affirm ancestral ideals even in a foreign land amidst an alien culture, they sat by the waters of Babylon more committed to the monotheistic ideal than they ever had been while in Israel. Why then was God still abandoning them? Now that the people had turned to God, why had the glory of Israel not returned? Even as some exiles began to return, and later as some reestablished a small Temple in Jerusalem, they still remained under foreign rule. (Israel was not to become autonomous until several hundred years later during the short-lived Maccabean rule of the second and first centuries B.C.E.)

If exile originally represented the justification of God's word, Israel's continued suffering appeared to represent the failure of God to act in history. Could God remain their enemy even as the people turned back to true worship? Israel's fate now resonated with a terrible silence from God, a silence that served to contradict the meaning of history established through the acceptance of the prophetic critique. If suffering were related to sin, why did pious generations remain in exile?

Israel's introspective attempt to understand the meaning of its own trauma was now raised to a new level of intensity. The final shaping of the Bible results from the internal debates that raged around this question of self-understanding and suffering.

In the Book of Job that national problematic is posed as a personal quest and through that representation achieves a new level of urgency.

> Job's question comes into being as the question of a whole generation about the sense of its historic fate. Behind this "I" made so personal here, there still stands the "I" of Israel.[6]

As the horrors build around him, Job, like the first generation of exiles, suffers in silent piety. Initially, the crisis does not overwhelm him. Seemingly, his received faith, the pious answers he gave to others in their tragedy, suffice to explain what is happening. With each test Satan brings, Job remains silent, faithful to the received tradition, knowing that God is good and that all can be explained. No further words are necessary.

> Then his wife said to him:
> Are you still holding fast to your piety?
> Curse God and die.
> Then he said to her:
> You talk like an impious, foolish woman.
> Shall We accept good from God
> and not accept evil?
> Yet even in all this, Job committed no sin with his lips.
> (Job 2:9-10)[7]

His friends, who share with him this received tradition, join him in silence: "They sat with him on the ground for seven days and for seven nights no one saying a word…"(Job 2:13).

Finally, Job breaks the silence, and in that speech shatters the piety that had fostered his acquiescence of suffering. As loss upon loss is heaped on him, Job, unable to contain himself any longer, howls in pain, and the security of all received knowledge is broken with that cry. Job experiences the anarchic world of pain and suffering where God's reassuring voice can not be heard, for amidst this mourning no meaning can be found.

Job, once faithfully quiet, testifying to the meaningfulness of the divine word, now speaks. The overwhelming lack of understanding, the impossibility of making sense of suffering is the source of speech. This new speaking of Job contains no refraction of the divine mystery; this is not the disclosure of meaning, but its negation.

Afterwards, Job began to speak and cursed the day of his birth.

Job spoke saying:

> Perish the day when I was born
> and the night which said
> a man-child is conceived...
> Why did I not die in the womb?
> Or perish as I came forth from it?...
> For then I would have lain down and been quiet
> I should have slept and been at peace...
>
> (Job 3:1-3,11,13)

Job's suffering has no meaning, and therefore points to the overwhelming silence of the universe. If life can not indicate the presence of God then it is no better than death. Just as the world of shadows exists in stillness, so too life itself has ceased to reveal divine speech. The silence of the grave is the same as the death in life which Job now experiences. God has absconded from the world—all is desert. Job is dead in life.

The human comes into being with the cry of a cursed painful birthing. The anguish represented by that first howl is the source of all expression. The shattered nature of existence—its incongruity—the terrible discrepancy between life's promise and reality demands a voice.[8]

And so Job cries out. It is a spear flung into an anonymous universe, a gesture aimed almost as much at himself, alone in a vast emptiness. Job's speech is a monologue, which takes no notice of the friends sitting near him, for the presence of others is insignificant in light of the absence of God. Job raises a fist to an empty world, and addresses the void. All is relentless and meaningless suffering.

> Indeed, my sighing comes like daily bread,
> my groans are poured out like water....
> I have no ease, no peace, no rest.
> What has come is agony.
>
> (Job 3:24,26)

It is not solely the pain, the spiritual and physical scars Job has suffered, that is the source of his complaint. What has happened to Job can not be explained, and so the promise of justice as the foundation of the universe is negated. The terrible absence of God is the salt heaped on Job's wounds. As Job sits facing the terrifying indifference of the universe, its silence and cruelty, he can only feel the cold reality of his own aloneness made even more intense by the daggers that constitute the rhetoric of his "friends." The divine word spoken at creation is a lie. The human cry echoes hollowly in the universe.

> If I called him, would he answer me?
> I cannot believe that He would hear my voice.
> For He crushes me for a trifle,
> And increases my wounds without cause.
> He does not let me catch my breath
> But fills me with bitterness.
> If it be a matter of power, here He is!
> But if of justice, who will arraign Him?...
>
> (Job 9:16-24)

Job's suffering puts the lie to the sense of order in the universe, to all received truths about the meaning of existence. Job now knows the terror of abandonment, the absence of the rule of goodness, and the blinding false vision of life offered by traditional faith. What he experiences, instead, is the terror of existence.

Guilt and innocence have been mocked. Goodness is punished, evil rewarded. One person builds, another destroys, and it is the destroyer who lives on. Nothing makes sense. The world is silent in the face of suffering. Traditional faith is negated as destruction and evil dominate existence. Life is not blessed, and the only salvation is death itself, for it alone, and not religious faith, brings peace.

Job's faith has been shattered by his existential condition. The world has lost all meaning. There is no cause for hope. If faith is the ability to see the world as revelation, then Job has lost all faith, for the universe utters no speech.

The religious verities that formed the language of traditional faith have a hollow ring, and can no longer address Job. The religious faith and language that brought order out of chaos, that gave meaning to life by placing humanity in the midst of a just and rational universe, is shattered by existential and historic experience. Only a cry of personal anguish can be uttered.

Of course, some will always attempt to hold onto the comfort of received truths by denying the reality of the suffering that confronts them. Over and over, Job's friends seek to buttress the truths of their ancestral belief in the face of Job's denial of God's justice. Bildad, for instance, baldly states these "truths" even knowing that they constitute an accusation against Job himself:

> For inquire, I pray you, of an earlier generation,
> and heed the insight of their fathers—
> for we ourselves are mere yesterdays and know nothing;
> our days, only a shadow upon earth—
> Indeed, they will teach and inform you
> and out of their understanding utter these words:
> "...God will not spurn the blameless man,
> Nor will he uphold the evildoers"
>
> (Job 8:8-9,20)

God is just, so Job's suffering must be a result of his sinfulness. It is Job, not God, who must be at fault.

The remarks of the friends cause even more pain than the physical suffering Job has undergone. The religious verities themselves have become a bed of thorns. Previously Job's flesh had been afflicted, now his friends puncture his soul. Job condemns their tortured arguments, calling on the same rules of justice that they have appealed to to punish them for the hurt they have inflicted.

> Have pity on me, O my friends, have pity,
> For the hand of God has struck me.
> Why do you persecute me like God?...
> When you say: How shall we persecute him,
> since the root of the matter must be found in me?
> I answer: Be afraid of the sword,
> for yours are crimes deserving of the sword,
> and you will learn that there is a judgement.
>
> (Job 19:21-22,28-29)[9]

In the final speaking, which is God's, the friends are in fact condemned to punishment. God witnesses that religious orthodoxy has not captured divine truth. Job's friends, who were confident that they knew the divine order of things, are upbraided (Job 42:7-9). Only to Job, who will not paper over the world's disorder with words, nor engage in theological apologetics, does God turn.

But Job, too, is faulted, although for a different reason. God's opening words to Job are harsh and condemnatory:

> Then the Lord answered Job out of the whirlwind, saying:
> Who is this that darkens My plan
> by words without knowledge?
>
> (Job 38:1-2)

Job's speech also has been false: he has turned his own suffering into a singleminded view of the universe. His constantly expressed wish to die denied meaning to all life and any blessing to creation. If his friends only saw God's goodness, Job only saw the underside of creation: misery, desolation, and the inexorableness of death. Thus Job had cried:

> But as a mountain falls and crumbles
> and a rock is moved from its place,
> as waters wear away stones
> and a torrent washes away the earth's soil,
> so do you destroy a man's hope.
> You seize him and he departs forever;
> You change his countenance and send him off...
> his flesh will be pained within him
> and his spirit will be in mourning.
>
> (Job 14:18-20, 22)

If the friends' rhetoric was a hollow mouthing of received wisdom that refused to acknowledge Job's suffering, Job's speech too was fragmentary, for Job could not see beyond his own suffering. His suffering was his world: it filled and overwhelmed him and blocked any chance to see beyond himself.

In the end, what is needed is a new integration, a vision, a theological matrix that will grant the reality of Job's suffering and yet affirm meaning. Here God's speech arises.

Out of suffering, divine speech once again is born. God's voice is heard. The primal word of creation is invoked. And, in the end, Job is overcome by God's addressing him while acknowledging his torment. Job's anguish had cut him off from God, now he realizes God can be present even here:

> I have heard of you by hearsay
> but now my own eyes have seen you.
> Therefore I abase myself
> and repent in dust and ashes.
>
> (Job 42:5-6)

Still, this new speaking of God is shrouded in mystery—it is entirely interrogative, openly asserting very little, leaving its discursive truths to implication and interpretation.

> Brace yourself and stand up like a man;
> I will interrogate you, and you tell me!
> Where were you when I laid the earth's foundations?
> ...Who settled its dimension?....
> On what do its supporting pillars rest?
>
> (Job 38:3-8)[10]

God overwhelms Job with questions, and so leaves him with only guesses, attempts to construct answers, never with the divine self-understanding itself. The mystery is not dispelled, nor is it negated; rather it is entered into. In God's speaking, we are introduced to an ambiguous vocabulary, the wellspring of theological discourse, that which can not contain truth, but only hint at it. We are confronted with a language of mystery—the divine word that is palpable silence—speech beyond words that we, as readers, are forced to turn into spoken language. God's speech is punctuated by gaps of silence, pregnant with meaning yet covered by mystery. It is for us to transform it into a spoken language of faith.

Some outline of a response seems to emerge. In both the opening and the ending of the book of Job, the mythologized Satan, Behemoth and Leviathan, the dread forces of evil, are given a power that surprises us. Caught up in the whirlwind, Job is overwhelmed not only by God's power, but by God's acknowledgment of these evil forces.[11] God as it were recognizes their terrible power. God's own potency is not some absolute, existing outside of time and the world, but forms the cosmos in relation to these other forces. God's word, too, gestates, becoming viable over time. In some way, only vaguely hinted at, the dissonance of existence is not only a human fate but, as it were,

God's lot as well. The history of man and the universe is a manifestation of this struggle.

If Job is given reassurance that ultimately a just and good God is at the heart of existence, we, who have seen God manipulated by Satan to put Job through a cruel testing, must be more doubtful about the ultimate rule of the divine order. We, as readers, meet an even deeper level of injustice than Job can recognize and acknowledge, and so we are left with the disquieting sense that Job's original faith had expected too much, that God's time is slower than a lifetime, that even for divinity there is no fleeing an imperfect world. There is no "up there" or "out there" to flee to, even for God; rather it is in life, in the midst of the contending forces of evil and pain, suffering and labor, that God is revealed. There is no way out, but only a battle to make the divine manifest.

And we readers come away with another realization as well: Job's integrity parallels God's truth. Job is the hero of the book because he is willing to face God openly and directly. Though he may have had to admit error in his reasoning, nevertheless, God applauds his untrammeled insistence on speaking his truth, his inability to accept pious verities as answers, his absolute honesty in attacking theological problems. Job's truth-seeking comes closest to God; Job's confrontation with his pain-racked condition evokes God's presence. The human who battles to understand God's beneficence parallels the God who wars with the forces of nature to establish blessing in time.

But have we been saying too much? Are we overrepresenting a twentieth-century perspective and obscuring the author's voice? Are these indeed the resolutions the book has been striving for, or are we engaged in a contemporary misreading of the book?

The gaps of time that separate us from the author of the Book of Job make it difficult for us to reconstruct his voice. The book is the most difficult of all the poetic works of the Bible and gives evidence of having been reworked by more than one hand. So to find the obscured original voice within it becomes a task that constantly reminds us of our distance from the author.[12] Yet we feel a remarkable closeness to the man Job. His questions are so like our own that we hear them as palpably as an inner voice. "The book is one of the special events in world literature, in which we witness the first clothing of a human quest in the form of speech."[13] The language of Behemoth and Leviathan may be an ancient rhetorical style that is not ours, but Job's cry surely echoes across time, in terror, and seizes us: "Where then is my hope? /My hope who can see it?" (Job 17:15).

The innovative speaking of the author of the Book of Job ends by offering only fractured vision. Job is restored to his former condition, though we imagine him to be a very different person at the end of his journey than he was in the beginning.

Israel, having heard God responding to Job, waits, too, for its restoration, watches in patience as the divine mystery unfolds even as it suffers its fate. It knows it has not deserved its pain, though the divine acknowledgment of Israel's condition is yet to come.

3

THE SUFFERING SERVANT

Isaiah offers an alternative response to the questions posed by the continued suffering and exile of Israel: the suffering servant is beloved by God.

Isaiah prophesied more than 120 years before the Babylonian exile, but a second part, by an anonymous exilic author to whom we give the name Second Isaiah, was attached to his work, as if Isaiah's book could not be seen as complete unless it included acknowledgment of the most terrible historic circumstance Israel had to live through. It is to the second Isaiah, who represents a remarkable climax of prophetic rhetoric, that we now turn.

Second Isaiah, like Job, is consumed by the problems posed through the continuance of Israel's exile. Second Isaiah, like Job, confronts the suffering of the innocent, the question of why the generation born in Babylonia is made to pay for sins it did not commit. So close is the problematic out of which Job and Isaiah speak that one can easily come to believe that they knew each other, perhaps even read each other's works. The Bible might be said to be a community of argument, a literary unit joined not by a common response, a common creed, but by a common set of questions. Certainly Job and Isaiah seek to respond to the same problem: how can a pious generation, duly chastised and repentant, continue to suffer? The downtrodden condition of Israel's existence now bears little relation to its sinfulness.

Isaiah therefore envisions a world filled with intense contradiction. The true servant of the Lord is not the person who is most glorified by the rest of humanity but the one who suffers. God's servant is beaten, disfigured and scorned, yet, ultimately, he is the most beautiful, close at hand to God. Although he suffers, he is innocent: his pain is the result not of his own sin but that of others.

In the biography of Jeremiah, the Bible had already presented a model for such an interpretation. Jeremiah was persecuted in the years preceding the destruction of Jerusalem. He was put into stocks and mocked by passersby. He was jailed and thrown into an isolation pit. But unlike Second Isaiah, Jeremiah did not see his suffering and scorn as a necessary part of his calling, rather his fate was a source of despair. Like the pained Job, he cries:

> O Lord, thou hast duped me, and I have been thy dupe;
> Thou hast outwitted me and hast prevailed.
> I have been made a laughing stock all the day long,
> everyone mocks me...
> A curse on the day when I was born!
> Be it for ever unblessed,
> the day when my mother bore me!...
> Why did I come forth from the womb
> to know only sorrow and toil,
> to end my days in shame?
>
> (Jeremiah 20:6,7,14,18)

What Jeremiah protested, Isaiah now understands to be a desirable fate. Isaiah, while still seeing a theological connection between sin and suffering, innovatively argues that there is no simple mathematical formula for the pain of existence. When there is evil in the world, the evildoer is not necessarily the one who suffers; sometimes it is the righteous. But the suffering of the righteous serves as expiation for the sins of the world.

And as in Job, the suffering people is personified so that the national question is presented as a personal one. At times, in Isaiah, we feel that the suffering servant is the prophet himself, at others, the remnant of Israel, and at still others the whole nation who are the righteous. Each individual's unjustified suffering represents what the people of Israel experience in their exile.

Isaiah declines to see a one-to-one connection between sin and punishment, but sees an ecological whole that is demonstrated through the unity of all existence over time. The righteous suffer because sin is abroad, their pain is a tearing through the abscess infecting the world.

Israel, God's chosen people, is in exile in order to fulfill God's larger plan. But Israel should not despair, for its outward circumstance is not a sign of its true fate. God's reality lies deeper than surface pain and derision. Israel's abject condition is a sign of its chosenness.

Isaiah, in overcoming the formulaic relation between obedience and blessing, sin and punishment, restores the mystery and majesty of God. Nothing in the world is as it seems. Everything has the possibility of transformation,

> Every valley shall be lifted up
> Every mountain and hill brought down;
> rugged places shall be made smooth,
> and mountain ranges become a plain.
>
> (Isaiah 40:4)[14]

All of nature can be turned upside down and inside out. The victory of the unrighteous is a superficial reality. Religious truth does not exist on the surface of things. Meaning is to be found at deeper levels—in a vision of the world transformed. Listening is not simply hearing, true vision is not attained with eyesight:

> Hear now, you that are deaf;
> you blind men, look and see...
> Walk through fire and you will not be scorched
> through flames and they will not burn you
> for I am the Lord your God.
>
> (Isaiah 42:18;43:2-3)

Do not accept that visible reality portrays the deeper truth of the universe. Do not say you are in exile, separated from God: know that though you seem abandoned you can be in touch with a deeper reality. Your fate is not to live in darkness but to be the true beacon of the world, the light unto the nations. Just as God's vision shapes all reality, your mission is to fashion the world.

> I have formed you, and appointed you
> to be a light to all peoples,
> a beacon to all nations,
> to open eyes that are blind
> to bring captives out of prison,
> out of the dungeons where they lie in darkness.
>
> (Isaiah 42:6-7)

Although in exile and seemingly powerless, Israel still has the power to mold reality, to create a moral universe and inscribe a new meaning to life. This is the level of meaning that always exists beneath the surface realities of power. You have a calling even as the conditions of your life suggest abandonment. Listen to that, serve God, and transform the world.

Interestingly, both Job's and Isaiah's responses to the problem of evil now force us to face human finitude and simultaneously a grand and mysterious view of creation and of the world. Job argues that humans can not see the larger picture, the overwhelming tasks that God is engaged in, Isaiah, that we can not envision the underlying realities that represent the true nature of creation.

There is no singleminded correlation between an individual's worldly condition and divine blessing. But while Job's suffering is ultimately inexplicable, it has no purpose; Isaiah sees the pain that the righteous suffer as necessary for the birthing of a new order. The true servant of God understands that this must be his fate and commits himself to this most selfless of attitudes, the recognition of the need for self-sacrifice, in order that the world might be transformed.

> But he was pierced for our transgressions,
> tortured for our iniquities;
> the chastisement he bore is health for us
> and by his scourging we are healed.
> We had strayed like sheep,
> each of us had gone his own way:
> but the Lord laid upon him
> the guilt of us all.
>
> (Isaiah 53:56)

Israel does not suffer for its actions, but because it is the lightning rod of the world, making visible and redeeming the evil practiced by the world. Israel suffers not for its own sins, but to instruct and to atone for the sins of the world.

In the end, the suffering servant will be acknowledged as the beloved of God. In the end, restoration will take place:

> After all his pains he shall be bathed in light;
> after his disgrace he shall be fully vindicated;
>
> (Isaiah 53:12)

Be patient, and the God who shaped all of reality at creation will transform yours in the end.

It is a mark of the similarity of the world from which the authors of Job and Second Isaiah emerged that in the works of each the personal and the communal constantly intersect. Job is the single individual who asks the question of the community of Israel, and the suffering servant becomes the personification through whom the community of Israel understands its fate. Just as Job and Isaiah do not deserve their fate, neither does the remnant of Israel—suffering does not represent guilt.

Job achieves the literary pinnacle of the Bible by entering into the layers of God's mystery; Isaiah, through his imaginative rhetoric, creates a new vision of the world and achieves a poetic height rivaling his contemporary. Both engage in a radical theological reorientation so that Israel can faithfully bear its suffering. For Job, the meaning of suffering is forever hidden in the mystery of God and the forces at work in the universe. For Isaiah, suffering has a redemptive purpose that will give birth to a new reality.

Both authors give us a legacy of the unseen God, the invisible One, who exists amidst deeper realities than those met by our senses. In fact, the person of faith knows that the realities normally encountered are surface truths which divinity shatters. So the psalmist sings:

> He lifts the poor out of the dust,
> He raises the needy from the rubbish heap.
> He seats them with the powerful
> with the powerful of His people.
> He sets a barren woman in her home
> as a mother happy with children...
> When Israel left the land of Egypt,
> when the House of Jacob left alien people...
> Mountains leaped like rams; and hills like lambs....
> He turns rock into pools of water;
> flint into fountains...

> The stone which the builder rejected has become the
> cornerstone...
>
> (Psalm 113:6-9; 114:1,4,7; 118:22)

And so the Bible comes full circle: the slave people remain God's chosen; they are still the bearers of God's unique message. In the darkness of Egypt, salvation came in time, so too the realities that now seem chiseled in hard stone will be overturned, the time of redemption will arrive. Wait upon the Lord who in the fullness of time mysteriously breaks through the harshness of all realities. Just as Job was finally answered, so will Israel be in its suffering and exile. Do not insist your anguish is a result of your own wickedness; God's accounting is more subtle than any accounting you may devise. Continue to be bearers of the light.

PART TWO

The Bar Kochba Revolution

4

THE FALL OF THE SECOND TEMPLE: The Persistence of Normative Theology

*In explaining the fall of the second Temple in
70 C.E. the rabbis and Josephus reflect the
more normative Biblical theology: 'because
of our sins were we punished.'*

Unlike the pagan world view that sees history as a succession of
wars among the gods, and so understands human destiny as
being controlled by forces outside human control, the most basic
underlying Biblical assumption is that the world is ordered.
Monotheism ultimately understands the world as resulting from a
single impulse, the creative hand of God. Since God is both good
and just, God's handiwork also must be beneficent and just. To
associate prosperity with the good life and conversely suffering
with punishment is the most natural outcome of this perspective.
While the last of the Biblical authors and poets would question
this simple equation, seeing God's hand even in suffering, the
more popular view was to hold on to the earlier and more
dominant Biblical perspective. On the one hand, the appeal to
mystery which animates the book of Job hints at a less-than-
all-powerful God. And on the other hand Isaiah's image of the
suffering servant could have appeal for an elite but not for the
common people struggling with daily existence and seeking a
God who could respond to their lot. It therefore should not
surprise us that it was the more normative Biblical theology, one
that connected sin and suffering in a direct way, that remained the
dominant theological perspective in Israel.

Ben Sira, for instance, writing at almost the midpoint of the Second Temple in approximately 210 B.C.E., could continue the wisdom tradition of an earlier Biblical theology and write:

> You who fear the Lord, wait for his mercy;
> do not stray or you will fall.
> You who fear the Lord, trust in him,
> and you shall not miss your reward.
> You who fear the Lord, expect prosperity,
> lasting happiness and favor.
> Consider the past generations and see:
> was anyone who trusted the Lord ever disappointed?
> was anyone who stood firm in him ever deserted?
> did he ever neglect anyone who prayed to him?
>
> (Ecclesiastes 2:7-9)[1]

The monotheistic assumption that God was present in the ordering of the world and will surely reward righteousness and punish evil is unquestioned here. This, long after the authors of Isaiah and Job had evolved their more subtle theology.

In fact, so persistent was this normative view that when Israel experienced the tragedy of the destruction of the second Temple by the Romans in 70 C.E., five hundred years after the Bible had recorded the destruction of the first, although there was a deep sense of suffering and crisis there was no great theological upheaval. Just as the first Temple's destruction was attributed to the evils of the generations immediately preceding the fall of Jerusalem so, too, this time, one could point to the sinfulness of the period prior to the Roman invasion. Josephus, the Jewish turncoat general who surrendered to the Romans, joined the Roman court and wrote the only history of the war, attributed the fall of Jerusalem to Jewish factionalism, arguing that Jews were defeated by internal strife. Josephus is our only source for the mass suicide of Jewish patriots atop Masada, the final battle in the first-century revolt against Rome. His version of this event has largely been confirmed by archaeological evidence, and though we may question the authenticity of the final speech by Elazar, the leader of the beleaguered defenders of Masada, Josephus' version calls upon a theme that undoubtedly constituted normative belief:

> For it is not of their own accord that those flames which were driving against the enemy turned back upon the wall constructed by us; no, all this betokens wrath at the many wrongs which we madly dared to inflict upon our countrymen. The penalty for those crimes let us pay not to our bitterest foes, the Roman, but to God through the act of our own hands.[2]

While it is true that Josephus is trying to justify the destruction wreaked by his Roman masters, his theological reasoning blaming the Jewish defeat on the sinfulness of the defenders would make no sense unless this perspective found resonance among his people. In fact, the rabbinic tradition is quite similar: in a widely quoted tale Rabban Yochanan ben Zakkai, the leading rabbi of the years following the destruction, attributes Israel's fallen state to its "failure to do God's will."[3]

Josephus in describing the fall of Jerusalem specifies the sinfulness as that of a hate-filled factionalism that led defenders during the siege to threaten the lives of fellow Jews, and Rabbinic theology remarkably echoes Josephus. The Talmud ascribes the fall of Jerusalem to *sinat hinam*—needless hatred among people—and understands the tragedy as resulting from internal Jewish strife. Although the Talmudic presentation of the background to the destruction of Jerusalem is a fanciful tale written much after the event, there is such a haunting confluence between Josephus' view and the rabbinic perspective that we can believe that a measure of historical accuracy is preserved. This later rabbinic legend personalizes the story of the fall and ascribes the immediate cause of Rome's military intervention to an insult by an aristocratic patron of the rabbis to a man named Bar Kamza. It seems that the noble intended to invite his friend Kamza to a party, but his servant mistakenly delivered the invitation to the wrong person—Bar Kamza. Bar Kamza, an enemy of the aristocrat, was pleased that a hand of friendship was finally being extended. When he arrived at the party, however, the noble was enraged by his presence. Though Bar Kamza pleaded that he not be embarrassed, the host threw him out. As the rabbis seated at the party did nothing to alleviate his humiliation, Bar Kamza went to the Roman authorities and mischievously reported that the Jews were concocting a revolt. It was then that Rome sent troops to Israel.[4] In this portrayal, it was rabbinic collusion in *sinat hinam*, the free-flowing and unnecessary hatred between Jews, that caused the war.

The same Talmudic passage goes on to describe the factionalism in the besieged city of Jerusalem, portraying the peacemakers, including the leading rabbi, Yochanan ben Zakkai, as victims of the radicals who seized control of the revolt, threatening death to anyone who advocated conciliation with Rome. Again, this accords with Josephus' description of the hate-filled internecine factionalism that gripped the besieged city.

What these texts have in common is the search for an internal cause for Israel's downfall. These authors could not imagine that the destruction could have been brought on Israel without Israel's own sinfulness being the reason for the fall. In this, they are adopting the prophetic theology enunciated in the Bible regarding the first destruction of Jerusalem. To this day, the view is embedded in Jewish liturgy in the refrain, "Because of our sins, we were exiled from our land...."

This prophetic outlook became a norm of rabbinic theology expressed in the phrase, *midah kineged midah*, every measure calls forth an equivalent and opposite measure. God's activity in the universe is likened to a scale in which the two balances are equal, the same image as our own ubiquitous one of blind Justice holding a balanced scale in her hand. The implicit notion is that any action on one side of the scale will call forth a commensurate response on the other. God's activity is always equivalent to human behavior: not only are good and evil rewarded and punished appropriately, but the fate held in store for a person is similar in kind to his or her sin or good deed. This formula is expressed typically in a Mishnaic teaching:

> By the yardstick which a person uses for himself it is in turn meted out to him...
>
> Samson followed after what his eyes yearned for, therefore the Philistines gouged out his eyes...
>
> Absalom was proud of himself, especially of his hair, therefore he was hung by his hair...[5]

The rabbis' concrete explicitness even radicalized this Biblical theology. The following text from Mishna Avot illustrates the point:

> Seven kinds of suffering come to the world for seven types of sin:
> —when some people tithe their grain and some do not, a famine caused by limited rain arrives, wherein some go hungry and others eat well;
> —when all have concluded not to tithe their grain, both a famine caused by limited rain and one caused by calamity, arrive;
> —when the tithe of the dough is not taken, a famine of complete destructiveness arrives;
> —pestilence arrives for the sins which are punishable by death though not executed by the judicial system, and for harvesting the fruit of the Sabbatical year;
> —the sword arrives because of the tribulations of justice, and for the perversion of justice, and because of those who teach the law incorrectly;
> —beasts of prey arrive because of false promises and the desecration of the Name;
> —exile arrives because of idolatry, incest, murder and for the lack of observance of the Sabbatical year. [6]

There is a neatness to this portrayal of the universe: all of our suffering is absolutely correlated to our behavior. (Since in all Israel some proportion of the population will have committed one or another of these sins, suffering is always explicable.) All things have their place within God's orderly rule; there is no inexplicable mystery. Goodness and bounteousness, evil and suffering follow each other with the inexorableness of natural law.

> Whoever observes a single commandment, good is bestowed on that person and his days are lengthened and he inherits the earth. And on those who do not do a single commandment, good is not bestowed, their days are not lengthened and they do not inherit the earth.[7]

The rabbis took this retributive theological outlook seriously; when they suffered, they examined their own lives for the sinful cause of their condition. In the most extreme instance, when they underwent martyrdom at the hands of the Romans, they believed that their suffering could only be caused by their sinful behavior:

When Rabbi Ishmael and Rabbi Simeon were already on their way
to be martyred, Rabbi Simeon said to his colleague, "Master, I lose
heart, for I do not know what it is I am giving up my life for."

Rabbi Ishmael replied to Rabbi Simeon, "In your entire life, did
not someone come to you for judgment, or with a question, and did
you not put him off until you could finish your drink? Or tie your
shoes? Or until you put on your clothes? And did not the Torah say,
'You shall not mistreat any widow or orphan. If you do mistreat
them, I will heed their outcry as soon as they cry to me, and my
anger shall blaze forth and I will put you to the sword, and your
wives shall become widows and your children orphans?' (Exodus
22:22-23).[8] What difference is there between a major or minor
mistreatment?"

And to this, the latter replied, "I am consoled, my teacher."[9]

The piety of these rabbis caused them to ransack their behavior
for even the slightest offense in order to shore up their faith in a
God who meted out reward and punishment justly. At times, as
rabbis, they had acted proudly or irresponsibly. Leadership is a
difficult role. For those who take it seriously it is always fraught
with guilt: the justification for their suffering lay in that sense of
sinfulness, in having fallen short. Here we are far from the world
view that animates the author of the Book of Job who continuously asserts innocence even while his friends seek to justify God's
punishing hand. Rather, these rabbis insisted on preserving an
earlier, more normative Biblical code that directly links sin to suffering, goodness to blessedness.

Why did these ideas have such persistence when the Bible itself
offered directions for alternative theologies? In part it may be said,
that clinging to the belief that there is a correlation between sin
and punishment permits the hope that blessing and a good life
will follow repentance and the turning to God. Monotheism's
most basic impulse is to overcome fatalism. If we resolve to turn
and change, then our historical fate will be altered too. We are not
passive victims of the forces that surround us: our deeds control
our destiny, whether for good or ill. God's punishing hand also
points to God's caring heart, and this Divine involvement in
human affairs holds out the promise of a fecund future. To
continue to insist on God's chastening rod, even at the most
dreadful moments, is to affirm the salvific direction of all history.

When we listen to and heed God's word we can effectuate redemption.

To be sure, such faith is constantly tested by the realities confronting believers. At times, the pain of suffering threatens to overwhelm theological conviction. Frequently, radical conclusions are drawn from such moments, for instance, that the breakdown of order must be due to the ushering in of the Messianic era. The pain now experienced represents the final death throes of the old order—a new age of justice is upon us. For some radical thinkers it was all too obvious that if every sin is counted by God, and if even common evils such as jealousy bring destruction then there is no hope of ever achieving redemption, since humans are sinful by nature. Rather, the time of the Messianic coming must be fixed: God will usher this era in, not as a reward for the good deeds humanity has performed, but out of God's mercy. The good acts of individuals or of Israel can not achieve this new epoch, because human nature will prove insufficient to the task. God's goodness transcends human frailty.

The suffering of Israel and the destruction of the Temple is the central concern of the pseudographic author of Fourth Ezra, who wrote at the end of the first century, just after the destruction of the Temple. "Why is Israel subjected to abuse by the nations, the people whom you chose given up to impious tribes?" Ezra asks. He accepts that Israel suffers because of sinfulness and that its fate is properly deserved. But he also realizes that when punishment of such magnitude is meted out for each sin, there is no hope for an end to the cycle of destruction. He therefore takes solace in the idea of Messianic redemption coming at a fixed time. The inevitability of a Messianic redemption (rather than one achieved through Israel's own acts) is what offers hope. The author even hints that the moment of redemption is not far off, that we may be experiencing the labor pains of the new era's birth, "for just as a woman about to bear [a child] strives to bring to an end the inevitable [anguish] of delivery, so also do these places strive to expel those things committed to them from the beginning. Then the things you want to see will be shown" (Ezra 4:23,42-43).[10] In fact, it is eschatology, the assured sense that history as we know it will come to an end, that our mundane story has a defined gestation period, and that a new age will soon be ushered in, that offers relief from the dismal present whose meaning can only be explained by a retributive theology whose effect seems so dismal.

This Messianism fueled the growth of the newly organized Christian sectarians. In Pauline theology, Jesus ushers in a new order, one that brings an end to the old history: the gift of his coming is one freely given by God and is not a reward for acts. Paul says:

> ...though you were dead because of your sins and because you were morally uncircumcised, he has made you alive with Christ. For he has forgiven us all our sins; he has canceled the bond which pledged us to the decrees of the law. (Colossians I, 2:13)[11]

Christian messianism sought to resolve the terrible tensions created by the normative Biblical and Rabbinic conceptions of retributional theology current among the great masses of Israel. In Paul's view, though we may be full of sin, faith in Jesus will overcome the terrible fate that awaits us. By emphasizing God's freely given gift of redemption any cause-and-effect connection between sin and punishment was severed. Christians thus announced a new testament, one whose theological premises are different than what animated the "old." But for Jews who remained loyal to the heritage of the Hebrew Bible such a response was not possible.

5 MARTYRDOM

Martyrs become the new typology of the hero, and the doctrine of reward and punishment is revised.

Christian, apocalyptic and rabbinic literature all demonstrate that the pressures of Jewish history were just too great for a doctrine that maintained a simple correlation between sin and suffering, good and blessing, to retain sole theological legitimacy. Subjugation by Rome, oppression by foreign rule, was unremitting. In the course of time, Jews could hardly be sustained by a theology of self-condemnation; they could not believe that every turn of the screw was due to their own lack of piety; on the contrary, they could observe the increasing faithfulness of their co-religionists even as the conditions of their existence worsened. A theology of self-abnegation and self-flagellation was replaced for some by the heroic sense of self gained through martyrdom. To understand this process fully, we need to go backwards in our story and review some Second Temple history.

The return from Babylonia was not as glorious as the prophets had predicted. Only a small number of Jews reestablished a settlement in and around Jerusalem and rebuilt an undistinguished altar. Full autonomy was not achieved during the first three centuries after the return. The period is marked by a succession of foreign rulers, first the Persians, then, after the conquest of Alexander, the Greek Kingdom in Egypt and, later, that of Syria. These are a dark ages of Jewish history. Little datable historical material is available from this period until the middle of the second century B.C.E. when the remarkable events of the Maccabean revolt occurred.

In 167 B.C.E., the Syrian Greeks, spurred by Jewish Hellenizers, sought to strengthen their colonial rule of Israel by outlawing

Jewish religious practice and by instituting the worship of the
Greek pantheon in the Temple. Not only was Jewish ceremonial
banned, but individual Jews were forced to publicly affirm the new
cultic practice and to violate their own religious obligations by, for
instance, eating forbidden foods such as pork. Defying a major
world power, risking death rather than compromise their faith, the
Maccabean revolt finally proved successful. Though many had
been martyred, their faithfulness was justified in the end.[12]

Writing their own narrative of these events, Maccabean historians portrayed themselves as steadfast upholders of the faith
and captured the essence of what had occurred in the legendary
story of the martyrdoms of Elazar, and of Hannah and her seven
children.[13] While the Syrian Greeks were forcing the violation of
Judaism on pain of death, Elazar and Hannah and her seven sons
sought martyrdom rather than eat swine's flesh. The Maccabean
historians recording these events justify what occurred in the final
speeches of these martyrs who say that their deaths will serve as
an expiation, an atonement for the sins of Israel and for the
apostasy of the Hellenizers, and that through their martyrdom
they will inherit the world to come.

> Thereafter they brought the sixth [son], and as he was about to
> die, he said, "Do not indulge in vain delusions! Through our own
> fault we are subjected to these sufferings, because we have
> sinned against our God. They pass belief! You, however, think
> not to escape unpunished after having dared to contend with
> God." (II Maccabees 7:18–19)[14]

This narrative of Maccabean martyrdom relies on a retributive
theology,"We are suffering....for sins against our own God," yet
we should notice two new emerging themes. The first is a clear
affirmation of the theology enunciated by Second Isaiah. Suffering
and death are not correlative with one's own sins but are an
atonement for the sins of the community. Although a relational
equation exists between sin and suffering, the martyr should not
be seen as a wrongdoer who is punished for his own sin: rather
martyrdom is a sacrifice, an expiation that brings redemption by
atoning for the sins of the larger collectivity.[15] Just as what is sacrificed did not commit the sin but rather the person who brings the
sacrifice, so too the martyr is not the author of his or her sad fate.

And in II Maccabees we find, for the first time, the theme of resurrection and afterlife as consolation for the martyr's death. The divine economy is not only displayed in this world but also in the next. Suffering is a temporary condition; afterwards, there is a final and just settling of accounts to look forward to.

This alternative theological viewpoint lives side by side with the view that the fate of the martyr is due to his or her own sinfulness. To be sure, the more righteous the person, the more closely God may examine his or her life. It is precisely the righteous who may be punished for the smallest of offenses. As we have seen, this is how some second-century rabbis explained the martyrdom of their teachers, arguing that Rabbi Ishmael and Rabbi Simeon died because they had delayed judgment when a widow or orphan came before their court.[16] But the Maccabean model that martyrdom was an expiation for the sins of the larger community could be drawn on in moments of peril.

Three hundred years after the Maccabean revolt, sixty years after the destruction of the Temple, in 132 C.E., the paradigm of the Maccabees inspired another Jewish revolt, that of Bar Kochba. That revolt, though, ended in failure and led to radical theological revision since this time martyrdom could not be seen as an atonement: in the end no redemption had come, all had been lost.

From 132-135 C.E. revolution raged in Judea. The rebellion was tenacious, and the war was especially cruel. To subdue the rebellion, Rome had to draft troops from as far away as Britain and Gaul. More than one quarter of all Roman legions were engaged in battle in the Land of Israel.[17]

During the previous three years (from 129-132 C.E.), the Emperor Hadrian had stationed himself in Egypt, preparing his troops for a major offensive in the East to shore up the border with Parthia (modern Iraq). On a side trip to visit the Roman garrison stationed in Jerusalem, he ordered that the city be rebuilt, renamed Aelia Capitolina, and that a temple dedicated to Zeus Jupiter be constructed in what had been the sacred precincts of the ancient Jewish temple.[18]

The Jews residing in Judea waited until Hadrian and his legions left for the East and then revolted to undo the sacrilege. The patriots saw themselves as new Maccabees cleansing the Temple.

The leader of the revolution, Bar Koziba, was given a new patronymic, Bar Kochba, son of a star, thereby incorporating the Messianic longings attached to the entire enterprise in his very name.[19] But though motivated by true religious passion, the revolt lacked any political sensibility. The eminent Jewish historian Salo Baron enunciated his retrospective judgment of the revolt declaring, "Only a frenzied messianic belief in a forthcoming supernatural intervention may explain this utter disregard of Realpolitik."[20]

Revolting against the might of Rome, Bar Kochba and his followers could convince themselves that victory was at hand because they viewed Jewish historical models as decisive. Jeremiah had foretold the rebuilding of Jerusalem and a mere generation after the terrible destruction of the first Temple, its destroyer Babylon was itself overcome and the altar in Jerusalem was rebuilt soon after. When the practice of the faith had been outlawed by the Syrian Greeks, had not the Maccabees defeated that world power? Had not the appropriate time now passed for the sins of the people to have been expiated and for the Temple to be rebuilt? Would not God favor the new pietists as God had answered the Maccabean cause?

But these new Maccabees were not as favored as their predecessors had been. Instead the revolt brought a toll of death and destruction far exceeding that which attended the fall of Jerusalem sixty years earlier.

The Roman legions poured into Judea to subdue the threat to their empire. Although the Jews inflicted serious damage on the Romans, they suffered enormous loss of life themselves, for Judea was subdued with such devastation that even pagan reporters were shocked. The Roman historian Dio Cassius wrote of the Jewish rebellion:

> Very few of them in fact survived. Fifty of their most important outposts and nine hundred and eight-five of their most famous villages were razed to the ground. Five hundred and eighty thousand men were slain in the various raids and battles, and the number of those that perished from famine, disease and fire was past finding out. Thus, nearly the whole of Judea was made desolate....[21]

Those who remained were caught in the Roman vise and suffered enormously, many dying as martyrs; those who could, fled.

Judea was almost depopulated of Jews, so that down to the twentieth century, even as Jews returned to the land of Israel, they were always a minority of the population.

> Before Bar Kochba's war we know the names of seventy-five settlements in Judea inhabited by Jews: after the fall of Betar there is no evidence of Jews continuing to live in a single one of them.[22]

The province was renamed Palestine, further severing its connection with a Jewish past, a measure that was to have lasting symbolic effect. And in the wake of the revolt, not only was Judea despoiled, but the practice of Judaism was outlawed. Never before in Jewish history had an act of piety led to such utter disaster.

The failure of the revolt created a deep crisis of belief. Had not those who died acted in defense of their faith? Had not the very effort to continue righteous Jewish practice been defeated? Why did this revolt not meet with the success of the Maccabees? Why was the Second Temple not restored as the First had been? Why was their piety not rewarded? Israel had not sinned, but had acted faithfully, yet now it was suffering mercilessly, and God's Torah was banned. Clearly, suffering and blessing had no relationship to faithfulness.

At least one rabbi, Elisha ben Abuyah, faced this new challenge squarely: seeing how deeply it contradicted traditional Jewish theological categories, he became an apostate and joined the Romans.

> What happened to that one [referring to Elisha ben Abuyah]?
> He saw a pig rolling the tongue of Huzpit the translator [one of the martyrs], and said,
> 'The mouth from which pearls issued should now lick the dust?'—and so, he left and sinned.[23]

Here legend has preserved the shattering nature of this crisis. Biblical models of divine justice, theological notions of the essential order and balance of the universe, of reward for the faithful and punishment of the sinful could not cope with the tragic reality of the martyrdom of thousands of Jews, among them

the most notable of the rabbinic leadership of that generation, and
the outlawing of the practice of Judaism itself in the wake of a pietistic revolt. Martyrdom had not brought atonement or salvation.
What was needed was a new theological formulation that could
explain this generation's terrible fate.

The ideological vacuum was filled by Rabbi Akiva, himself one
of the organizers of the Bar Kochba revolt and one of the martyrs
of the Roman suppression. Rabbi Akiva turned his own death into
an act of heroism and triumph, seeing martyrdom not as a punishment, but as a great religious act: the righteous are precisely the
ones who suffer and are martyred so that their last hours on earth
may reach the noblest of spiritual heights. Because of their guilt-
lessness, because of their piety, they are granted this special moment. Suffering and martyrdom are God's gifts to the righteous so
that the highest religious level, the giving of one's life to God, may
be achieved. To be martyred is to die nobly and happily.

> While the case of Rabbi Akiva was being adjudicated before the
> hated Tyranus Rufus, the time of reciting the Shema* arrived.
> Rabbi Akiva began to recite it and broke into a broad grin.
> "Old man," called the Roman,"you either don't understand
> what's going to happen to you, or you're a masochist."....[24]
> "I understand and I'm not a masochist. Rather all my life I have
> been reciting the verse: 'And you shall love your God with all your
> heart, with all your soul, and with all your life'—
> I have loved Him with all my heart,
> and I have loved Him with all my possessions,
> but I have not been able to offer my life.
> And now the time has come to offer my life and I am at peace
> with myself,[25] should I not recite the Shema, and smile broadly?"[26]

To be a martyr is to fulfill a religious command; to accept death
with joy is to be beloved by God, to die a holy death is the ultimate
religious fulfillment. Akiva goes beyond any notion of martyrdom
as a punishment for sin, or even of martyrdom as atonement or
purification, both of which concepts we have seen earlier in
rabbinic sources and in the Second Book of Maccabees. Even
those who accepted Isaiah's image of the suffering servant and

---

*Deuteronomy 6:4-9, the central declaration of Jewish liturgy.

sought to go beyond any exact equivalence between martyrdom and their own sinning, still retained some relationship between sin and suffering. Somewhere—perhaps in Israel, perhaps in humanity—sin must be present for which the suffering is atonement; there must have been some polluting characteristic for which the martyrdom is purification.[27] But Akiva's bold new thrust, on the contrary, states that it is especially to the righteous that martyrdom is granted. Martyrdom is a gift, not a punishment or a sacrifice. One is blessed to be a martyr. What more holy way to end one's life than by sanctifying God's Name?

Akiva's theology gained wide currency because martyrdom was not just the fate of a few leaders, but of the mass of Jewry as well. The common Jew continued to defend the faith and observe the commandments in the face of adversity. These people needed to know that they were dying for the sake of heaven.

In a sermon preached some years after the rebellion (but whose inner voice bears an authentic immediacy and heartfelt power), Rabbi Nathan, a youthful observer of the events of the Bar Kochba revolt, praised the common people who defended their faith and sacrificed themselves for the sake of the Torah:

> Who is referred to when God says, "...showing kindness to the thousandth generation [i.e. eternally] to those who love Me and keep My commandments" (Exodus 20:6)?
>
> Those are the people of Israel, who live in the land of Israel[28] and martyr themselves for the commandments.
>
> "Why are you led out to be killed?"
>
> "Because I circumcised my son."
>
> "And why are you led out to be burned at the stake?"
>
> "Because I read the Torah."
>
> "And why are you being led out to be crucified?"
>
> "Because I ate Matzah."*
>
> "And why are you being flagellated?"
>
> "Because I shook the lulav."**
>
> "And I said unto him,'What are these striped marks on your hands?'and he said,'That which I received in the house of my beloved'" (Zechariah 13:6).
>
> "These stripes make me love my father in Heaven.[29]

---

*   The unleavened bread eaten on Passover
** The palm branch carried in the fall harvest festival—Succot (Tabernacles).

The martyrs who suffer apparently without reason are consoled with the assurance that because they demonstrated trust in God even in this most extreme circumstance, they are truly faithful and are among those blessed by God. To be martyred is to become God's beloved.

In accordance with this position, the Book of Job is reinterpreted. In this new reading, Job is seen as someone who has been tested and not lost faith, and so in the end he is granted a vision of God and restored to blessedness. Job's plight is viewed as akin to that of the martyrs, and he becomes an archetype for them.

> That day,[30] Rabbi Joshua ben Hyrcanus taught:
> Job served God only with love,
> as it is written, "Though he slay me yet would I
> await Him"(Job 13:15).
> But that verse might be interpreted in the very opposite way, for some read:
> "Were he to slay me, I would no longer await Him,"
> therefore it is written, as well,
> "Till I die, I will not lose faith in Him"* (Job 27:5).
> Thus we know that Job served God with love.
>
> Rabbi Joshua interjected, "Would that the dust be removed from your eyes, O Rabban ben Zakkai.
> For all your life you would teach that Job worshipped God only out of fear, as it is written, 'And the man was upright fearing God and distancing himself from evil' (Job 1:1), and Joshua, your student's student, has shown that he served God out of love."[31]

Represented here is an historical awareness that Yochanan ben Zakkai, speaking to the mourners of Jerusalem after 70 C.E., had seen the destruction largely in terms of punishment for sin. In rabbinic thought, to worship God out of fear is to be concerned with reward and punishment. Thus, we are told that initially the rabbis conceived of Job as being primarily concerned with issues of retribution—after all that is an essential aspect of Job's questioning God's justice. The generation of Bar Kochba now understood Job differently: Akiva regarded Job as a hero, a true lover of God, who did not believe that there was a connection

---

* The two interpretations are based on the alternative readings for the Masoretic text. The *Keri*, the oral text, reads *lo* with a *vav*, meaning 'Him.' The *Ketib*, the written text, is *lo* spelled with an *aleph* and thus means 'not.'

between earthly consequence and religious performance. Those who reconstructed Jewish life after the destruction of the Second Temple could still attach themselves to a theology that connected suffering and death with sin, but for those who lived in the second century, the connection was severed. Death and martyrdom did not result from sins that either the person or the community had committed. Rather martyrdom was a gift: if one came through the test of martyrdom faithfully, if one willingly suffered and died for God, then one was considered a true religious servant. What appealed to these second-century interpreters was the Job of the ending of the book, the Job who understands that God and His activity in the world is mystery, the Job who would worship God whatever his fate.

Akiva's students now reinterpreted the tradition in light of Akiva's martyrdom and the new theological understanding of a faithful death. They grounded the new outlook in tradition and attributed Akiva's viewpoint to the patriarchs themselves. Just as Job had been reinterpreted by Akiva, now all the great Biblical models were seen as having prefigured Akiva's outlook.

Rabbi Meir, one of Akiva's closest students, interprets each of the Shema's threefold affirmations: "And you shall love the Lord your God, with all your heart, with all your soul, and with all your might," as referring to the willingness to give up your possessions and even your life for God's sake. He ascribes each of these qualities to one of the three patriarchs. Each of the founders of Judaism represents a different religious characteristic. Abraham is the archetype of the one who loves humanity and loves God, displaying the absolute quality of heartfelt love; Isaac, offered up as a sacrifice, is naturally seen as the one who willingly suffers and dies for God; and finally Jacob, the one who left home as a penniless fugitive, symbolizes the nonattachment to material goods, the worship of God with all one's wealth.

> ...Rabbi Meir taught:
>
> Is it not written, "You shall love the Lord your God, with all your heart?"(Deuteronomy 6:5). Love the Lord like Abraham your forefather did, as it is written, "and you, O Israel, my servant, O Jacob, you whom I have chosen, the seed of Abraham who loved me" (Isaiah 4:8).

"And you shall love the Lord your God…with all your soul,"—as Isaac did, who arranged himself as a sacrifice on the altar, as it is written, "And Abraham sent forth his hand and took the knife" (Genesis 22:10).[32]

"And you shall love the Lord, your God,…with all your might,"—submit yourself before Him as Jacob, your forefather did,* as it is written, "I do not deserve all the grace and constancy which You have done with Your servant, for I crossed the Jordan with only my walking stick, and now I have become wealthy enough to support two camps" (Genesis 32:11).[33]

Everything is to be offered up to God: personal wealth, one's heart, one's life. To undertake these renunciations was to make the ultimate statement of faith.

Having created a new ideal, all of Judaism was now to be reinterpreted through Akiva's model.

---

* The Hebrew is a pun on the similarly-sounding *meod*—might—and *modeh*—acquiescence and acceptance.

 **THE CHILDREN OF THE MARTYRS**

The generation after Akiva radicalized his theology, seeing this world as a place of pain and suffering and looking toward the next world for significance.

Not only had the students of Akiva grounded his new theological outlook in the tradition, but they now expounded and radicalized the implications of this new ideology. For many of his students, the experience of suffering became a demonstrable sign of piety, and earthly concerns were viewed negatively, for the Divine was not to be met in things of this world but only in a future world experienced after death.

Rabbi Simeon ben Yohai, perhaps the most radical of Akiva's students, taught that the religious life could be achieved only through suffering:

> Suffering is beloved by God, for three things were given to Israel which are desired by the other nations of the world, and Israel received them only through suffering. They are: Torah, the Land of Israel, and the world to come.
> —Whence do we know that Torah came through suffering?
> From the verse, "To know wisdom and *musar*..."(Proverbs 1:2).*
> The meaning of the word, *musar*, can be derived from a related verse: "Blessed is the person who is chastened** by God and learns from your Torah."
> —Whence do we know that the Land of Israel came through suffering? From the verse,"The Lord your God chastens you....so that the Lord your God may bring you into the good land" (Deuteronomy 8:5,7).***
> —Whence do we know that the world to come is achieved

---

* The rabbis always identify Biblical "Wisdom" with "Torah."
** Hebrew root = *ysr*, same as *musar*.
*** R. Simeon b. Yohai is playing on the word *ki* which is found in both verses 5 and 7, interpreting it to be a statement of cause. The verb used here is the same, *ysr*.

through suffering? From the verse, "For just as God's command is a candle and His Torah a light, so the way of life is chastening instruction* (Proverbs 6:23).

What is the path which leads to the world to come [eternal life]?—Is it not the very same chastening—suffering?[34]

Redemption can only be achieved through suffering. Instead of earthly blessing being a sign and a reward of virtue, painful living now becomes the mark of the religious life. Only through the denial of this world, achieved by a life of suffering, do we release ourselves from material care and attach ourselves to God. The faithful ought to focus on how to achieve a future existence and give up any sense that the material world has any worth.

A generation later, Rabbi Jose the son of Rabbi Judah summarized this school of theology when he said,

> Suffering is beloved by God, for His name is added to the one who suffers, as it is written, "...The Lord your God, who causes you to suffer"** (Deuteronomy 8:5).[35]

Closeness to God is marked by suffering. The person who suffers has a special relationship with God and takes on God's name as a patronymic.

Rabbi Huna, a third-century teacher, shows what a radical rereading of the Bible this new exegesis involves, by reinterpreting the way the world is understood as blessing in the creation story of Genesis:

> "...And behold it was very good" (Genesis 1:31),
> —this refers to suffering.
> And is suffering such a good thing?
> Rather, through it, a person achieves the world to come.[36]

God's grace is not to be found in the material blessings of this world, but rather suffering brings closeness to God. Blessing is not of this world but of the next. The mistake of the revolt of Bar Kochba was to put faith in things of this world, but history is not where we find God, for God is not of this world, but of the next.

---

* *Musar*, as above.

**The verb used here for suffering *ysr* is the same used in the previous citation. In both cases the double meaning of *ysr* as instruction and as chastening is played on. The play is probably etymologically the case, instruction being conceived of as the whipping the teacher gave to discipline his students. (My teacher, Ernst Simon, is the source of this insight.)

> The Divine voice responded:
> You are blessed, O Akiva,
> for you are called to the future world.[37]

With that sentence the Babylonian redactor ends his recounting of the martyrdom of Rabbi Akiva. For him, as for Akiva's students, the lesson to be learned from the great master's death was to leave off the things of this world, including the search for God in history. Suffering is a means of divestment from this world, an entree into the next, and therefore the instrument of salvation.

Expectations of a future life were not new to Judaism, rather they now came to the fore in a way that completely severed the connection between life in this world and blessedness. God's hand was simply not to be seen in the goods of this world nor in its history. The story that unfolded here and now was of no significance save as a test for the world to come.

> Rabbi Jacob said:
> Whenever the Bible ascribes reward for the performance of a commandment it is referring to the resurrection of the dead.
> With regard to the respect due a mother and father, the Bible writes, "so that your days may be lengthened and so that good may be bestowed on you in the land which God has given you" (Deuteronomy 5:16); and in regard to sending away the mother bird before taking the nestlings, it is written, "so that good may be bestowed on you, and you may have length of days" (Deuteronomy 22:7), but if his father told him to go up to the crown of the tree and bring down the nestlings, and he went up to the crown, and sent away the mother, took the children but on returning fell down and died, where is the good that was to be bestowed on him?—where is his length of days?
> Rather good is bestowed in the world which is fully good, and length of days in the world which is eternally long.[38]

This world is a place of happenstance, of broken dreams and shattered visions, a place devoid of the real imprint of God. Here there is no justice, no correlation between deed and consequence; pass through this world in faithfulness so that you will enter into the real presence of God in the next world.[39]

> In the Torah scroll [betorato] of Rabbi Meir it was written,
> "and behold it was very good"(Genesis 1:31 referring to the
> creation of the human),
> —and behold death, it was good.[40]

Rabbi Meir argues a radical substitution. By punning on the similarly sounding Hebrew, me'od—very, and mavet—death, he is turning Genesis on its head. For while the overwhelming import of the first chapter of Genesis is that we meet God's blessing in this world, amidst creation itself, Rabbi Meir teaches that God's goodness lies beyond this world. Death is a blessing, not a curse, allowing us to leave a place of pain and suffering and enter the next world where God dwells. Now death becomes the glorious reward for the righteous, the hallway to the world to come. God, in his goodness, blesses us with death. There can be no more radical overturning of the biblical notion of creation.

Of the students of Akiva, Rabbi Simeon ben Yohai achieves the most extreme and consistent formulation of the new theological orientation, drawing out not only its theoretical implications but also radical practical ones as well.[41]

Although the later redactions of Simeon's biography found in rabbinic sources are full of legendary material and can hardly be trusted for historical accuracy, they are nevertheless striking in capturing his singleminded turning away from everyday life:

> ...The Romans decreed...that Simeon ben Yohai, who had spoken against Rome, should be killed. He and his son hid themselves in the house of study. Each day his daughter would bring him flat cakes, a jug of water, and a bedroll. When the persecutions grew tougher, he said to his son, "The woman may not withstand torture... perhaps she will be captured and reveal our hiding place."
>
> They went away and hid in a cave. A miracle occurred and a carob tree and a well of water were created. They stripped themselves and sat with sand up to their necks, studying all day long. When it was time for prayer, they dressed themselves and prayed; afterwards they stripped once again in order not to wear their clothes out.
>
> They sat in the cave for twelve years. Elijah suddenly came and appeared at the entrance to the cave and said, "Who will inform the son of Yohai that the Emperor is dead and the decree repealed?"

They left the cave and saw someone who was tilling and planting. Simeon said, "They leave the eternal life in order to do temporal things." And so everywhere they looked, everything was immediately devoured by fire. A divine echo said to them, "Have you gone out to destroy my world—go back to your cave!"

They returned, and for twelve months sat once again saying, "The evildoers are judged in hell for twelve months."

A divine echo called, "Go out from your cave."

They went out, and anywhere that Rabbi Eliezer, Simeon's son would destroy, the father would rebuild. He said, "It is sufficient for the world, that the two of us are together."

As Friday evening approached, they saw a certain old man who was holding two bundles of myrtle, scurrying at dusk. They said to him, "Why do you need these?"

"To honor the Sabbath."

"Would not one have been sufficient?"

"One is for the word 'remember,'* the other if for the word 'keep'."**

He said to his son, "See how beloved the commandments are to Israel," and his mind was at peace.

Rabbi Phineas ben Yair, his son-in-law, came out to meet him, took him home and began to heal his body. He saw that he had sores all over his body and began to cry, tears pouring down and irritating the wounds, "Woe is me that I have seen you in such a state."

He replied, "How wonderful it is that you see me in such a state. For would you not see me in this state you would not find me to be the person who I am."[42]

Life in the desert, the hermetic existence in a cave, the experience of death-in-life, has now become the proper place to receive instruction into the spiritual dimension. Fleeing from Rome, from the war and its consequence, Simeon and his son learn to reject the tragedy of temporal existence. Only total immersion in the life of Torah makes existence bearable. The hermetic life of the cave becomes a spiritual ideal, and the negation of the world, even to the point of physical denial and suffering, becomes the condition for living the life of Torah—eternal life. The story ends, after all, with Rabbi Simeon announcing that he has achieved his

---

* Used in the Exodus version of the Ten Commandments, Chapter 19.
**Found in the alternative version in Deuteronomy Chapter 5.

estate because of having suffered. The material world does not display God's blessing, only in Torah can we find the divine voice:

> If while walking on the way, one stops one's study of Torah to remark, "How beautiful is this tree—how handsome that plowed field,"—the written word considers it as if one had committed a capital crime.[43]

Torah has replaced the world as a map for finding the Divine. Creation is no longer the stage where one can meet God: it does not contain the ability to reveal the ultimate source of holiness.

Any involvement in this world is a diversion from that which we truly ought to attend to. Thus Simeon bemoans the fact that humans are required to do any physical act to keep them alive.

> Had I been at Mt. Sinai at the time of the giving of the Torah, I would have beseeched the Merciful One to create humans with two mouths, one so that a person could always speak the words of Torah, the other to do all his necessary things.[44]

To spend one minute away from Torah, even to take care of those affairs necessary for existence, is to divert oneself from eternity. All aspects of life unrelated to the study of Torah are secular events, transient and inconsequential diversions from our eternal purpose.

The failure of the Bar Kochba revolution impressed on the survivors the knowledge that God is not to be found in this world, that the world of work and of history, indeed of all sensuousness, is closed off from Divinity. God is to be found in eternal time, encapsulated in the word.

For the generation living after Bar Kochba, the world and the word had split. No longer were they intertwined leading one to the other, but nature, history, daily toil, and indeed action of any kind were only secondarily the world of the divine—God was essentially manifest in Torah, in the word, in the quiescent life. Torah, not physical reality, become the central aspect of creation. Many of this generation even negated the practical work of sustenance, thus overturning the earlier model of scholar-laborer.[45]

> The Torah was given only to those who eat Manna.
> How is that possible since clearly the Torah was given to each generation?

If you sit and study and do not know where your food and drink are coming from, or how you will be able to clothe yourself then you are considered among those who eat Manna, and for whom the Torah was given. Second to these are the Priests, who eat from the fixed offering.[46]

The mendicant is the new priest, for like the latter, he only lives off the offerings of the people. The new class of beggar-scholars has now replaced the priests as those who are especially close to the divine, for of all people they have separated themselves from engagement in the affairs of this world. They have even surpassed the priest in the scale of piety because the priest is assured some kind of fixed income while the mendicant-scholar is not. The life of studying Torah provides a new Temple and a new religious service with its own specially dedicated class of officiants—the rabbis themselves.

Labor in the world is no longer regarded as a positive endeavor, and the praise once afforded it is now reserved for the work of the word. Rabbi Elazar ben Shamua, a student of Akiva's, reinterprets the entire concept of work as found in the Bible to denote the study of Torah so that any positive view of work is transformed into a praise of Torah.

> Every person was created to work, as it is written: "A person was born to work" (Job 5:7).
>
> But from this verse I would not know whether the work meant here is labor to be accomplished through speech, or that of a craft. However, when it says: "The soul of a man will work for him, his mouth shall be like a hand"(Proverbs 16:26),* I know that a person was created to work with his mouth.
>
> Still, I would not know whether this referred to the work of Torah or perhaps simply to any sort of speech, however, when it says, "May this scroll of Torah never depart from your mouth" (Joshua 1:8), I know that a person was created for the work of Torah.[47]

Rabbi Noharai, a younger colleague, joins in this opinion and explicitly draws out its practical implication: teach your children Torah rather than a trade.

---

* Punning on *achaf*, usually translated as compel and changing it to *caf* meaning palm.

To be sure, many of the most prestigious rabbis of this generation opposed the radicalization of this perspective. Rabbi Meir, for instance, insists that it is incumbent on a father to teach his son a craft,[48] and Rabbi Judah Ilai argues that, "One who does not teach his son a trade makes him into a professional robber," but this opposition is based on practical considerations, not on ideology: to burden the community with a class of beggars is wrong. Even these rabbis who argue that one must teach one's child a dignified trade to be self supporting nevertheless denigrate the world of work. Rabbi Meir says: "Lessen your preoccupation with business, and busy yourself with the occupation of Torah."[49]

And Rabbi Judah adds,

> He who makes Torah essential and work unimportant, is himself made important in the world to come. And he who makes work essential and Torah unimportant, is himself made unimportant in the world to come.[50]

An anonymous Mishna sums up the ideal enunciated by this generation as that of a life spent studying Torah with only the most minimal worldly contact:

> This is the way of the Torah:
> you should eat a morsel of bread with salt,
> and you should drink only a measure of water,
> and you should sleep on the ground,
> living a life of suffering
> and slaving over the Torah.
> For if you do this, then "it will be satisfying and good for you"
>   (Psalm 128:2).
> "Satisfying"—in this world,
> "and good for you"—in the world to come.[51]

The life of Torah stands in complete opposition to any participation in the life of this world, save for the most basic sustenance. The pious life is one of suffering, of meager existence.

The world, God's creation, is no longer the setting where one can meet God. Turning away from the world, the rabbis substitute a different arena in which to meet God. Divorcing oneself from this world, one gains the world to come.

7

TORAH, NOT HISTORY

*Akiva's students make the study of
Torah the central Jewish value.*

Having ruthlessly suppressed the revolt of Bar Kochba and his followers, the Emperor Hadrian now finished the task he had originally set for himself. Jerusalem was turned into a completely foreign city renamed Aelia Capitolina and Jews were forbidden to enter therein. A temple to Zeus Jupiter was built on the ancient site of the Jewish Temple.[52]

But the Romans went further: wreaking vengeance upon this rebellious province, they now embarked on the obliteration of Jewish teaching and practice. Where once Jews had been exempted from the Roman ban on circumcision, they now were included in the proscription. The teaching of Judaism was altogether suppressed; synagogues and Jewish courts were closed. The transmission of Torah, of any Jewish religious teaching, became a capital crime. The public recitation of the Shema, the central declaration of Jewish faith, was outlawed.[53]

The observance of Judaism became an underground activity marked by great danger and subterfuge, as Rabbi Judah Ilai reports regarding the reading of the Torah on Shabbat:

> During the time of persecution,
> we would carry the Torah
> from the courtyard to the roof,
> and from one rooftop to another
> in order to be able to read it.[54]

Under these extreme conditions of religious persecution a strategy for Jewish survival had to be devised: decisions were made as to what could be compromised and what had to be fought for, even to the point of martyrdom. The leaders of this generation had to stipulate what was to be preserved at all costs and what was less essential, what could be celebrated only underground and what needed public demonstration. Rabbi Nathan himself, who so extolled the martyrs,[55] remarks on the need to compromise even if it meant violating some of the commandments. He reinterprets a psalmic verse to justify this need:

> "It is a time of acting for the sake of heaven when your teaching is violated, for I love your commandments more than the finest gold" (Psalm 119:126-27).
> —Rabbi Nathan interpreted the verse to mean: why is "your teaching violated?"
> —because it is "a time of acting for the sake of heaven."[56]

In other words, defending the faith in its hour of trial may necessitate compromising some commandments, and indeed in the case of one of the most central, the Sabbath, he makes this explicit: "Violate one Sabbath, that you may observe many Sabbaths later on."[57]

In these times when Jewish survival itself was at stake, even quintessential Jewish religious acts such as the observance of the Sabbath must be compromised.

While there was debate over whether to engage in such desecration and about which commandments had to be upheld under any conditions, it is crucial to note that in the tales of martyrdom there is a remarkable consistency. The stories later generations told of the arrest of the great rabbis by the Romans always occur when they are engaged in the public teaching of Torah. It was the continuity of the study and teaching of Torah which was seen as the key to resisting the Roman regime. The great Rabbi Akiva himself was martyred for continuing to study Torah and lecture publicly. Once again later legend dramatizes the tale while conveying an important theological message.

> Our Rabbis taught:
> Once the evil kingdom* decreed that Israel should not study Torah, whereupon Pappas ben Judah came upon Rabbi Akiva publicly gathering people to study the Torah.
> "Akiva, are you not fearful of the government?"

*A euphemism for the Romans.

"I will tell you a metaphorical story," he replied. "There was once a fox who was stalking the riverbank. He saw some fish dashing for cover from place to place.

'Why are you running about?' said the fox.

'To escape from the men who are casting their nets to catch us,' they replied.

'Would it not be better for you,' said the fox, 'if you came up to dry land, and we could then live peaceably together as our ancestors once did?'

The fish responded, 'Are you really the one whom they call the wisest of all the animals? You're nothing but a fool. If we are afraid of our natural habitat, should we not be even more fearful of a habitat which is deadly for us?'

"And so," Rabbi Akiva continued, "it is with us. Now that we are afraid when we study Torah of which it is written, 'it is your life and the length of your days' (Deuteronomy 30:20),[58] would we not be even worse off, if we were to just walk away, and stop studying the Torah?"

And our Rabbis further related:

Not very long thereafter, Rabbi Akiva was arrested and jailed. Rabbi Pappas was jailed too, and was placed in the same cell as Rabbi Akiva.

Rabbi Akiva queried him, "Pappas, what brought you here?"

"How fortunate for you, Rabbi Akiva, that you were captured for the sake of the Torah."

"How unfortunate for me, Pappas, that I was captured engaged in silly things."[59]

Whatever else, these legends of martyrdom contain a historical memory of a time in which the transmission of Torah itself became a prime value, the chief instrument of survival, the place where the rabbis took their stand. With the Temple destroyed, Jewish survival depended on the continued transmission of this teaching and for the sake of the continued study of Torah these religious masters were willing to risk their lives.

After the tragedy of the destruction of the Temple in 70 C.E., the agenda of the rabbis had been the normalization of Jewish life. The past offered a model of destruction followed by reconstruction. During the first exile, Jeremiah had told the people that in seventy years the Temple would be rebuilt and indeed it had been. Jeremiah had instructed the people to build houses and live a life of normalcy in the interim period.[60] Now, too, after the destruction of the Second Temple, Rabban Yochanan ben Zakkai and his circle at Yavneh had counseled the normalization of Jewish life despite the enormity of the tragedy they had just suffered.[61]

Interestingly, Yochanan was a priest and many of his closest associates numbered priests and levites.[62] Their primary concern was to preserve Jewish life in a period which looked forward to rebuilding of the Temple in two or three generations.[63] Most of the legislation which can legitimately be ascribed to Yochanan attempts to preserve ceremonies originally limited to observance in the Temple and that would be lost if they were not observed now outside the Temple precincts.[64] Thus, the lulav (the palm branch carried on the holiday of Succot) and the shofar (the ram's horn blown on Rosh Hashonnah), which had been associated with the Temple service, were now adopted as a norm for all Jews to be observed as a ritual everywhere. Similarly, the formalization of prayer, which was the work of Rabban Yochanan ben Zakkai and the rabbis at his court in Yavneh, was fixed to correspond to the times of sacrifices no longer offered, and was replete with invocations for the restoration of Temple life. Thus, it was not so much a replacement of the function of the Temple as an extension of a priestly program which looked toward a time of reconstruction.[65]

Yet in the process of preservation something new and almost unintended occurred as well. The process of codification needed to preserve the tradition for a historically redemptive time, the disquisition and ordering necessary for programmatic reconstruction, produced a measure of religious vitality and comfort in itself. Surprisingly, there was a way in which studying about the Temple was as involving as a pilgrimage to the actual Temple. Whether derived from the pilgrimage or the study of the teaching, the central message of Judaism was communicated. Gradually, the study and teaching that had been undertaken as an intense preparation for a hoped for redemption came to be seen as redemptive in itself.

The sixty years between the destruction of the Temple and the Bar Kochba revolution were among the most hermeneutically and legally creative in Judaism's history. The fabric of Jewish life was interwoven with study, creative interpretation, and legal disquisition. Thus, when the rabbis of the generation of Bar Kochba had to decide which were the most central Jewish institutions to protect, the study and transmission of Torah stood out as the essential instrument of religious preservation.

A conscious recording of this new set of priorities, indeed what may very well be a record of the decision to make the study and teaching of Torah the focus of resistance against persecution, may survive in the following account:

> While Rabbi Tarfon and the elders were in session in the attic of the house of Natza in Lydda, the following question came before them: which is greater, study or action? Rabbi Tarfon responded: action is greater. Rabbi Akiva responded: study is greater. They all then agreed: study is greater for it leads to action.[66]

The decision arrived at in this secret meeting of the rabbis in an attic in central Palestine was to have a profound effect on that generation and on all subsequent Jewish life. Despite the threat of persecution and martyrdom, the public teaching of Torah and the transmission of authority from one generation to the next must continue at all costs. The teaching, not any single commandment or act, was the foundation on which Judaism rested. Here the rabbis would take their stand. Akiva's martyrdom was an act repeated again and again.

> . . . They found Rabbi Hanina ben Teradyon holding court[67] and occupying himself with the Torah: publicly gathering assemblies and keeping a scroll of the Torah in his bosom.
>
> Immediately, they captured him, wrapped him in the scroll of the Torah, placed bundles of branches round him and set them on fire. They then brought tufts of wool, which they had soaked in water, and placed them over his heart, so that he should not expire quickly.
>
> His daughter exclaimed, "Father, that I should see you in this state!"
>
> He replied, "If it were I alone being burnt, it would have been a hard thing to bear; but now that I am burning together with the Scroll of the Torah, He who will have regard for the plight of the Torah, will also have regard for my plight."

> His disciples called out, "Our Master, what do you see?"
> He answered them, "The parchments are burning,
> but the letters are soaring on high. . . ."[68]

The truth of Torah does not exist in its physical reality, that part can burn: the Torah's truth lies in an etherealized existence, as the connecting link between heaven and earth. The martyred rabbi, himself having become one with the Torah, is transported by it from earthly to heavenly existence, and through this martyrdom a vision of a transfigured Torah is revealed.

The Temple was no more, nor would it be speedily restored. Now Torah itself would bring the faithful into the presence of God. The fiery letters of the Torah dancing ghost-like in the air, forming a chain between heaven and earth, can be the intercessor between the two. The disembodied letters of the Torah form the ladder to heaven.

And the reverse image is equally true—Torah is the means of drawing God into this world—through it the earthly can become the heavenly, the seat of the Divine. So it was reported in the name of the martyr Rabbi Hanina:

> . . . should two people sit together and engage in a discussion of Torah, the Shekinah, God's presence, itself, rests amongst them, as it is written: "Then, they that feared the Lord spoke often one to another; and the Lord listened and heard it, and a book of remembrance was written before him, for they that feared the Lord and pondered His name." (Malachi 3:16)[69]

Study of Torah becomes the bridge between this world and the next, forming not only a substitute for the Temple, but even replacing creation as a pointer to the divine. The mundane is not the home of the divine encounter, but what is required in order to reach God is the transformation of the everyday through words of Torah.

By studying Torah one can live out an other-worldly existence, one can taste the world to come here on earth, one can live in God's dwelling. Through Torah the secular meal may be transformed into a sacral event, something hitherto only accomplished through sacrifical offerings on the altar of the Temple.

Rabbi Simeon says:

Three who eat at one table, yet do not speak over it words of Torah, are to be considered as if they ate from the sacrifices offered by the dead, as it is written:

"Every table is covered with vomit,

filth that leaves no clean spot"(Isaiah 28:8).

But, three who eat at one table, and do, indeed speak over it words of Torah, it is as if they had eaten from God's very table, as it is written, "He told me, that this was the table that stood before the Lord"(Ezekiel 41:22).[70]

The mundane meal now becomes the altar of the Lord, food takes on the quality of sacrifice through the power of the words of Torah spoken over them. The Torah, as it were, reestablishes the space the Temple occupied. Through Torah, holiness is once again restored. The closeness to God, previously available only in the precincts of the Temple and lost with its destruction, once again, returns to earth across the sacred bridges of Torah. To study Torah is to be transported to heaven, to live out the next world in this one.

This replacement of Temple function by Torah is made explicit in a statement reported anonymously in one source and in the name of Rabbi Simeon in another:

... the study of Torah is more beloved by God than burnt offerings. For as a person studies Torah he comes to know the will of God, as it is said, "Then shalt thou understand the fear of the Lord, and find the will of God"(Proverbs 2:5).

Hence, when a sage sits and expounds to the congregation, Scripture accounts it to him as though he had offered up fat and blood on the altar.[71]

No longer is even the hint of a meal necessary to make one feel that this is the altar of God; the words of Torah alone become the living sacrifice.

For this generation, the study of Torah became the central religious act. They saw their masters martyred for continuing to teach Torah, and they understood their basic charge, their very commission as rabbis, to be a call to continue the teaching of Torah. After the martyrdom of Rabbi Akiva, a contemporary of his, Rabbi Judah ben Babba,[72] risked his own life by ordaining five of Akiva's younger students so that the process of transmitting Torah could continue:

Once the evil kingdom decreed regarding the
Jewish people that anyone who ordained would be killed,
and that any city in which ordination took place
would be obliterated.
What did Judah ben Babba do?
He went and sat between two large mountains,
between two cities, Usha and Shifraim, on the county borders,
and there ordained five elders: Rabbi Meir, Rabbi Judah Ilai,
Rabbi Simeon Yohai, Rabbi Jose Halafta, and Rabbi Eleazar ben
Ahamua [Avya adds Rabbi Nehemiah to the list.].
Ahamua
[Avya adds Rabbi Nehemiah to the list.]

Realizing that they had been discovered, he said to them, "My
children, flee."
They said to him, "Teacher, what will be with you?"
"I shall be in their path as a stone that cannot be turned."
It is said, that they had hardly gone, when the Romans pierced
him like a sieve with three hundred lances.[73]

Jewish legend preserved a sense that these five, who were most
responsible for reconstructing Jewish life in the aftermath of Bar
Kochba, had been indelibly marked by their experience of their
master's martyrdom for the sake of Torah. Tempered by the fires
raging around them, they were charged to continue the teaching
at any cost. Not surprisingly, Torah became for them the central
Jewish religious value.

RABBINIC JUDAISM:
The Heritage of
Bar Kochba

*While Jewish generations that followed retreated
from some of the more radical statements of the
disciples of Akiva, their theological revision
formed the underpinning of the fundamental
works of Rabbinic literature.*

During the three years that followed the quashing of the Bar
Kochba revolt the Hadrianic persecutions continued in full force,
and then, with the death of the Emperor, conditions began to
improve. Antonius Pius, the new emperor, repealed the restriction
on circumcision and allowed for the resumption of Jewish life.

Yet Judaism had lived through a traumatizing and transforming tragedy. Necessarily, restoration included the assimila-
tion of what had occurred during the crisis. The rabbis who now
gathered to lead the resumption of Jewish public life were the
same ones whose apprenticeship took place amidst the war and
martyrdoms. In part, their authority stemmed from their teachers'
sacrifice and their success in preserving Judaism through the time
of crisis.

These rabbis' formative experience of Jewish leadership had
been forged in the oppression and suffering following the revolt.
As underground leaders they had been trained to keep Judaism
alive under Roman occupation and power, and their experience
had taught them to find the purpose of existence beyond the realm
of power. They realized now that Jews would not overthrow the
Roman Empire; Jerusalem would not be liberated; the Temple
would not be quickly restored. They also discovered that holiness

had been found beyond the realm of governance and politics, that what held the people together during the crisis was not the Messianic hope of restoration that had sparked the Bar Kochba revolt, but rather the continuous study of Torah, which served as a portable sanctuary that could exist autonomously amidst political defeat.

What had been forged was a new Jewish self-understanding: that politics and war led to tragic failure and that the spiritual essence of Judaism could exist beneath the realm of power. These rabbis did not see history as the field on which the divine drama was played—history, dominated by Roman might, was secular, without religious significance. What was important was trans-historical, eternal, that which could be discovered beyond all seeming reality. For had not the war been lost though the cause was right? Armies and battles, victories and war did not exhibit God's saving hand, rather the experience of God's beneficence was found beneath the plane of history. Had not the conventicles, secretly gathered around a rabbinic master passing on the teaching, done more for Jewish survival than the defeated Bar Kochba with his peasant armies and ill-fated dreams? Had not Judaism survived in the underground even as Rome's might marched through the streets?

The catastrophe of the revolt, the devastation wrought by Hadrian's legions, the subsequent persecutions and attendant martyrdoms clearly showed that Rome was not Babylon and that there would be no reconstruction of the Temple seventy years after the destruction. Judaism now taught a different story whose moral was that a return to the life of piety would not effectuate historic events. After all, had not this most recent devastation been wrought on those who tried to defend the faith and purify Jerusalem? The mistake had been to identify God's blessing with the realm of the worldly and transient. Involvement in history led to disaster; in the world of power and politics one could hardly discern the workings of the Divine.

Under these circumstances, the rabbis realized that the true center of Jewish life lay in the cultivation of inwardness. In turning to study Torah, the pious found the arena in which to meet the divine. There, one could taste of the world to come even while living out this earthly existence.

The rejection of the validity of history by the generation following the Bar Kochba revolt involved a thorough theological reorientation. The study of Torah replaced all other values; it replaced not only the work of this world, but all other commandments as well. Rabbi Simeon ben Yohai, for instance, teaches that studying should not be interrupted even for the recitation of the Shema, the central credal statement of Jewish faith.[74] Although the Shema is said only at a fixed time, and not stopping at this moment would mean that one would have failed to say the Shema, nevertheless, studying should not be halted. In contemplating Torah the student is transported to another realm, seated under God's wings, and therefore a person ought not to interrupt these probings even for prayer, for through study one has already attained the highest spiritual plane.

Torah even took precedence over the commandments themselves. When Rabbi Elazar ben Shamua taught Torah, he would not go out to the Succah, the tabernacle built to celebrate the autumn harvest, though food was distributed while they studied, and the Rabbis had ordained that food must be eaten in the Succah during the holiday.[75] He believed that a person should not break off from study even for the celebration of the festival.

In a more limited way, this perspective is incorporated in an anonymous teaching that describes the conflict between studying and a wedding ceremony or funeral.

> If two rabbis are sitting and studying Torah and a bride or a coffin passes in front of them,
> if there are enough people accompanying the procession, they should not interrupt their studies.
> But if not,
> they should disport before the bride and accompany the dead.[76]

For the authors of these passages, even the celebration of life's special passages takes on a relative value in relation to Torah.

Other rabbis were not willing to join with the radical replacement of every command or every deed by the study of Torah itself. In fact, the text that contains the above mentioned quotation also reports its immediate contradiction by citing an illustrative incident in the life of Judah Ilai:

Once, as Rabbi Judah bar Ilai sat teaching his disciples a bride passed by.

"What was that?" he asked them.

"A bride passed by," they replied.

"My sons," he said to them, "get up and attend the bride." For thus we find concerning the Holy One, blessed be He, that he....fixed Eve's hair and outfitted her as a bride and brought her to Adam, as it is said, "And he brought her unto the man . . ." (Genesis 2:22).[77]

Rabbi Judah ben Ilai steps in when he feels that the value of studying Torah has begun to override even the most basic humanity. He insists on interrupting study to celebrate a decisive moment in another's life. Joining a wedding celebration is understood to constitute the fulfillment of a biblical command.

What these passages illustrate is the way in which the priority of Torah study became a matter of controversy in the generation of reconstruction: How much time should it take? What is its relative importance? For some, study has become more essential than participation in other religious acts, even those celebrating the most intense moments of life. They would agree with the anonymous Mishna which enumerates the commandments that have eternal significance, and concludes, "But the study of Torah is greater than all of them."[78] The full implications of Akiva's martyrdom and his assertion that the study of Torah was the single most important priority for national survival was being drawn to its logical conclusion.

To be sure, there was no unanimity in this view of the primacy of Torah study, in fact many rabbis who lived during and after Bar Kochba opposed many elements of this theological outlook. For instance, Rabbi Judah the Prince, although having studied with the masters of the generation after Bar Kochba, more closely reflects the traditional concerns of the Patriarchate (the head of the Jewish community in Israel), than the philosophy of his teachers.[79] "So it was taught by Rabbi Judah the Prince: action has precedence over study."[80]

Similarly, Rabbi Judah's student, Rabbi Yochanan, seeks to vitiate the teaching of Rabbi Simeon ben Yohai, analyzing the passage in which Rabbi Simeon asserts that one is not to stop studying when the time for prayer arrives, and arguing: "This law applies only to Rabbi Simeon ben Yohai and his companions, who made the study of Torah into a profession."[81] Thus Rabbi Simeon and his circle are relegated to a position of uniqueness and irrelevance; their total dedication to Torah set them apart and we, who are less fully involved than they, are to operate under a different set of priorities.

Equally fascinating is the way later tradition reworked the legend of the martyrdom of Hanina ben Teradyon. They imagined the following conversation taking place in the prison where he was detained:

> When Rabbi Eleazar ben Petara and Rabbi Hanina ben Teradion were arrested, Rabbi Eleazar ben Petara said to the latter,
>
> "Happy are you, for you have been arrested on one charge, woe is me for I am arrested on five charges."
>
> Rabbi Hanina replied:
>
> "Happy are you who have been arrested on five charges, but will be rescued; woe is me who though having been arrested on one charge will not be rescued. For you have occupied yourself with the study of the Torah as well as with acts of benevolence, whereas I occupied myself with Torah alone."[82]

Here the tables have indeed been turned. The policy of the time of persecution, emphasizing the teaching and study of Torah as a central priority, is now seen as having been punished by martyrdom. Those who made action as well as study a priority are set free from prison. Rabbi Hanina, his companions, and by inference, his teacher, Akiva, sinned in their reinterpretation of Jewish ideology and in some sense desecrated sacred elements of Judaism by denigrating involvement in this world.

We see, then, subsequent generations trying to once again reorder the priorities of Jewish values and reinterpret the legacy of Akiva and his students. Yet the ideology that made the study of Torah paramount and that discounted participation in mundane activity continued to have enormous appeal. Living in exile, with a history of repeated persecution, Jews found comfort in meeting their God in the pages of the books they copied, studied, and commented on so diligently.

Judaism did not develop all of a piece. The Talmud, as well as other records of the tradition, sound a cacophony of voices, attitudes, and schools of thought. In Judaism's peculiar development, each historical layer and school of thought was reported so that there is no single or final encapsulation representing an authoritative Jewish creed. New theological outlooks simply coexisted alongside the old, never fully replacing them.

Yet the theology of the generation after Bar Kochba was not merely one school of thought among many, for it was their system of thought that became institutionalized. Until then interpretation had been transmitted orally, but these rabbis were responsible for recording the authoritative interpretive texts.

> The author of the anonymous portions of the Mishna is Rabbi Meir,
> of the Sifra* [83]—Rabbi Judah Ilai,
> of the Sifre—Rabbi Simeon Yohai,
> and of the Tosefta—Rabbi Nehemiah;
> and all of them follow Rabbi Akiva. [84]

This dictum reflects the prodigious editorial work these rabbis engaged in, the centerpiece of which was the publication of the Mishna by their students. Upon its publication, shortly after the close of the second century, the Mishna was received as the authoritative compendium of Jewish law, and all subsequent Jewish legal authority traces its development from the Mishna. Thus, the teaching transmitted by the generation after Bar Kochba and their students became the pillars of the tradition, frequently more studied and probed in subsequent eras than the Bible itself. Although the Mishna was edited by Rabbi Judah the Prince and sometimes reflects his more conservative theology rather than the radical reconstruction of Akiva's students, nevertheless there is no doubt that the rabbis most frequently mentioned in the Mishna are those of the generation after Bar Kochba. Similarly, it is clear that the subject matter and concerns of this work were shaped by them. [85]

Their theology triumphed in yet another way: the publication of these texts introduced a new level of intricacy into Jewish tradition, and Jews in future ages would find it difficult to understand their culture unless they devoted themselves to studying the

---

* The *Sifre* is the midrash, early rabbinic commentary on Deuteronomy, the *Sifra* is the midrash on Numbers.

corpus of rabbinic literature. Such study became a primary motif of Jewish religious life.

The same historical forces that influenced this era, leading it to take the theological position it did, were to influence later Jewish life again and again. Until our own time, each new persecution would teach Jews, once more, that their salvation was not in the historical drama now playing out its script, but in a world beyond.

For instance, while individual acts of martyrdom became a crucial theme in the second century, the practice of mass martyrdom, suicide exercised by whole communities faced with persecution, is first recorded by the Jewish chroniclers of the First Crusade (1098). These eleventh- and twelfth-century texts incorporate the theological stances displayed by the Biblical authors and by the generation of Bar Kochba.

The communities of the Rhine, faced with hordes of Christians demanding their conversion and threatening their lives, were willing to engage in mass suicide rather than undergo baptism. They took the lives of their own children for the sake of their faith, for the Sanctification of the Name of God. They interpreted what was happening both as punishment for sins and also as the achievement of a state of righteousness that would assure them paradise.

The chronicler's description of their martyrdom is a powerful story of the cruel fate these communities met. Mothers slaughtering their children to save them from forced conversion, Crusaders bursting upon roomfuls of Jews and murdering every man, woman, and child. But the rhetorical flourishes the chroniclers give their story are modeled on earlier images. Thus, for instance, the sacrifice of Isaac forms the literary background for a heartrending tale:

> There was a certain young man named R. Meshullam ben R. Isaac. He called out loudly to all those standing there and to Zipporah his helpmate: "Listen to me both great and small. This son, God gave me. My wife Zipporah bore him in her old age and his name is Isaac. Now I shall offer him up as did our ancestor Abraham his son Isaac." Zipporah replied: "My lord, my lord. Wait a bit. Do not stretch forth your hand against the lad whom I have raised and brought up and whom I bore in my old age. Slaughter

me first, so that I not witness the death of the child." He then replied: "I shall not delay even for a moment. He who gave him to us will take him as his portion. He will place him in the bosom of Abraham our ancestor." He then bound Isaac his son and took in his hand the knife with which to slaughter his son and made the benediction for slaughtering. The lad answered amen. He then slaughtered the lad. He took his screaming wife. The two of them departed together from the chamber and the crusaders killed them....[86]

The victims of the Crusades in trying to comprehend their fate were not theological innovators but drew their self-understanding from ideas permeating Rabbinic literature. These victims may have gained comfort from the idea of placing themselves within the tradition. On the one hand they say, "Our sins brought it about that the enemy overcame them [the Jewish defenders] and captured the gate."[87] On the other hand, at the moment of their dying the chronicler puts these words in their mouths:

For the moment the enemy will kill us....but we shall remain alive; our souls [will repose] in paradise, in the radiance of the great light, forever.... Ultimately one must not question the ways of the Holy One blessed be he and blessed be his name, who gave us the Torah and commanded us to put to death and to kill ourselves for the unity of his holy name. Blessed are we if we do his will and blessed are all those who are killed and slaughtered and who die for the Unity of His Name. Not only are they privileged to enter the world to come and sit in the circle of the saintly... What is more, they exchange a world of darkness for a world of light, a world of pain for a world of happiness, a transitory world for a world that is eternal and everlasting.[88]

The rabbinic glorification of martyrdom, with its emphasis on other-worldliness, is fully incorporated in the mentality animating this chronicle: death is seen as a release, as a means of achieving a higher goal.

The martyrdom of Akiva and his rabbinic colleagues became the perspective by which Jews throughout the Middle Ages arrived at their own self-understanding. These medievals poetically elaborated the story of the saintly deaths of Akiva and his colleagues and made it one of the most central liturgical moments of the liturgy of the Day of Atonement, the holiest day of the Jewish calendar (Eilah Ezkara).

Other rabbis and thinkers might try to modify the stance of Akiva and his students, but the opinion of the latter dominated Jewish history. The outlook of Akiva and his students was incorporated and institutionalized in the publication and dissemination of the normative texts of rabbinic Judaism. And the history of subsequent Jewish persecution (the martyrdom of the generation of Bar Kochba was but a rehearsal for what was to loom so large in the fate of Jewry in the Middle Ages) made the constant return to this theology necessary.

9 THE MEDIEVAL AND MODERN HERITAGE

*Later Judaism was formed by the
primacy of study as a religious value,
and utilized the theology of Akiva and
his students to understand and respond
to subsequent Jewish suffering.*

The generation after Bar Kochba transformed the Jewish people into
the "people of the book" and, in the long night of exile, the elaboration of "the book" was frequently to have a greater reality for Jews
than the terrible actuality of life outside the House of Study.

This ability of Torah study to act as a defense against the
external crises that Jews suffered and to function as a primary
instrument of salvation endured throughout the Middle Ages and
well into the twentieth century. To analyze the full breadth of
medieval Jewish theology would overwhelm this work, but a few
brief examples will demonstrate the continuity of ideas.

Moses Maimonides is universally considered the greatest
Jewish medieval thinker, perhaps the greatest Jewish philosopher
of all time. His own life embodied the communal and personal
suffering that was the lot of many Jews in the Middle Ages: born
in 1135, in Cordoba, Spain, he and his family were forced into exile
by a conservative Moslem revolution and wandered for years
through Spain and North Africa. Having settled in Fez, they were
forced to move on when religious persecution once more hounded
them and Maimonides' teacher was martyred. Settling for a short
period in Israel, they moved again, this time perhaps for financial
reasons, to Egypt, where Maimonides again found himself bereft
when his brother, who served as both his business partner and
companion, died on a trading voyage.

This twelfth-century Jewish thinker expounded the most significant philosophic reconstruction of Judaism in the Middle Ages. In his system, contemplation and understanding are given pride of place and become the central value, the essential goal of life. The acquisition of knowledge and understanding is considered to be the essence of our humanity. In fact, so significant is intellect to the Maimonidean system that it becomes the sole point of correlation between the divine and the human. The very first chapter of Maimonides' *Guide to the Perplexed* argues that the only possible meaning of the divine image in the human is the intellect:

> It was because of...the divine intellect conjoined with man, that it is said of the latter that he is "in the image of God and in His likeness...."[89]

If the intellect constitutes the sole similitude between the human and the divine then it makes sense that intellectual activity can ultimately be the only kind of redemptive life for Maimonides. In fact the *Guide to the Perplexed* does not mention either Messianic fulfillment or even a special role for Israel, but instead, repeatedly places the intellectual contemplation of God as the end of human activity, equating intellectual contemplation with redemption itself.

Thus, the last chapter delineates four different kinds of human beings and describes the highest level:

> The fourth species is the true human perfection; it consists in the acquisition of the rational virtues—I refer to the conception of intelligibles, which teach true opinions concerning the divine things.[90]

For Maimonides the highest achievement the human is capable of is intellectual understanding, which is, ultimately, the knowledge of God.

Maimonides even argues that the person who achieves intellectual perfection avoids suffering. (*Guide to the Perplexed*, III, 51) Students of Maimonides have debated how to understand this assertion, two differing interpretations being possible: either the person who achieves intellectual understanding will behave in such a way as to avoid disastrous consequences, or, intellectual attainment will give one the skills to overcome the sense of suffering by putting one's own condition in proper perspective.

> ...in the measure in which the faculties of the body are weakened and the fire of the desires is quenched, the intellect is strengthened.... The result is that when a perfect man is stricken with years and approaches death, this apprehension increases very powerfully, joy over this apprehension and a great love for the object of apprehension become stronger, until the soul is separated from the body at that moment in this state of pleasure. Because of this the Sages have indicated with reference to the deaths of Moses, Aaron, and Miriam that the three of them died by a kiss.... Their purpose was to indicate that the three of them died in the pleasure of this apprehension due to the intensity of passionate love....which in true reality is salvation from death....[91]

Here we find encapsulated the themes that have been discussed throughout this section. It is knowledge which constitutes salvation. Through the achievement of understanding, a person exits from the trials of history into the greater reality—even overcoming death—leaving this world while lovingly contemplating God. History and the lived life have less significance than the achievement of this eternal truth. One can imagine that Maimonides had learned in his own painful life that it was only intellectual attainments, portable as they were, which could be carried in exile and which could serve as a joyous substitute for the worldly suffering constantly encountered. Maimonides expanded the meaning of Torah to include all intellectual attainments, both secular science and philosophy and religious texts. God is known both through creation and through revelation. But though the concept of Torah has taken on new meaning, the centrality of study as a means of contemplating God constitutes the same idea which animated the thought of the earlier rabbis.

In the High Middle Ages, Jewish mysticism vied with philosophy for acceptance as the ground of Jewish religiosity, and Jewish mystics, like the philosophers who were their rivals, engaged in a major reinterpretation of Judaism. Yet just as for Maimonides there is significant continuity of ideas even as he formulated the tradition in a new way, so too the mystics, while developing a new understanding of Jewish spirituality, also embodied some of the essential ideas we have discussed here: the central place of Torah, of study and of intellectual understanding.[92] Gershom Scholem, the great historian of Jewish mysticism, points out that unlike the Christian world where mystics were frequently outside the normative life of the Church, among Jews mysticism was most often the theology of the elite, the rabbinically learned community. Not surprisingly then the medieval Jewish mysticism which Scholem describes is a contemplative one, seeking theosophical understanding of the Godhead.[93]

In the Zohar, the classic text of Jewish mysticism, Torah is identified with God's Kingship, which is the connecting link between the purely spiritual and the physical world. In this system, Torah is not discarded as a central value, but is now understood as forming the very means of attachment (devekut) to God.

The chief concern of these mystics is to arrive at a proper understanding of the nature of God. It is a mysticism in which intellectual play and mental contemplation have significant roles. In fact, many mystical texts center on developing an intellectual system in which to understand God and God's emanation into this world. There is a direct parallel between classic rabbinic study and what was understood as mystical contemplation: it is right understanding which is salvific.

These themes are continuous throughout the history of Jewish mysticism. Even the eighteenth-century Eastern European Hasidic movement, which is often understood as a revolt against the Torah-centered approach of the ruling rabbinic leadership, exhibits the same tendencies. For instance, the first book published by the movement, the Toldot Yaakov Yosef argues that:

> According to what I received from my master [The Baal Shem Tov, the founder of the movement] the essence of occupying oneself with Torah and prayer is to attach oneself to the inner spirituality, the infinite light, in the letters of Torah and the liturgy...for knowledge of the future, and understanding of all events will come from the Torah....[94]

Through attachment to the letters of Torah one achieves union with the Divine. Although the sentences have been stripped of intellectual content, the letters still form the ladder to heaven and so through the proper contemplation of Torah one achieves enlightenment. The full elucidation of the themes of Jewish mysticism is a task which contemporary scholars are engaged in. The subject is much more complex than the way I have presented it here. But any analysis of mystical themes needs to keep in mind the degree to which intellectual concerns form a central motif of these texts.

The legacy of Akiva and his students is that Torah and intellectual contemplation are the way to God. It is a theology summed up at the turn of this century by the Hebrew national poet, Hayim Nahman Bialik, who wrote an encomium to the place the study of Torah had in Jewish history. The poem achieved immediate acclamation and is still taught in many Jewish classrooms.

If thou wouldst know the mystic fountain whence
thy brethren going to their slaughter drew
in evil days, the strength and fortitude
to meet grim death with joy, and bare the neck
to every sharpened blade and lifted axe,
Or leap into the flame of ascending fires
and saintlike die with "Ehad"* on their lips.

If thou wouldst know the mystic fountain whence
thy stricken brethren crushed and overcome
by hellish pains and fangs of scorpions
drew, patience, firmness, trust—heaven's comfort,
and iron might to bear, relentless toil,
with stooped shoulders to bear a loathsome life,
and endlessly to suffer and endure...

If thou wouldst know, O humble brother mine—
go to the house of study grown old and hoary,
...see it, in the long nights of desolating winter
or in the scorching, blazing sunny days,
...If God has left there still a remnant small,
thine eyes shall even to this day behold
through somber shadows cast by darkened walls
in isolated nooks or by the stove,
stray, lonely Jews, like shades from eras past,
dark, mournful Jews with faces lean and wan.

---

* "Ehad" is the last word of the "Hear O Israel, the Lord Our God, the Lord is One," which is recited before death, especially before martyrdom. The last letter is always drawn out, as if it were a dying breath.

Yes, Jews who bear the weight of exile's yoke,
forgetting toil in brittled Talmud pages
and poverty in tales of bygone days,
who rout their cares in psalmic songs…

This house is but a little spark, a remnant
saved by a miracle, from that great fire,
kept by thy fathers always on their altars.
Who knows—perhaps the torrents of their tears
translated and ferried us to this new place?
Perhaps with their prayers they asked us of the Lord,
and in their deaths bequeath us a life,
a life that will endure forevermore.[95]

Bialik, the twentieth-century secularist, stands outside the House of Study. The world of piety and Torah is not his. Yet even he insists that only in continuity with Torah can Judaism survive. The new evolving Jewish culture must be stamped with Jewish intellect. Modern secularist Jews must continue in the same intellectual vein as their pietistic forebears. Jewish survival in the exile depended on Torah. In the House of Study one could cling to an ark against the storms of persecution. There one found the spark of life, a remaining cinder of the Temple, whose light must be kept burning and then passed on. And now this spark must yet keep the people warm in their travels and new beginnings.

PART THREE

The Holocaust

THE HOLOCAUST

Introduction

In 1492, tragedy once again struck the Jewish community: it was exiled from Spain. What made the event especially painful was the memory of the unique cultural contributions that community had achieved. In fact, though, banishment had become a well rehearsed part of Jewish life in Europe: France, England, parts of Germany, some city states in Italy had all expelled their Jews.

But the discovery of the new world which that date also heralded was significant for Jewry in quite a different way. It signaled the breaking out of a new world all over Europe. Jews were still to experience many of the abuses that had been their fate throughout the Middle Ages. In fact, in 1648, Polish Jewry suffered enormous losses during the Chmelnicski uprising, and the community became so downtrodden that it never again recovered the privileged status it had experienced till then.

The changes brought about by Enlightenment thinking profoundly effected first Western European and then Eastern European Jewry. The assumption of the status of citizen, the acquisition of equal rights, and the guaranteed entrance into the community at large created a new set of conditions for Jewish life. It was possible to think that Jewish identity had permanently changed and that a new era of human existence had been ushered in which would be characterized by mutual understanding and brotherhood.

To be sure there were signs that these new conditions had also given birth to a new disease—modern anti-Semitism. Pogroms and blood libels in Russia, the election of an anti-Jewish mayor in Vienna, the Dreyfus incident in France all pointed to the danger of utopian thinking. Poets, artists and philosophers could see through the fabric of their society and adumbrate what would come. A Kafka would prove hauntingly prophetic. But most people could reasonably believe that modernity had ushered in a new era, that humanity had profoundly changed, and that scientific progress pointed to the evolution of new social patterns.

The Holocaust put the lie to these assumptions as it put the lie to so many other self-delusions. The Holocaust has become the datum which now shapes the core of our self-understanding.

10 DESCENT INTO CHAOS

What happened in the Holocaust is different from what occurred in other persecutions of the Jew and transforms both Jewish and human self-understanding.

The Holocaust is the closing parenthesis for much of Jewish life; it kills the spirit as well as the body. Whoever enters the kingdom of night cannot emerge whole, cannot remain the same person but must be deeply transformed. And as much as all of humanity is affected, the Jew even more so: the remnant of Jewry that emerges from the war does so having been thrown and shaped and fired into new form. We who live after are different from those who came before.

For the Jew, the relationship with God, one's own self-identity as a member of this people, and the connection with the rest of humanity are fundamentally and profoundly changed. One cannot be a Jew without being touched at the most fundamental level by images of the Holocaust. And insofar as being a Jew is a paradigm of the larger human family, humanity itself is transformed. Good and evil, holy and unholy, divinity and secularity all take on new colorations of meaning.

So much turned to smoke in that conflagration, so much disappeared, physically and spiritually. From one perspective, the Holocaust is part of a continuum of persecution in Jewish history

But that says too little, for tragically the Holocaust extends beyond that history and confronts us with a new dimension. Here we are forced to painfully say, "Would that the destruction had achieved only the level of the past," for then so much and so many would have been saved.

Our generation has been forced to witness mass destruction on a previously unimagined scale; our conscious and our sub-conscious have now absorbed visions of unparalleled evil.

The extent of the death toll almost cannot be enumerated; it certainly can never be fully pictured. It is so immense that the base numbers for accounting are figures rounded out to the nearest million: six million Jews dead, a million and a half children among them. The effort to list all those who died is doomed to failure. Millions of people, whole cities, towns, and villages are lost in some black hole of history, their stories untellable, for the only ones who knew them are themselves victims. Had Hitler won, undoubtedly every Jew alive would be dead. In Prague the Nazis assembled a museum of Jewish artifacts so that a world without Jews might appreciate what had been accomplished in their destruction.

Here one goes beyond any localized pogrom or even national tragedy. In less than ten years French, Dutch, Belgian, Danish, Greek, Czech, Polish, Hungarian, Rumanian, Italian, Latvian, Lithuanian, Ukrainian, and, of course, German and Austrian Jewry ended, and the litany can go on. All of Europe, stretching from the Atlantic well into Russia, was decimated of its Jews.

Along with this physical annihilation was cultural strangulation. The history of European Jewry, a 2,000-year epoch with numerous golden ages, ended. The story of a whole language, Yiddish, is over. The rich fabric of European Jewish life, of scholars and poets, of talmudists and story tellers, of theologians and violinists, of thespians and comics, is gone. The fecund symbiosis of Jewish culture and the German language, the world of Freud and Buber, of Kafka and Einstein, is aborted. And the Eastern European Jewish community—the Maskilim and Hasidim, socialists and hebraists, rabbinic masters and secular novelists of the largest Jewish community the world has ever known, are gone. The Bund and the Musar Yeshivot whose clashing sounded the voice of Jewish renaissance are both now stilled. That unique cultural life will never throb again.

The vastness of the devastation belongs to our modern era, overwhelming all other tragic memories. The totality of the Nazi destruction cannot be captured by any of the previous names we have used to describe Jewish persecution: pogroms, purges, inquisitions, mob actions are names out of an older Jewish history. The English language demands a new more horrifying name: Holocaust—the systematic burning of an entire people.[1]

The vastness of this decimation has meant that almost every Jew of European origin has some family member—whether sister, uncle, or cousin—who was killed in the Holocaust. Every Jew now residing in the United States or Israel or South America or Australia whose family originated in some European country was affected. North African and Middle Eastern Jewry also felt the proximity of the Nazi threat. Almost every Jew alive has been touched in a deeply personal way that almost makes each one of them a survivor.

More, the extinguishing of whole cultures has meant that Jewry is not only physically bereft but spiritually deprived. No longer are hundreds of Yiddish poets and novelists upbraiding their people, telling their stories, teaching them how to live and love. A vital religious center was swept away as well: nine of every ten rabbis living at the time died.

Not only are European Jewry and their world gone, but an element of the Jewish past has been expunged. Our history is no longer the same, for we now know that the Jewish past itself was unable to guide the victims through this tragedy. Turning to the past, depending on historical precedent in fact, helped the work of devastation. Worse, the Nazis consciously bowdlerized and used the Jew's past as a means of destruction. They intentionally played on the methods Jews had adopted over the centuries to mitigate the horror of persecution in order to effectuate the "Final Solution." Jews had learned to live through a thousand years of European persecution by bribing officials, ransoming captives, befriending powerful government ministers, or by having a friend in court who in some cases was himself Jewish. The Nazis anticipated these responses and subverted them to their own ends.

The Nazi authorities purposefully encouraged Jewish hopefulness that bribery would stop the transports, first as part of a
general policy of lulling the population into docility so as to more
easily manipulate them, and, secondly, as a means to extract
wealth from Jews before their destruction. But in the end, no
matter what their status, all Jews were transported and stripped of
their possessions.

> It goes without saying that all this bribery failed to change the
> ultimate fate of the doomed Jews. Whatever success the bribes may
> have had was only temporary. In the last analysis bribery was only
> another form of spoilation of Jewish property by the Nazis. Jews
> themselves deliberately gave up their possessions into the hands of
> their oppressors in the fervent, though futile, hope that perhaps,
> somehow, at the very last moment, delivery might yet come....[2]

The historian Isiah Trunk takes the argument further: the very
establishment of Jewish councils by Jewish communities, the very
attempt to bring order into the chaos caused by the Nazi invasion
aided the German policy of extermination. When Jews took a
housing census so that space in the ghetto could be rationally
apportioned and refugees provided for, they generated a death list
for the Nazis. When Jews set up factories in the ghettoes to earn
money for food and medical supplies and to prove their
"usefulness" to the Germans, they ended up by sewing Nazi
Wehrmacht uniforms. In perhaps the ultimate irony of this horror,
scrounging for materials, they turned old Talesim — ritual prayer
shawls—into uniform linings.[3] Never has the past been so
demonically used by the persecutors. Never has the past been
such a poor compass for the present.[4]

Of course, not only Jewish values were mocked. Everything of
significance took on ironic meaning through Nazi use and
therefore their worth becomes questionable to us. Any sense of
culture as humanizing is caricatured by the knowledge that an
orchestra played Strauss waltzes to greet the arrivals at
Auschwitz. And we must wonder about our commonplace beliefs
in humanism and scientific progress, knowing the uses Nazis
wearing white lab coats made of modern instruments of
civilization. Mengele the angel of death, standing on the arrival
platform, deciding who shall live and who shall die, was a medical

doctor. In the camps he conducted experiments for the "advancement of science." His techniques carried out on human guinea pigs, practiced without anesthetics, led to the maiming and death of most of those experimented on. Yet he thought of himself as a man of science, advancing civilization.

Indeed, it is the abuse of modern technocratic culture which helps form our singular sense of horror at what the Nazis achieved. This total devastation could only be accomplished by the complete mobilization of the full force of a modern technocratic culture. The overwhelming extent of destruction would not have been possible without the tools of modernism. All aspects of culture were marshalled for death, rather than for progress. Killing by rifle was too inefficient, too slow, too messy, too personally involving. Instead, the clinical efficiency of chemical annihilation and the precision of science was mobilized for destruction. A death camp might exhibit the sanitary standards of the modern laboratory.

> The gas chambers and crematoria were set up so diabolically that the victims really did not become aware of their fate until the last minute. Everything was sparkling clean in the huge crematory. Nothing pointed to the fact that only the day before thousands had been gassed and cremated there.
>
> Nothing was left of them, not even a speck of dust on the armatures.[5]

We read with horror as this pursuit of cleanliness is given a special meaning in ridding the hospital barracks at Auschwitz of lice:

> Then Mengele came. He was the first one to rid the entire women's camp of lice. He simply had an entire block gassed. Then he disinfected that block, put in a bathtub, and let the inmates of the adjoining block bathe there. And it went on like that. After this procedure a compound was free of lice. But it began with the gassing of the 750 women in the first block.[6]

Culture, science and medicine are mobilized for murder; all life-affirming values have become instruments of death. Hygienic control, "cleaning up," is accomplished by the off-hand death of 750 people. In such circumstances, cleanliness, health, science, progress, and even life itself have lost all meaning. Civilization ceases its orienting function, becoming a servant of maniacal evil.

All that signifies hopefulness in the modern world becomes an instrument of death. All language is turned on its head.

At times the bureaucracy of death would take on aspects of a well-managed business. Exacting records had to be kept. People had to be numbered, and their disposition accounted for, as one would inventory stock in a factory.

> Personal data, day of death, and cause of death had to be entered with great precision. If there was a typing error, they might become terribly angry.[7]

The office had to be properly managed; no mistakes were allowed. Yet, the exactitude serves as a bizarre cover:

> Most of the recorded causes of death were fictitious. Thus, for example, we were never allowed to enter, "shot while escaping" in the book; I had to write "heart failure." And "cardiac weakness" was the cause listed, not "malnutrition."[8]

And those who went straight from transport to crematoria were never numbered or recorded.

Proper accounting, orderly management, methods of efficient production take on disembodied meaning. Modern bureaucratic culture lulls us into a sense of order, but as soon as we begin to focus we discover the void. One "doctor," whose task was to choose chronic patients from the infirmary for death by phenol injection, always chose some extra people in order to "round out the figure."[9] Thus proper accounts are kept!

Seen from the vantage point of the Holocaust, all our perspectives, our planes of sight, become so entangled that the world becomes surreal. The continuity of reality is sundered when every value previously held precious and infused with lofty purpose now ironically becomes an instrument of cruelty.

For as one moves closer to this well-ordered factory and begins to focus more clearly, understanding dawns that all this proper management, all this surface normality, is directed to nothing less than the transformation of human beings into waste products. We experience a profound disorientation and dislocation, an uncontrollable dizziness, as all hopeful signposts are turned towards this grotesque end. As Richard Rubenstein has put it:

> The stench of the corpses and the use of people as raw material to be turned into feces....was the chief industry of the camps. There

were, of course, subordinate industries, such as the turning of the fat of the Jews' bodies into....`pure Jewish soap'...their skin into luminous lampshades.... Nevertheless...the whole enterprise was directed primarily to the manufacture of corpses. The decaying corpses represented the final transformation of human beings into feces.[10]

This turning of human beings—Jews—into something other than human is programmatic. For the Nazis, along with attempting the "Final Solution" of the Jewish problem, the complete biological elimination of the Jewish people, also aimed at the complete dehumanization of the Jew. Rubenstein remarks,

In Nazi propaganda, the Jews are identified with lice, vermin, and insects, the very organisms for which an insecticide like cyclon B was most appropriate.[11]

To create a super-race, the Nazis took a part of humanity and set about consciously making them less than human. What is intended is more than physical devastation; what is wanted is not only physical extermination, but the ridding of the Jew of any association with humanity. This demanded the identification of the Jew as lice and disease, as repulsive, loathsome waste. This "spiritual" task was central to the Nazi treatment of the Jew. This program began to be implemented in the very first days of occupation, as the Nazis rolled eastward, and reached its height in the work camps and concentration camps.

Not only were Jews to be killed but on the way they were to be stripped completely of their humanity. The Jews were so deeply humiliated that in the end they were made to become their own despoiler. Humiliation was an essential element of the Nazi program. Bruno Bettleheim reports[12] that the Nazis carefully initiated you into a world of terror and loss of self-respect, then they had you. Similarly another survivor reports:

One lady walking in the street wearing a Persian lamb coat was dragged to Gestapo headquarters. There she was ordered to take off her underwear and scrub the floor with it. Then, made to put the dirty, wet underwear back on, she was thrown into the street without her coat. It was very cold, and she caught pneumonia and died.[13]

The Nazi radar discovered what was most cherished, that which would result in the greatest loss of personal dignity, of self-respect. One woman who always had thought of herself as pretty describes how she felt as the long red hair she had lovingly combed was forcibly cut off with a razor, nicking her bald scalp:

> When he finished, he picked a handful of hair from the floor and waved it in front of me. "This is all there is! You Jews.... How do you like yourself now!" he shouted. "Proud swine! No pride left now! Jew!" He led me back to the cell and threw me on the floor.... I put my hand to my head and felt the bareness and nakedness of my head, and tears came. I could never be quite the same again, it seemed impossible. So it is gone, I thought. There is nothing left for me to protect.[14]

The Nazis made sure that nothing sacred remained, that everything valued was despoiled. Anything sacred was purposefully trampled on and disported. Warsaw Jewry was ordered to enter the ghetto on Rosh Hashonnah, the New Year, and transports to concentration camps were organized on or before Jewish holy days so those left behind would have no holiday. Nothing sacred would remain untouched by spoilation.

> The refinements of cruelty were reserved especially for pious Jews and rabbis, whose traditional Jewish garb—hat and long coat—and whose beard and sidelocks identified them as quintessentially Jewish.... The Germans deliberately chose observant Jews to force them to desecrate and destroy the sacred articles of Judaism, even to set fire to synagogues. In some places the Germans piled the Torah scrolls in the marketplace, compelling the Jews to set fire to the pile, dance around it, singing, "We rejoice that the shit is burning."[15]

Referring to Jews as swine, the Nazis proceeded to turn rhetoric into reality. Concentration camps provided the most intense way to accomplish this. The victims were to be turned into objects of loathing, into excrement—totally humiliated. Terrence des Pres has accurately called this aspect of the camps "excremental assault":

> The fact is that prisoners were systematically subjected to filth. They were the deliberate target of excremental assault. Defilement was a constant threat, a condition of life from day to day, and at any moment it was liable to take abruptly vicious and sometimes fatal forms. The favorite pastime of one Kapo was to stop prisoners just

before they reached the latrine. He would force an inmate to stand at attention for questioning, then make him "squat in deep knee bends until the poor man could no longer control his sphincter and 'exploded,'" then beat him; and only then, "covered with his own excrement, the victim would be allowed to drag himself to the latrine."[16]

There was no escaping the filth that was everywhere.

There was one latrine for thirty to thirty-two thousand women and we were permitted to use it only at certain hours of the day. We stood in line to get into this tiny building knee-deep in human excrement. As we all suffered from dysentery, we could rarely wait until our turn came and soiled our ragged cloths, which never came off our bodies, thus adding to the horror of our existence by the terrible smell which surrounded us like a cloud. The latrine consisted of a deep ditch with planks thrown across it at certain intervals. We squatted on these planks like birds perched on a telegraph wire, so close together that we could not help soiling one another.[17]

And the horror of these conditions increased manifoldly because of illness.

Everybody in the block had typhus....it came to Bergen-Belsen in its most violent, most painful, deadliest form. The diarrhea caused by it became uncontrollable. It flooded the bottom of the cages; dripping through the cracks into the faces of the women living in the cages below, and mixed with blood, pus and urine formed a slimy, fetid mess on the floor of the barracks.[18]

Having destroyed all that was of value, having despoiled all that was sacred, having reduced the victims to filth and so humiliated them they could no longer think of themselves as men and women, the final tie with anything human had to be broken before they were totally eliminated. The most basic of human relationships, that between mother and child, child and parent, was then severed.

In April 1943, transports began to arrive from Warsaw. Because of the armed struggle at that time raging in the Warsaw ghetto, these unfortunates were treated with exceptional brutality. Women with children were singled out, led up to the fires, and after the executioners had their fill of watching their terror-stricken victims, the children were killed and tossed into the flames. While one batch was thus being finished off the others stood by, waiting their turn. Time and again, children were torn from their mother's arms and cast alive into the flames. Their fiendish tormentors would urge the mothers to jump heroically after their children, then taunt them for their cowardice when they failed to follow through.[19]

Furthermore, the victims would be forced themselves to become tormentors.

> The SS men guarding the prisoners amused themselves by chasing the twenty men of the work detail into the water hole.
> They had to jump into the water and swim. Then they ordered a prisoner named Isaac—he was called Isaac the Strong in the camp—to drown his comrades. Finally, they also ordered him to kill his own father. In the act of drowning his father, Isaac went berserk and started to scream....[20]

And so one's humanity was undone.

The Holocaust is a kingdom of night, the triumph of irrationality, of madness, of vicious and unmitigated evil, of a reality incomprehensible to those who experienced it and to those who come after. Here we are faced with a demonic silencing of the spirit, a silencing that no system of valuation, no framework, can comprehend.

The image of madness is an appropriate one, for something inside us has snapped. A sense of human rationality, a belief that human conscience can set limits, a faith in ourselves, in our innate sensibility, is lost. Now we know that the "impossible is possible,"[21] that all is possible; the range of human possibility has been diabolically expanded. We know we are capable of depths of evil previously unimagined.

> In the end, it was ruse, deception, cunning beyond anything the world had ever before seen, which accomplished what hunger and disease, terror and treachery, could not achieve. What defeated us was Jewry's unconquerable optimism, our eternal faith in the goodness of man, our faith that even a German, even a Nazi, could never have so far renounced his own humanity as to murder women and children coldly and systematically.[22]

Jewish experience is a microcosmic exemplar of a universal nightmare. Our sense of what it is to be human has been deeply attenuated. We meet such an intense reality of evil in the Holocaust that we are forced to incorporate a new and different understanding of what humanity is capable of.

And with this new knowledge all optimistic liberalism evaporates. Any simple trust in the basic and inevitable goodness of human beings is forfeited, any faith in the long-range victory of a general and progressive meliorism is dispelled. We now know the depth of humanity's capacity for evil. We are different because of the Holocaust, terribly different.

Elie Wiesel remarks,

> But I will have acquired the certitude that the man who measures himself up against the reality of evil always emerges beaten and humiliated.[23]

In the end, we are defeated by the Holocaust; we who would hear and read about it are after all diminished by the experience. We cannot view the Holocaust without being shattered; it is a jagged rock of history that we can only pass by, grazing and wounding ourselves.

Richard Rubenstein, the first American theologian to attempt to come to grips with the Holocaust, summed up this sense of negation by saying,

> There are no innocent men.... Civilization begins, not with the recognition by brothers of their impeccable virtue, but with the first and awesome discovery of their ineradicable guilt. In the beginning was the deed—the guilty deed. The man who confesses his own potential for murder, and that of his religious tradition, is far more likely to master this potential than the one who refuses this terrible truth about himself.[24]

We now know the depths of depravity to which the human species can descend. The range of human possibility, the depth of evil revealed by the Nazis, goes beyond anything previously imagined. Indeed, the inability to imagine anything so horrible limited the victims' ability to defend themselves.

The Nazis attacked the Jew to fundamentally transform the meaning of what it was to be human—to create a master race—and they succeeded, achieving the opposite. Having surveyed the human depravity demonstrated by the Nazis, we can never again relate to our own humanity in the same way: we can never trust ourselves; we must inevitably think less of ourselves. Some may assimilate this knowledge easily, but it is no wonder that a person who experienced the horror, having seen what life had turned into, would choose to stay with the dead.

> I once walked through a barrack filled with corpses, all of them stripped. Then I saw something moving between the corpses, and that something wasn't nude. It was a young girl. I pulled her to the outside and said, "Who are you?" She said she was a Greek Jewess from Salonika. "How long have you been here?" "I don't know." "Why are you here?" And she answered, "I can no longer live with the ones alive. I prefer to be with the dead." I gave her a piece of bread. By nightfall she was dead. [25]

Humanity had been undone.

11 THEOLOGICAL ASSESSMENTS

The tragedy of the Holocaust causes us to question the tradition of the significance of what it is to be a Jew, the meaning of providential care and the nature of our humanity. The Jew's ability to relate his or her own history to divine purpose is amputated here.

When we look up from contemplating the events that constitute the Holocaust, we feel overwhelmed and spent. We have no means to integrate what we have seen; language has exhausted its ability to comprehend. All our inherited patterns of thought are incapable of explaining this event. Just as trite and simplistic consolation can be more offensive to a mourner than silence, so too have inherited litanies that consoled previous generations become a mockery when offered in the context of the Holocaust.

Previous Jewish theologies and modes of comprehending tragedy exhibit a hollowness and irrelevance when used to explain this destruction. Rather than serving as balm for the soul, they are more like salt in a wound; to offer them is not only inappropriate but increases the pain of the victim.

Were we being destroyed "for our sins"? Would self-accusation as sinners explain away the destruction? Elie Wiesel describes a recitation of such a traditional confessional in the camps on Yom Kippur — the Day of Atonement:

> Then came the Vidui, the great confession. There again, everything rang false, none of it concerned us anymore. Ashamnu, we have sinned. Bagadnu, we have betrayed. Gazalnu, we have stolen. What? Us? We have sinned? Against whom? By doing what? We have betrayed? Whom? Undoubtedly this was the first time since God judged his creation that victims beat their breasts accusing themselves of the crimes of their executioners. Why did we take

responsibility for sins and offenses which not one of us could ever have had the desire or the possibility of committing? Perhaps we felt guilty despite everything. Things were simpler that way. It was better to believe our punishments had meaning, that we had deserved them; to believe in a cruel but just God was better than not to believe at all. It was in order not to provoke an open war between God and his people that we had chosen to spare him, and we cried out: "You are our God, blessed be your name. You smite us without pity, you shed our blood, we give thanks to you for it, O Eternal One, for you are determined to show us that you are just and that your name is justice!"[26]

The devastation wrought during the Holocaust is so vast, the evil so intense that it becomes a cruel mockery of God and of the victims to believe that it was in the least inspired or approved by God. What kind of God would we then believe in?

If those who died and suffered were sinful, the sin was that of being human. The victims were saints and sinners, heroes and cowards. A million-and-a-half children were killed; Eastern European Hasidic masters and Western European assimilated Jews all died the same death; socialists, Yiddishists, Talmudists, and pietists all went up in smoke. Who deserved this terrible fate? No rationalization could make us think of God as anything but cruel, a God we certainly would abandon if we believed that he had a hand in killing six million of his people. For what sin? For what ultimate plan? To enumerate any sins that might have caused such an event is only to increase the horror of the suffering, and to blaspheme both God and human.[27]

Nor does this demonic spoilation, this Nazi hell, allow us classic images of martyrdom, for the nature of the persecution of the Jew is changed. Although the Nazis' anti-Semitism developed out of the medieval image of the Jew,[28] the medieval attacks in the Christian and Moslem worlds were by and large fundamentally religious in character: one could escape through conversion, and one died by choice, for one's faith. But modern anti-Semitism is racial in character, one has no choice: it is simply one's fate. A new totalist enemy determines all by genetic record. The medieval German Jew, for instance, faced with the fanaticism of the Crusades, eschewed the option to convert and died for the "sanctification of God's name." This haunting faith, demonstrated again and again,

gave Jewish history its heroic quality.[29] But those who died amidst
the Holocaust included many who had been raised as Christians
or who, in fact, had chosen conversion. More were highly
assimilated, having given up any association with things Jewish.
So many of them died for a word whose meaning they did not
know. The Nuremburg laws defined as Jewish those who did not
have the slightest association with Jewishness, but whose genes
were somehow "tainted" by Jewish blood.[30] Many of the victims
did not "choose" to die as Jews: they did not know what they were
dying for. This is not a choice of fate, a martyrdom. There is almost
no more poignant image emerging from the camps than that of the
"Jewish" Catholics of Theresienstadt who daily celebrated mass
and who regularly studied New Testament with Leo Baeck, the
"Rabbi of Theresienstadt" who was expert in Greek, while on their
way to die as "Jews." Never before, in all the long history of medieval persecution, had persecuted "Jews" died as Christians.

In the twentieth century, both the persecution of the Jew and
Jewish self-understanding changed radically. Jews were not
persecuted for religious reasons by the Nazis, though their
demonic image of the Jew depended on inherited religious
imagery. Further, the persecution was enforced not by the Church
but by the State. Nor did Jews respond to what was happening to
them in religious categories. By and large, Jews did not retreat to
the synagogue to fast and confess their sins that they might be
saved. They did not "choose" to be martyrs.

For all who would die in the ghetto and in the concentration
camps, any element of choice was eliminated. Standing at the gate
to Auschwitz, Dr. Mengele, with the barely detectable motion of
his swagger stick, decided who shall live and who shall die. The
victims were treated like animals going to slaughter, hardly to be
expected to understand why they were dying. Here the only
choices were the whims of the oppressor. Had this community the
opportunity to choose, its members would have chosen life.

> There was an episode in the Kovno Ghetto that taught us a great
> deal.
> When that ghetto was being set up, the Germans brought us
> 5,000 white certificates with orders to distribute them only among
> laborers and artisans. At that time there were 29,000 Jews in the

Kovno Ghetto and we were well aware of the German's purpose in having us distribute those grim white certificates. So we were faced with the tragic question of how to distribute them. Were we to accept the fact that death transports awaited all the intellectuals, the women and the little children in the Ghetto? A terrible dilemma confronted us. Suddenly an idea was presented—I do not know by whom—to burn all the certificates and tell the Germans that we refused to distribute them. In other words, "Do what you will." We knew well enough what they would do. But as soon as the idea became known in the Ghetto, dozens of people came to us speaking on behalf of hundreds of the common folk, common folk in the best sense of the term, and said to us, "You want to send us to death. What right have you to do that?" They did not speak about the generations to come. They spoke a very prosaic language, but it was the language of their instinct to live. There were only two alternatives in the Kovno Ghetto. One was to delay matters as long as possible. Almost any price would be paid to gain time. The other alternative was to go out against the Germans with bare hands, in other words to do something that in realistic language meant collective suicide. And I ask you, has anyone the right to decide that a community must, even for considerations of honor or any other lofty motive, commit suicide?[31]

These Jews wanted to live, not die; they did not want to be noble martyrs, dying and suffering in defense of the faith. Few of them believed this was a test issuing from God.

In the end their dying, too, was unromantic. Death by dysentery and disease[32] has no poetic quality.

At one time or another, everyone suffered from diarrhea or dysentery. And for prisoners already starved and exhausted, it was fatal more often than not: "Those with dysentery melted down like candles, relieving themselves in their clothes, and swiftly turned into stinking, repulsive skeletons who died in their own excrement."[33]

To die of typhus buried in one's own excreta, to be so starved that one dies eating one's own shoes, to die of bloating, having continually drunk water to ease the endless gnawing pain of hunger, is to depart without dignity. These deaths can never be glorified or romanticized. This was not martyrdom, this was utter negation. One did not die for anything. One died because one was named Jew, for no other reason, for no other purpose. There is no rationalizing these senseless deaths, they cannot be explained. Elie

Wiesel reports that he once asked the critic Alfred Kazin whether he thought the Holocaust had any meaning. The latter replied, "I hope not."[34]

Past litanies do not illuminate the Holocaust nor offer comfort and solace, and Jewish theology offers no guide to understand this event. In fact, to hear records of those who died reciting the old litanies is wrenching: a cantor, Fishel Bieter, called out as he died, "I accept this with love, if I must be an atonement-offering for the Jewish people.... I do not feel any pain for I am an atonement offering...."[35] We can hear these words and have only admiration for those who were able to say them with their dying breaths, but we cannot say them. We who come after, who know the vastness of the destruction and the overwhelming nature of what occurred, would find it a sacrilege to utter these words. To say that the Holocaust was an atonement would mean that six million Jews, having no choice in the matter, died for the sins of humanity. Yes, humanity sinned, but the sin was against the Jew. Did we have to die to prove that evil lives within the human heart, that modern technological humanity can multiply the horror of previous epochs? Do we have to die millions of deaths more in order to prove this point again?[36] We cannot say the victims were an atonement; the tragedy was too immense for such a simple response. For us to use such words is at best hollow, at worst obscene.

The Jew's ability to relate his or her own history to divine purpose is amputated here. For all our experience of tragedy, nothing prepared us for this tragedy; for all that we knew of persecution, what occurred went beyond our comprehension. Some chasm between ourselves and the world opened before us; some abyss between ourselves and our past appeared. We awake from our nightmare, yet it is still night: the surreal terror remains. We are surrounded by the silence of the deepest darkness: we have a new knowledge of what humans are capable of and of how limited divinity is. The time before we acquired this knowledge seems almost paradisiacal.

This sense that the conditions of Jewish life had radically changed, that all that went before has been overturned was captured by the Yiddish poet Jacob Glatstein, who immediately after the war, in 1946, wrote a masterful poem of theological protest:

Not the Dead Praise God

We received the Torah at Mount Sinai
and in Lublin we gave it back.
Not the dead praise God —
the Torah was given for the living.
And as we all together
stood in a body
at the Granting of the Torah,
so truly did we all die in Lublin.

The entire imagined people stood at Mount Sinai
and received the Torah:
the dead, the living, the yet unborn.
All the Jewish souls responded:
We will harken and obey!...

And as we all together
stood in a body
at the Granting of the Torah,
so truly did we all die in Lublin.
From everywhere pious souls came flying:
those who had lived out their lives
and the youthfully dead;
the persecuted, those tested in all fires,
the yet unborn.
All the departed Jews,
from Grandfather Abraham on,
were in Lublin at the Holocaust.
And all who stood at Mount Sinai
and received the Torah
took upon themselves the sacred deaths.
The souls clamored:
"We want to be dead together with our people,
we want to die once more."
Mother Sarah and Mother Rachel,
Miriam, and Deborah the Prophetess,
who perished praying and singing;
Moses, who so much did not want to die
when his time came,
died once more;
and his brother Aaron,
and King David,
and the Rambam, and the Vilna Gaon;
the Maharam and the Marashel,

the Seer and Akiva Eiger...
Accompanying each sacred soul
died hundreds of souls
of pious, already departed Jews...

An extinguished desolate Sinai smoked
above the gas chambers
and pious departed souls...

It is you after all,
you were the hushed, desolate, returned Torah.
You stood on Mount Sinai
and wept your tears into a dead world —
from the beginning to beginning to beginning.

And this is what you cried:
"We received the Torah at Mount Sinai
and in Lublin we gave it back.
Not the dead praise God —
the Torah was given for the living."[37]

It is fitting that Yiddish, a language that suffered a fatal blow in the devastation of Europe, should in its dying breath express the enormity of what had occurred, the severance of the Jewish people from its past. Yiddish, which had formed the most intimate connection between God and Israel, Yiddish, which had been the holiest of Jewish secular languages, now became the language that bore the burden of expressing the pain of amputation, the anger and hatred God's desertion evokes. Glatstein speaks of the abrogation of the covenant between God and Israel, for the contract between the two has been violated in the vastness of the destruction. Had the faithfulness of generations that transmitted the name "Jew" and kept alive the burden of history come to this?

Where was God at Auschwitz? If ever there was to be Divine intervention was it not demanded at this moment? Were not enough prayers mouthed by the victims to warrant Divine response? Were the words not offered with the proper intent? Was this not the right moment to intercede?

If God's providence, the divine relationship to particular human beings and their fate, has any earthly relevance at all, should not the manifestation of that care have been at this hour? If God's word and meaning permeate the world, if God's order is at the heart of creation, if God's presence is affirmed and articulated in history, if Divine providence acts in time, why was God absent at Auschwitz? Auschwitz was a place devoid of God's presence, and if the Divine was absent here then where does God dwell?

The world was filled with cries and whispers of death. No one heard the cry of the wounded, the shock of the slaughter of family after family. The gas chambers were hermetically sealed. And God, too, hermetically sealed himself, in silence. It is a silence terrible and overwhelming, engulfing and overcoming us. We are stopped in our tracks. Some inner part of our being is severed. Some ongoing conversation is ended. We are alone.

Martin Buber, "the philosopher of dialogue," himself a refugee of Nazi Germany, is painfully aware of this silence, this radical cleavage from God. He calls this moment "The Eclipse of God," a terminology that has biblical roots and was later developed by Jewish mystics. God hides his face, Providence withdraws into herself, and this absence leaves behind a world in chaos, the primordial state before God entered into relation with the world, at the beginning. Buber acknowledges God's absence in the Holocaust and seeks to connect it with these Biblical images:

> The Bible knows of God's hiding His face, of times when the contact between heaven and earth seems to be interrupted. God seems to withdraw Himself utterly from the earth and no longer to participate in its existence. The space of history is then full of noise, but empty of the divine breath. For one who believes in the living God, who knows about Him, and is fated to spend his life in a time of His hiddenness, it is very difficult to live.[38]

Buber knows the suffering experienced in the Holocaust is so vast, the evil so deep that one can never argue there is a redemptive quality in it. To attempt to excuse such suffering theologically would be heartless.

Buber faces the terrible silence, the awful absence of God. He recognizes the Holocaust as a moment when God disappeared from history, as an hour when prayers were unanswered. The Holocaust was a time of God's withdrawal from creation; a moment when holiness had no power on earth.

Yet this is no resolution either. For is not the hiddenness of God, God's absence when creation was turned into hell, a moment of absolute terror? Can we face a God who has withdrawn while death was rampant in the world? Can we pray to such a God? Can we enter into relationship with this Disappearing One? Does not our sadness overwhelm us? Has not something inside us been broken?

Can a mother ever again join with the father who turned his back while their son or daughter died? Can there ever be a return to "normality"? Would not that failure always define their relationship? Forever joined by tragedy, would they not then be alone and separate? We can not leave off asking these questions simply because we have found a new terminology to describe this state—"the eclipse of God."

Buber himself feels the pain of God's absence and would confront God with the horror wrought by the Divine absconding:

> ... how is a life with God still possible in a time in which there is an Auschwitz? The estrangement has become too cruel, the hiddenness too deep. One can still "believe" in the God who allowed these things to happen, but can one still speak to Him? Can one still hear his word? Can one still, as an individual and as a people, enter at all into a dialogic relationship with Him? Dare we recommend to the survivors of Auschwitz, the Job of the gas chambers, "Give thanks unto the Lord, for He is good; for his mercy endureth forever"?(Psalm 106:1)[39]

The words of the psalmist choke in our throats. How is prayer possible in our own time? What meaning is there in our listening for God? Is not our story together ended? Buber understands the terror of our unanswered cry in the night.

And yet Buber, in responding to these events, seeks solace: he tries to salvage something of the old relationship, and turns to the figure of Job, Job who also suffered endlessly, and in that figure Buber seeks a paradigm for our own time. Buber analyzes God's response, God's appearance at the end of Job's tale:

> And he [Job] receives an answer from God. But what God says to him does not answer the charge; it does not even touch upon it. The true answer that Job receives is God's appearance only, only this: that distance turns into nearness, that "his eye sees Him" (Job 42:7) that he knows Him again. Nothing is explained, nothing adjusted, wrong has not become right; nor cruelty kindness. Nothing has happened but that man again hears God's address.[40]

In other words, we must seek to find God's presence again and this should be our solace. If the Holocaust represents God's absence, then all we can ask for now is to face God once again.

But even as we feel the groping, stuttered quality of Buber's painful and awkward attempt to reestablish a life of faith after the Holocaust, we have to ask if Buber has not said too much. Is not something still being papered over? What is restored by simply hearing God's address again? Does God's mysterious return solve anything?

Perhaps Job's tale can end with a reconciliation between God and the sufferer achieved through God's reappearance and the restoration of Job's fortune, but that ending cannot work for us. For us there can be no restoration, no easy reconciliation. The hurt remains, nothing can make up for the vastness of the destruction. Job might be reconciled to a primal order at the heart of creation that cannot be immediately apprehended, but we cannot: too much has happened for that.

What ultimate plan could justify the death of so many millions? What ultimate end could explain the horror our eyes have seen? Would God's "presence" really be sufficient to answer our protest? What good would any "answer" be now? Does one really want to be with a God who has such "answers"?

For the implication of God's appearance at the end of the Book of Job is that Job's suffering is part of some larger picture, a piece in a master plan that only time can reveal, that is the burden of God's speech in the whirlwind. But we can not believe that the Holocaust is a part of some ultimate order; we can not have faith in the ultimate meaning of these events.

Buber, too, seems to understand that our situation may be different from Job's and hints at the nagging quality of the question in a closing paragraph:

> No, rather even now we contend, we too, with God, even with Him, the Lord of Being, whom we once, we here, chose for our Lord ... In such a state we await His voice, whether it comes out of the storm or out of a stillness that follows it. Though His coming appearance resembles no earlier one, we shall recognize again our cruel and merciful Lord.[41]

Buber recognizes that something fundamental has changed in our understanding of God, that the reconciliation in our own time cannot be the same as the one in Job. God's appearance now will "resemble no earlier one." Any new revelation will, first of all, have to deal with the cruelty of God. Our pain will always color the way we relate to God; the hurt must be included in any definition of the Divine we may have. We can only see God through the veil of our suffering.

But what understanding is this? What does it mean to worship a cruel silent God? What teaching does such a God represent? What kind of religious faith takes as its primary assumptions cruelty and despair? Is not living with a "cruel silent" God as shattering as any possible loss of faith? Is not the rule of a cruel silent God the Kingdom of the Absurd?

Buber, having gone to the brink of the abyss, ends his essay. It is the poet and concentration camp survivor who goes over the brink. Elie Wiesel has one of his characters say:

> A few years later, I saw just pious men walking to their death, singing, "We are going to break with our fire, the chains of the Messiah in exile." That's when the symbolic implication of what my teacher had said struck me. Yes, God needs man. Condemned to eternal solitude, he made man only to use him as a toy, to amuse himself. That's what philosophers and poets have refused to admit: in the beginning there was neither the Word nor Love, but laughter, the roaring, eternal laughter whose echoes are more deceitful than the mirages of the desert.[42]

The religious knowledge flowing from the Holocaust is madness. We are overcome with a sense of absurdity and irrationality as we gaze around at the ruins. If God's word pervades the world, is not what is revealed the triumph of chaos? If history reflects God's will in some way, then what is the message of our time? Our story has no meaning. This world is the creation of a cruel and silent God.

The disparity between the religious promise of blessing and the cursed reality of our recent history has brought us to a breaking point. The palpable absence of God in our own time violates such an essential core of our understanding of the Divine that we are forced to acknowledge that something has snapped. We cannot orient ourselves within a redemptive story anymore. And so Wiesel's world is a pastiche of madmen and insanity, phantasmagoria become reality. Who else but a madman would oversee such a nightmare? What else but cruel mocking laughter can describe God's relation to his creation?

Such is Wiesel's vision of the new revelation. This is the knowledge of God imparted by the Holocaust.

And if we have lost faith in God, surely we have lost faith in humanity as well. What society could we build that would prevent such horror from happening? Every moment we must be watchful, for in the next we might be led back into this black hole again. Can we genuinely believe that people in the twenty-first century will be better human beings than people in the twentieth? Already we have seen evidence of the opposite: genocide has become the path of this century—millions of people slaughtered in Third-World wars, hundreds of thousands killed by the advanced armaments developed and sold by the great powers. Even being a victim gives one no special moral claim to future good behavior as we have seen recently freed peoples commit the same acts they only just suffered themselves. Our history since the Holocaust has contained sufficient cruelty and injustice so that we can not say that the Holocaust is some exceptional moment, rather it is a revelation of who we truly are.

Richard Rubenstein argues that the Holocaust has destroyed hope, that there are no redemptionist ideologies possible after the Holocaust. We cannot believe in a God who will save us nor can we believe that salvation will come from humanity. There is no one in whom to put our trust; we can only walk on with the knowledge of our own inhumanity. And he offers this, as the only true salvation.

> Having lost everything, we have nothing further to lose ...we have passed all illusion and hope...we have lost all hope and faith...nothing is asked for, nothing is hoped for, nothing expected....[43]

Yet what is life like without hope? Can we live in a universe inhabited by a mad God? Can we simply accept that life and the world we live in is absurd and go on from there? Can we look toward nothing else?

12 MANNA

*Even amidst the worst horrors of the
Holocaust there was a measure of holiness:
the will to live was asserted, care was
displayed, heavenly bread passed on.*

> He told me his story, and today I have forgotten it, but it was
> certainly a sorrowful, cruel, and moving story; because so are all
> our stories, hundreds and thousands of stories, all different and all
> full of a tragic disturbing necessity. We tell them to each other in the
> evening, and they take place in Norway, Italy, Algeria, the Ukraine,
> and are simple and incomprehensible like the stories in the Bible.
> But are they not themselves stories of a new Bible?
> —Primo Levi, *Survival in Auschwitz*, p. 59

A sound stirs in the awful silence. A fragment of a sacred hymn
rises upward amidst the curling smoke of Auschwitz sung in a
small delicately thin voice amidst the stillness of the night. "Yet in
the midst of this terrible home of tribulation there flashed a
mysterious spark."[44] So the Hebrew writer Aharon Applefeld,
himself a refugee from the conflagration in Europe, phrases his
objection to survivors who often leave out of their accounts the
most important element of their report of survival.

In the midst of the darkness something awakens, some stirring is
felt. One cannot name it. It is not Providence. Yet it is of a piece with
what one previously knew as religious.[45] One chooses it to live.

> But this was the sense, not forgotten either then or later: that
> precisely because the Lager was a great machine to reduce us to
> beasts, we must not become beasts, that even in this place one can
> survive, to tell the story, to bear witness; and that to survive we
> must force ourselves to save at least the skeleton, the scaffolding,
> the form of civilization. We are slaves, deprived of every right,

exposed to every insult, condemned to certain death, but we still
possess one power and we must defend it with all our strength for
it is the last—the power to refuse our consent. So we must certainly
wash our faces without soap in dirty water and dry ourselves on
our jackets. We must polish our shoes, not because the regulation
states it, but for dignity and propriety. We must walk erect, without
dragging our feet not in homage to Prussian discipline but to
remain alive, *not to begin to die.*[46]

One chooses to live, and pursues small daily acts, seemingly inconsequential, yet absolutely necessary for survival: "Hammering
in a nail above his bunk from which to hang up his shoes... concluding tacit pacts of non-aggression with neighbors...."[47]
Asserting a basic will to live constitutes the most fundamental
uprising against the Kingdom of Death. Retaining some sense of
the human amidst a world of degradation is revolutionary. In a
world in which reduction to filth is a conscious policy, concern
with cleanliness, despite the fact that one could never really be
clean, is a protest whose echo is so loud that one's unconscious
remains awake even as one shuffles to the roll call of the camps.
Undertaking the assertion of dignity entailed in these daily acts
are the very means by which one retains a sense of being human.

Choosing not to emigrate, but to be transported to the camps,
Leo Baeck was in his seventies when he was interned in 1943. The
man who was the "Rabbi of Theresienstadt" had been the head of
the German-Jewish community and insisted on sharing its fate. At
one point, while interned in the concentration camp, he contracted
dysentery, whose symptom is a chronic diarrhea. Since the disease
was epidemic and to get to a latrine in time to relieve oneself was
almost impossible, Rabbi Baeck, like others, was in constant fear of
soiling himself. Instead, he fasted three days.[48]

Life itself was wrung out of that moment, a human worth,
which goes beyond mere survivalism yet makes life possible,
asserted. This is an insistence that there is a realm beyond the
camps, a meaning different than the values established by the
Nazi overlords: the dignity at the heart of the human being laying
claim to life's sacredness and so defeating the rule of the Kingdom
of Night.

Terrence des Pres, the social scientist who has combed the survivor literature, reports that there was a kind of thin coffee served in some camps in the late afternoon. Even though this was part of needed nourishment in a starvation diet, people used the liquid to clean themselves rather than for drinking. Anyone who failed to clean himself soon died. "It was an almost iron law: those who failed to wash every day soon died."[49]

> Why should I wash? Would I be better off than I am? Would I please someone more? Would I live a day, an hour longer? I would probably live a shorter time, because to wash is an effort, a waste of energy and warmth.... But later I understood.... In this place it is practically pointless to wash every day in the turbid water of the filthy washbasins for purposes of cleanliness and health; but it is most important as a symptom of remaining vitality, and necessary as an instrument of moral survival.[50]

The smallest act of assertion of self-dignity, even washing with dirty water, was in itself a radical opposition to Nazism, for it maintained the worth of life over the systemization of death.

In the Warsaw ghetto, a rabbi, Isaac Nissenbaum, understood this to be a religious principle:

> Now is the time of sanctification of life and not of martyrdom through death. In previous generations our enemies sought to capture the Jewish soul and Jews sought martyrdom to sanctify God's name; now the enemy seeks the physical destruction of the Jew and it is the duty of every Jew to protect life and watch over it....[51] Previously, Jews obeyed the command of martyrdom, now they must sanctify life.[52]

In previous generations martyrdom may have represented the most complete form of Jewish defense of the faith. But now, when the Nazis sought the death of all Jews, the preservation of life represented an act of faith. To maintain the continuity and worth of life: this was the revolutionary act of opposition, here was holiness.

People performed a new and terrifying acrobatics: balancing the need to preserve one's own life and the need to maintain human values of dignity and help, a shadow of ethical and religious intentionality. Here, in the midst of death, life was proclaimed. People discovered an oasis of the spirit that contradicted all that surrounded them. In the concentration camps, Judaism discovered its most ancient truth: the divine presence in the gift of life and the locus of the holy in the sanctification of life.

Nurture is found through the deed that reaches toward a hope that has no reason to be, the life-asserting act that embodies the sacred, the sharing that cherishes life, and the spirit that yet hovers above the chaos. In the wilderness Nazism had condemned the world to inhabit, something is revealed: the silence speaks. The echo of the Biblical "Here I am" is uttered as an inmate faces a fellow victim with terror and hope.

In the very heart of darkness, a spiritual awakening stirs: "moral survival": living gains its power by reaching beyond mere existence. In the underbelly of the beast, in 1942, in Berlin itself, after the implementation of the "Final Solution" had begun and while the "invincible" Nazi empire was at its height, Rabbi Leo Baeck studied with the last two Jewish students in Germany. The teaching was yet being generated across time. Secretly the hands were laid on these two who were to be ordained. Something was given, something passed on—a hand reaching across the darkness.

The generation of human life beyond the animal existence to which Nazism had condemned it was asserted by this affirmation. The determinateness of life, the inviolate insistence on hope, the standing with one's neighbor, the affirmation of a world beyond— these were as necessary for existence as the physical bread that one scurried for in order to survive.

Terrence des Pres sums up his reading of survivor literature this way:

> There is a power at the center of our being, at the heart of all things living. But only in man does it assume a spiritual character. And only through spirit does life continue by decision... The luxury of sacrifice — by which I mean the strategic choice of death to resolve irreconcilable moral conflicts — is meaningless in a world where any person's death only contributes to the success of evil.[53]

To continue to live—to will life into being—one's own and one's neighbor's, and then to act on that conviction is to rescue something from a world one had thought lost; it is to recover a hint of holiness.

To romanticize the life of the spirit lived under such dread conditions is all too easy at a distance. Let no one mistake what was needed to survive. One had to have a keen eye indeed to separate life from death.

> Survival without renunciation of any part of one's own moral world...was conceded only to very few superior individuals, made of the stuff of martyrs and saints.[54]

To preserve life—one's own life—one had to economize emotions of pity and sympathy, not allow normal feelings to take over, for if you would allow yourself to truly feel, you would be overcome by unbearable pain. One had to close one's eyes, not take on one's neighbor's hurt, notice the dying only so that you would be there when the moment arrived to remove the dying person's clothes.

> It is man who kills, man who creates or suffers injustice; it is no longer man, who having lost all restraint, shares his bed with a corpse. Whoever waits for his neighbor to die in order to take his piece of bread is, *albeit guiltless*, further from the model of thinking man than the most primitive pygmy or the most vicious sadist.[55]

Nevertheless, even as you must close off the normal pores of sympathy, even as you must look out for yourself in order to survive, at the right moment you also need the ability to reach out to the other, for that creates the oases of humanity nurturing life in this terrible desert. This is the paradoxical rule emerging from the Kingdom of Death.

One did not perform such acts constantly or foolishly. One hoarded one's energies, which must not be wasted on those who would surely die. But at crucial moments, people acted to give each other the gift of life and thus laid claim to a world beyond the camps. The survivor always had to make these life and death decisions. A person had to live on the razor's edge. But complete moral selfishness, mere survivalism, was a sinking into the abyss, just as the bleeding heart that soon burst. To know how to hoard and how to help, how to be self-sustaining and sustained by others, this was the macabre dance of survival one had to learn. The repetition of stories of help, and the very phrases used to describe them, constitute an uncanny litany of survival.

Yet, how little sometimes suffices to save a perishing man: a glance, a word, a gesture. Once I gave a fellow prisoner a boiled potato and he never stopped thanking me for having saved his life. Another time I helped someone to regain his feet after he had fallen during a march. He not only reached our destination alive, but survived the war; and he maintains that without my help he would never have gotten up, he would have been killed where he lay.[56]

And in almost the same language, the survivor Primo Levi writes:

I believe that it was really due to Lorenzo that I am alive today; and not so much for his material aid, as for his having constantly reminded me by his presence, by his natural and plain manner of being good, that there still existed a just world outside our own, something and someone still pure and whole, not corrupt, not savage, extraneous to hatred and terror; something difficult to define, a remote possibility of good, but for which it was worth surviving.[57]

What is overwhelming in the tales recounted by survivors is how small these necessary acts of sustenance seem. These deeds go beyond offering biological nourishment, the satisfaction of caloric or protein needs, but rather include symbols of spiritual kinship that prove most important in keeping life alive. Terrence des Pres quotes a marvelous incident capturing this point—the giving of a birthday gift in the concentration camp:

Ilse, who worked on the day shift, came back by noon... She turned away from me so that I could not see what she was doing, and dug into her pocket. "I have brought you a present!" she announced triumphantly. There on a fresh leaf was one red, slightly mashed, raspberry.[58]

Obviously, the single raspberry is not sustenance in any ordinary sense, yet in the act of gift-giving, life itself is given. The gift has no practical significance, it offers no real nourishment, but it represents another kind of necessary nurture: the feeding of one's inner being. It is an expression that love and care are still possible despite all the attempts of the enemy to perpetuate a world that daily reduces life to the level of animality. A person can create a moment of human joy and sharing, and then life itself becomes the gift snatched from the enemy's grip.

That people respond to the bestiality and the horror of the Holocaust with a loss of faith and a sense of despair is natural: "If this is what the world is capable of....if this is what man can do to man....if this is the face of the cruel God....if this is the fate of the 'chosen' people....then I want no part of it. I will take care of myself alone and hope for nothing."

Anyone confronting the horror of the Holocaust understands the honesty of this response. The Holocaust involves a knowledge of overwhelming terror; it shakes our faith in all the work of man and of God.

Yet there is another world disclosed by the death camps, a world not of the "master race" but one to be found in the small quiet voices of many of the victims. The Nazis dedicated themselves to obliterate this chorus, yet its quiet melody can be heard still.

Terrence des Pres quotes an exalting moment when people were called back to life by the power of a tune:

> Pain and...fear...kept us awake. A cloudless sky, thickly set with glittering stars, looked in upon our grief-filled prison. The moon shone through the window. Its light was dazzling that night and gave the pale, wasted faces of the prisoners a ghostly appearance. It was as if all the life had ebbed out of them. I shuddered with dread, for it suddenly occurred to me that I was the only living man among the corpses.
>
> All at once the oppressive silence was broken by a mournful tune. It was the plaintive tones of the ancient "Kol Nidre" prayer. I raised myself up to see whence it came. There, close to the wall, the moonlight caught the uplifted face of an old man, who, in self-forgetful, pious absorption, was singing softly to himself.... His prayer brought the ghostly group of seemingly insensible human beings back to life. Little by little, they all roused themselves and all eyes were fixed on the moonlight-flooded face.
>
> We sat up very quietly, so as not to disturb the old man, and he did not notice that we were listening.... When at last he was silent, there was exaltation among us, an exaltation which men can experience when they have fallen as low as we had fallen and then, through the mystic power of a deathless prayer, have awakened once more to the world of the spirit.[59]

It is a sad, terrifying tune that, lost in itself, can turn upward and leap across the abyss of abandonment and death. This painful song of the spirit rises out of the deep, and upon hearing it, people are raised from their death-in-life. There is a world of the spirit, that despite all Nazi efforts, was never fully stamped out, never fully captured. It is a dimension that has the power to survive the camps long after Nazism itself died.

Eliezer Berkovitz sums up this perspective by arguing:

> It is true that nowhere on earth and never before in history could one experience the absurdity of existence as in the German death camps; but it is also true that nowhere else in this world and never before could one experience the nobility of existence as there and then ...it is our conviction that in our generation nowhere on this earth have man's conscience and his faith in a transcendental meaning of existence been defended and vindicated as nobly and as heroically as in the ghettoes and the concentration camps, in the very dominion of their worst denial and degradation.
>
> ...If man's ability to perpetrate incomprehensible crime against his fellow bespeaks the absence of God, the non-existence of divine providence, what shall we say of his equally incomprehensible ability for kindness, for self-sacrificial heroism, for unquestioning faith and faithfulness?[60]

Just as a mournful tune has the power to cross the abyss, so too in the desert we discover the bread of affliction, the simple act that, like partially baked bread, barely has time to rise, and yet sustains us in our journey.

A survivor, Nathan Eck, is our chief source for the words of Rabbi Nissenbaum, quoted earlier regarding the need to sanctify life. The interpretation he and his fellow students listening to their master while confined in the Warsaw ghetto added to that command is most illuminating:

> Previously when the enemies of Israel sought the Jews' soul, the latter preferred to give up the body instead of handing over the soul which was sought. In our day, when the enemy had decreed the end of our bodily existence, it has become accepted among Jews to do everything, even to sacrifice some of our soul, of our ethical life, so that the enemy should not receive what it wants: the life of the Jew; and so we heard it from the mouth of R. Nissenbaum: previously Jews observed the commandment of martyrdom—the

sanctification of God's name—in our time it is incumbent on them
to observe the command to sanctify life.[61]

Survival depended on the courage and determination to
continue, to persevere willfully and ruthlessly, to blind oneself to
the crying needs that surrounded one everywhere. An etherealized moral existence, the lives Jews led as "luftmenschen," led to
death. One needed very pragmatic resources in order to live. Yet
those who gave up all morality, all search for holiness amidst the
Satanic Kingdom, also died. Those who survived were able to
strike a balance between the immoral demands made by the need
to survive and the need to preserve a measure of human dignity.
Those who knew how to sacrifice the Jewish past while yet being
suffused by it lived. The qualities needed to take one's stand
amidst the living were a curious combination of self-assertion and
selflessness, of a willingness to dirty oneself in the sewers and yet
search for holiness amidst all that dirt. This is not only metaphoric.
The defense of the Warsaw ghetto was organized in the sewers,
and Allied troops discovered in the liberated camps a prayer
book, written from memory, on a roll of toilet paper.

In the sewers of Europe, in the barracks of the concentration
camps, the deeds of Jews became a melody whose echoes only
now are being faintly heard. It is an ancient tune sung in a new
key. As Leo Baeck wrote on scraps of paper saved from Terezin:

> It is the song of men who follow God through the wastes and
> desolations and through the dark valleys of existence, of those who,
> as Hosea said, "respond" in the wilderness, as Jeremiah said, "go
> after" God in the wilderness.[62]

Now I will tell you of first things: God, earth, and heaven.

*In the beginning was abysmal chaos, darkness, and barrenness,
when the spirit of God began to stir in the face of the deep. Then light
began to dawn.*

*In the beginning was chaos, a swirling amorphousness that preceded
everything, in which all is included and towards which everything is
drawn to return once again. And because as we are products of this chaos,
in our conception, birth, life, and death, we recapitulate its history and
add to it. We contain in ourselves the most primal element; it is the deepest part of our own story. Our psyches are formed out of this terrible deep.*

But at some nebulous moment, which is the mystery attendant on the origin of the universe, light emerged. Reaching into itself and hurtling outward, it raced across the black emptiness, it wavered and danced, broke free and sent its message across the cosmos.

And more lights emerged and flew past each other, some stopping and pulling towards one another, seizing each other, sometimes wrestling, sometimes dancing together.

And this hurtling and wrestling, this light-filled dance, this too is a part of us.

For it is out of the antinomy of this hurtling outward and pulling downward, of this darkness and this light, of this tangible heaviness and this free-falling that the pulsations of history are born.

Drawn to one another then seeking surcease, the oscillation yet always resumes: the eternal yearning for restfulness is overcome again and again by the disorder of the world. Once more, we face the chaos that contains everything, and again we look toward the light flashing across the empty sky. And so night and day alternate, suffusing each other.

In the beginning was the darkness and chaos, but in its midst were born light and spirit.

Nurture the Spirit, lest the chaos return.

PART FOUR

After

Introductory
Comments

To come after is to be thrust into remembering. The story of the past inevitably becomes in some measure our own story. Who we are, the perspective with which we view the world, the fundamental beliefs ordering our existence are outlooks formed by the collective memories that have shaped our world.

Reading books on the Holocaust, leafing through photographs, watching films, we become traumatized: we are haunted by indelible images, speechless in face of the horror, like those who lived through it who could not comprehend what was happening to them. Twentieth-century means of documentation make the reality of the Holocaust unforgettable: the nightmare constitutes our own dreaming. Through photography and film we become visual witnesses to these events—images burn into our consciousness, engraving icons on our deepest mental recesses. Autobiographical reminiscences, memoirs, and histories based on the vast archival evidence captured at the end of the war are now published in such profusion that the Holocaust is the most documented of all historical tragedies.

At the time of liberation, Allied commanders insisted that their soldiers tour the camps so they could see what they had been fighting for. The soldiers were so affected that for many, their lives were transformed by this experience.[1] Though removed even further from the events, we, too, like they, while reading the accounts of survivors, even the driest of histories, or looking at photographs, or watching films, cannot but be shaken by what confronts us. Recalling these events, we are caught up in a vortex of pain, our minds numbed by the overwhelming horror. To experience the camps even as an observer is to be transformed; we are forced to face a different reality than the simple verities our own life of ease presents us with.

Just as so many survivors can justify their lives after the Holocaust only by witnessing,[2] by telling the tale, so must we, in relating our stories, include the Holocaust. We carry with us the burden of not forgetting. We have become a survivor people, our collective consciousness is formed by these events. The meaning of God, of history, of hope, of the Jew, of Israel, of humanity—all are seen in a new light because of what happened to us.

13 HUMANITY

Our ideas of what humanity is capable of and assurance in the progress of Western civilization are transformed by the Holocaust.

Our faith in humanity and in ourselves is affected by the events of the Holocaust, especially since it was one of the most "advanced" countries—the land of Goethe, Kant, and Beethoven—which gave birth to Nazism.

First of all, we can not relegate this evil to acts done by a "primitive" mentality. We can not simply fool ourselves that with the proper education, through science and enlightenment, the world will be improved and evil like this will become unthinkable. What we have learned is that technology, science, culture, and learning may be harnessed to write the most shameful pages of history. The Nazi rector, Martin Heidegger, one of the most respected philosophers of this century, signed the dismissal of the Jewish professor Martin Buber, who in turn was one of Germany's most respected theologians. The world of learning was no refuge from madness.

The collapse of the academy exemplifies the corruption of all cultural institutions by Nazism. Hitler was no mere dictator interested in venal profit, he was an ideologue instituting a new regime. In the end, killing Jews had become more important than survival, a demonstration of the way in which Nazism had succeeded in transvaluating all values.

There is a photograph taken at the time of liberation, a picture from one of the camps. Bald, pallid, emaciated figures stare at their liberators as they perch weightlessly on barbed wire fences, their striped pajamas hanging loosely on their wasted frames. Half alive, half dead, they tell a tale of another world. What dominates the photograph is their bewildered eyes staring out from hollowed skulls.

Margaret Bourke-White, who took the picture, says that she was trying to depict the joy of liberation, the expectancy of these people who had just come back from hell, but no one who sees the picture is first struck by an expression of hope. Rather one sees in their eyes an accusatory questioning. You are human, too, tell us how this could happen?

How did it happen?

Those of us standing at some distance from the Nazi dominance of Germany and much of Europe never will be able to comprehend these events, even as the historical facts increasingly are documented and interpreted. This is especially the case since Nazism cannot be relegated to acts committed by a few psychopaths or a ruthless dictator, but was a movement cheered on by millions of inhabitants. The destruction of the Jews was an event made possible through the participation of soldiers and police, doctors and businesspeople.

There were those who participated only passively and silently. After the war they would say that they did not know Jews were being killed. Jews had been beaten in the streets on *Krystalnacht*, but they did not know there was a pogrom against Jews. Jewish stores where they had shopped before the war were marked now with outsize stars of David and bore signs urging a gentile boycott, but they did not know of the war against the Jews. No Jews were to be found in Germany anymore, but they did not know what had happened to them. The people living near Auschwitz who smelled the human flesh burning also claim they did not know what was happening. So very few knew.

We should not simply sweep aside this "not knowing"; this multifaceted "not knowing" bears some scrutiny. There were Jews working in the labor camp attached to Auschwitz who also did not know until the very end that the chimneys they saw daily were carrying human ash into the sky. They needed not to know in order to have the will to survive, the energy to work. And ordinary people, gentiles, needed not to know (while another part of their brain knew full well that Jews were being persecuted) in order to continue with their daily lives, because something inside told them that if they would in fact attend to what was happening, they would not be able to go on with their lives; they would not be able to continue as loyal citizens, patriotic members of their state. To know would have been to put too much at risk. It was simpler to believe parts of the state's ideology: Jews really didn't belong here. They had introduced a foreign element into German society, they had cheated and weaseled and finally weakened the fiber of the German nation. Better they should be sent off packing. Where they were going was other people's business. If some old acquaintances disappeared, well they may have been good people, but they were part of a larger body that needed to be transported.

How easy it is to bifurcate the brain, to know and not to know, to have information but not process it, especially if one can accept part of the ideology, the language, that makes such horrors possible. People insulate themselves from making all the connections consequent to the knowledge at hand. Though having deductive capabilities, people leave off the calculation before the final sum is reached.

In a democratic age, the way the barbarian rules is through such not knowing, through a refusal to process all the data. Hitler used the instruments of Western legalism to accomplish his ends. He assumed power by constitutional means. His government was properly installed. When in power, legalism reigned: the Nurenberg laws defining Jews as outside the pale of first-class German citizenship were properly legislated, enforced by a Western-trained judicial system. Thus, the vocabulary used by the state incorporated the most heinous definitions but were fully legal and generally supported. What was accomplished in the end, the so-called "Final Solution," could not have been done save through what had been set in motion earlier for all to see. Nazi power depended on the complicity of all those who knew but did not know; they provided the cultural background that made genocide possible.

But the ultimate horror, the reduction of millions of humans into non-persons and the carrying out of mass murder, could not have taken place without the more intimate involvement of large numbers of men and women who took active roles in the destruction. Hannah Arendt has talked about the banality of evil. One of the factors she has pointed to as peculiar to the Nazi Holocaust is that in Germany there was a triumph of bureaucracy and that bureaucrats kept on functioning in the same manner regardless of the task at hand. In some measure their defense— that they were just carrying out orders—was correct.[3] The stationmaster could put his stamp on the manifest, whether the baggage car contained cows or Jews. He simply did his job. At best the stationmaster, while knowing who was being transported and towards what end, signed that paper because he needed to keep his job, because that was what he was accustomed to doing. He felt it was his way of keeping out of "trouble," or he might even have felt that what he was doing was "patriotic." But the warrants being signed were for the massacre of Jews, not for the usual freight.

This passive participation, fueled by cowardice or quiet resentment against the Jews, is only a part of the story of destruction. There were the stationmasters who happily signed the papers sending the Jews to their death. There were the German and Austrian citizens who joyfully lit the fires of the synagogues and rampaged through the streets breaking the glass of Jewish shops on *Krystalnacht*. And there were those who insisted on demeaning every Jew they met.

Then there were the people at the heart of the beast, the classic Jew haters: the Dutch burgher who informed on Anne Frank and her family hiding across the way, and the Ukrainian and the Pole who enthusiastically rounded up Jews, beating and then shooting them, and who some times had to be restrained by the Germans themselves, because their penchant for killing Jews put too much of a strain on the system—more methodical and less personal methods had to be found if the genocide of the Jewish people was to take place. There were the Nazi soldiers who ripped off the beards of old people with their bayonets, carrying away skin as well as hair; there were men who fired their rifles with a deathly rhythm forcing Jews to dance on Torah scrolls; and there were the officers who extracted every piece of gold from people being sent to their deaths. At the very center of the destruction were the SS soldiers who lined the way to the ovens and drove the victims into the "showers," supervising the cleaning of the area after one group had been gassed, before the next was ushered in. There were the commandants of the camps and their staffs, the medical officers who committed gruesome experiments on Jews, the Eichmanns who eagerly rounded up each Jew and were genuinely upset if one escaped their grasp, who felt they were doing heroic work in ridding the world of its Jews. Some of them were psychopaths, some of them were people filled with hate, some of them were criminal types who would be the bullies in any regime. What is surprising is how many of them appear to be average people. So many of those located in hiding long after the war lived ordinary lives for tens of years after the Holocaust, just as they had probably lived quietly before.[4]

In fact, it would not have been possible for the SS to recruit soldiers to work in Auschwitz and other concentration camps, it would not have been possible for the German army to organize the ghettoes and supervise the rounding up of Jews had not a cultural transformation taken place in which Germans had ceased to see Jews as human beings, objects of shared sympathy.

The center of Nazi ideology was a belief that it was creating a master race, ridding the world of the less-than-human, the insects and vermin that preyed upon the superior Aryan people. That the origins of the camps lay in the extermination of the mentally ill and homosexuals was not accidental, because the genocide of the Jewish people was part of a program which attempted to fashion a new human race. Humanity was imperfect and needed to be scientifically perfected. Those who were involved passively and those who were active participants both believed they were creating the better Germany, clearing Germany of the nest of vipers. The perfection of the Aryan race was a means for the perfection of all humanity. There was a kind of secularized perversion of religious values: salvation was to come by getting rid of the corrupting other, in separating off the vermin Jew. The vision of a higher calling permeated the rhetoric of Nazi Germany. What was taking place was a purification in order to achieve a more advanced order. Racial politics were attached to Darwinian social theory. While Nietzsche, in using the latter to talk of the evolution of the superman, may have meant something quite different, the Nazi ideologists were able to adopt his philosophy for their purposes.

What made the Nazi destruction of the Jews unique, what transformed it from pogrom into genocide, was the harnessing of the rhetoric of science and technology and the ideological thrusts of modernity to an atavistic hate. Nazism was attractive in part because it was able to use and draw the language of modernity, of what had been considered advanced. Nazism was a specific outcome of the modernist dream of the self reinventing itself; it contained a vision of a scientific reordering of reality to achieve a new perfection. In fact, elements of the Nazi hierarchy were upset that Jews were initially killed randomly. They saw this as barbaric. Jews were to be destroyed systematically, in a technologically advanced way. Their destruction was not to be a matter of sudden emotional flings or random pogroms, but it was to be well thought out and planned. Himmler apparently had a weak stomach for actual murder and vomited upon visiting Auschwitz and seeing the result of the destruction there. He, therefore, lectured his troops that theirs was the greatest sacrifice for Germany because they must conquer their inner inhibitions in order to do what was right—destroy the Jewish people. Personal feeling had to be overcome to do what was "right"—genocide. The use of gas was not only a means to quicken the destruction—death by firing squad was too slow—but to give a veneer of a scientific activity and therefore satisfying the Nazis' need to see themselves as engaged in a higher purpose.[5]

What Nazism articulated and used for its own ends were some of the underlying faiths that are themes of modernity: the break with the past and the need to extirpate traditionalist religiosity, a faith in science and technology as the means of creating a new and better future for all humanity, a belief that science itself can yield a system of values, and a preoccupation with the self, whether that be one's individual self, one's family, one's race, or one's nation.

Nazism was able to organize the instrumentalities of the state around feelings of resentment, anger, superiority of the self, and the demeaning of the other.[6] They were able to translate this resentment of the other and glorification of the self into a quasi-religious vocabulary, thus investing their ideology with ultimate authority. People who gazed at Hitler reported that they sensed something close to an epiphany,[7] and the destruction of the Jews could be felt as an inner command, a "sacred" duty. At his trial in Jerusalem, Eichmann insisted that he was a religious person, though not a Christian.[8]

Ever since the French Revolution, secular movements have clothed themselves in religious garb, attaching to themselves messianic and frequently apocalyptic fervor. In this century, that has been true of Marxist and Fascist regimes alike. Nazi ideology combined notions of racial purity with a progressivist modernist rhetoric. The vision of the "Master Race" was the triumph of a certain kind of secular vision taking on the coloration of religious faith, that of humanity reinventing itself.[9]

What was demonstrated was how delicate and fragile the ethical heritage of the West is. The moral climate of the West is the attainment of centuries and millennia of development, but modernity has created the conditions in which the ties to it can easily be swept aside. Modernity emphasizes its newness, its own separation from past constraint, and idealizes the need for experimenting with new permutations. On the one hand, science and technology are said to yield their own values, ones that ought to rule in the social sphere, as well. On the other, the loss of traditional values leaves one only with the interests of the self as paramount—self-exploration, and self-expression. With the ascendancy of these values the stage has been set for sweeping away the delicate instrument of human sympathy and the victory of the most horrifying glorification of the collective self, a culture that sees genocide as its central mission.

Perhaps, the most radical yet subtle expression of anti-Nazism was practiced by Jews who, while living in the ghetto, taught their children the song "All Men are Brothers." That German poem whose meaning was now forgotten by the culture that gave it birth was sung by those who were most tormented, most violently rejected by that culture. Was not the most fundamental opposition to Nazism a simple religious vision that each human being is precious, a traditionalist faith in the absolute worth of all human life? Did not a sense of humility, that "I" cannot contain all, cannot know all, constitute the first step in the opposite direction of the consequences of Aryan superiority?

Isn't this then the heart of the matter? That what was lost in Nazi Germany, what led to the destruction of so many and to the ruin of the fabric of moral culture, was a fundamental Biblical sense of the sacred—the belief that there is value in the human person, that the mystery at the heart of the universe is contained in the other. In the sense of otherness and beyondness that is encountered most concretely in our relationships with people and that forms the basis of Jewish religious faith[10] and the faith of her daughter religions, Christianity and Islam, do we not encounter the elements that stand eternally opposed to Nazism? One trembles to say something banal in relation to this evil, yet does not Nazism represent a loss of a fundamental religious value and the triumph of certain secular motifs that are common aspects of twentieth-century culture—the substitution of traditionalist faith by elements of the new modernist faith?

We come to realize that the belief in the self at the heart of modernity is also misplaced.[11] Enlightenment, education, culture, science will not produce well-balanced individuals who will do what is right. Instead, with the loss of restraint of traditionalist societies, modern nations have been freed to commit the most terrible horrors in the history of humanity.

The Enlightenment bore two different and opposing conceptions of the human. Hobbes argued that left to their own devices, people would descend to the level of the animal, so that without the proper ordering of society, humans would be ruled by the law of the jungle. The contrary position is that of Rousseau, who argued that each person was essentially good, but that society was the corrupting influence. Modernist faith has largely followed the latter: the self was thought of as ultimately good. What was needed was a societal revolution that allowed the individual to flourish. The Holocaust, though, has unveiled the true heart of humanity. At our center lies an ability to commit evil of an almost unimagined degree. We have seen the nature of human beings and found that the most ordinary amongst us can transport millions to their deaths, can cruelly experiment on human subjects, and can quickly explain away his neighbor's being beaten or dragged away in the night. The theory of the inherent goodness of the human being was daily disproved in Nazi Germany: conscience proved no guide, and one's inner voice placed no limits on what could be done.

But if Rousseau's argument was shown to be a romantic conceit, so has Hobbes' been proved wrong, for what made Nazism possible was the use of state power for evil ends. The rule of law was not an instrument that protected people against the jungle but the means for creating the machinery of death. The near total genocide of the Jewish people would not have been possible without, on the one hand, the ability to use all aspects of cultural communication to reduce the Jew to non-person, and on the other, the ability to mobilize the full weight of the modern bureaucratic state to carry out mass murder. So efficient did the process become that Hungarian Jewry was decimated in only the last hours of the war. And so central had the destruction of the Jews become to Nazi thinking that the extinction of the Jews had become equal in moral weight to national survival. The transformation of values had succeeded.

It would be misconceived to think of what happened in Germany and Europe as a singular event, an exception in history, a black hole that we cannot understand[12] but that cannot be repeated. Coming after and knowing what happened, we realize that the evil committed is a part of who we as humans are, that the evil at our door can be unleashed in the most "advanced" of cultures. It is all too easy to ascribe guilt to a collective "they," and in turn feel innocent and believe that the story of the Holocaust has no inherent lessons to teach us about ourselves. As passivity, bureaucratic acquiescence, and feelings of superiority are attitudes we all engage in, we are capable of behaving in the very same manner as citizens in Germany did. What happened in Nazi Germany is a human artifact. People did it, and all bear the same burden of humanity. Ignoring aspects of life going on around us because we cannot be bothered is the stuff of everyday life. Feeling that our lives, our culture, our environment is superior to others' is

among the most natural of human impulses. Emotions of resentment, anger, self-centeredness occupy our daily lives. We all
participate in the secularized currents of modernity and all have to
be watchful of the way it creates a destructive system of values.
What so easily happens through the negation of religious rhetoric
is that a new and menacing culture is substituted—an ideology
that glorifies the self and desacrilizes the other.

Our knowledge of the horror committed by fellow human
beings defines our sense of who we are. We must understand that
what the Nazis did is within the spectrum of being human, for the
success of the Nazis resulted from the participation of quite
average citizenry. Somewhere on that spectrum of evil we will
find our own image.

To recover our humanity, to find some surcease from endless
guilt, we seek to identify with the victims: to try to understand
their horror, to feel as one's own a measure of their pain.

Hannah Arendt argues that what makes the Holocaust bearable
is the knowledge that some people acted decently: that there were
non-Jews who hid Jews, countries such as Denmark where masses
of people worked to save Jews, and that there were even Nazi soldiers who said no to their superiors. "Humanly speaking, no more
is required, and no more can reasonably be asked, for this planet
to remain fit for human habitation."[13] What needs to be added to
Arendt's accounting of the righteous gentiles is the story of how
the victims remained human.

Spiritual resistance, the insistence that the Nazis would not
obliterate all goodness, the preservation of the sacred in at least
some relationships, this is what enabled some people to survive.
And for those who did not survive, this inner resistance denied
the enemy victory, at the very time the Nazis would strip them of
any semblance of holiness. Under the oppressive brutality of Nazism, these acts of grace were frequently not morally one-sided. But
by stealing of the bread off a dead neighbor, using those morsels to
stay alive and once passing a piece to a companion, something
beyond nourishment was shared.

Through our sympathetic reading of the tale of survival, we
seek to recover the belief in our own humanity, but in having

entered the kingdom of night we have lost something, as well—we know the evil that is at the center of our existence. We know the cost of our own survival. Even as we seek to do good we bear witness to the enormous power of destructiveness always welling within us.

The will to live, to survive, demands a certain selfishness. You must know how to fight for your life. How to steal from the dying, if need be, if that is what will keep you alive; how to use guile, how to trust few people. The will to live demands the ability to make terrible and difficult decisions; it means that you will act in a way others may understand to be immoral because you know that is what you need to do to survive. Delicate souls will not make it. And life must overcome death. An etherealized moral culture, one that knows not how to fight evil, how to survive, will not last to tell the tale, to proclaim its alternative message.

Yet if one simply allows toughness to rule, if one in fact becomes completely ruthless, then all is lost. The secret of surviving is knowing how to maintain the balance; it is a delicate and dangerous act, but it is all we are left with. Without grace, without moving toward the hand dimly stretched out to us, we will be overcome by the darkness within and fall as we will if we go forward unthinkingly, without care for ourselves. We have learned these truths in the depths of our being.

The survivor shuffled away from the camps to build a new life. What had gone before could never be forgotten, for try as one might, one was repeatedly awakened in the dead of the night bathed in a cold sweat. Nightmares continued to stalk sleep, the inner eye recalls surrealistic images of horror. Even as the survivor moves to new ground, the ravages humans are capable of, or the terror humans impose can never be forgotten.

At every moment, a memory of human destructiveness surrounds us. Even as one gathers one's energies to begin a new story, to will life into existence once more, one carries along the knowledge of terror.

> The survivor, then, is a disturber of the peace. He is a runner of the blockade humanity erects against knowledge of "unspeakable" things.[14]

But, in the darkest hours, even in the moment of greatest horror, some glimmer could be seen, something akin to what was
once called holy could be found. No one who forgot that principle survived.

The testimony of the survivor, the new knowledge that is
imparted, leads inevitably to a diminution of hope, but not (as
Richard Rubenstein would have it) an end to all hoping. There is a
constant battle to assert the good, to create moments of holiness.
Were we to give in to despair, were we to believe that such
moments, because they are transient, because they frequently do
not lead to salvation are not worthwhile, then we would lose all.
Yes, it was the righteous gentiles who were frequently caught and
sent to the death camps, themselves. Yes, it was rabbis and
intellectuals who were deported first. But even in defeat, if we
have any story to tell it is that people resisted becoming as evil as
the Nazis. A measure of another world was preserved by them,
and we choose to be the inheritors of those stories: of Jewish
theaters set up in the ghettoes, of Dutch families who sheltered the
Anne Franks, of prisoners who saved their rations for a Passover
seder in the camps.

The bestiality in the human heart is a given. Yet the sympathetic
spirit beats there, too. We know more than any previous generation, that the workings of that sensibility is a fragile creation, sand-
castles constantly despoiled by the tide.

In the beginning there was chaos, but there was also the spirit of
God hovering over the face of the deep. The great artists of the
twentieth century are aware of the chaos at the heart of humanity
and at the heart of the world. Kafka may be this century's most
significant literary figure for having portrayed that madness most
insightfully. Yet what is forgotten in that secular artistry is the
possibility of holiness and that this too is at the heart of the human.
We all have the potential of becoming Nazis, and we all have the
ability to become Jews who carry a larger vision. We can corrupt
religious values and turn the wish for salvation into an instrument
of destruction, but we can also achieve the knowledge of life's
sacredness, the affirmation and nurture of the other, the building
of a society that allows God to rest in its midst.

Coming after the Holocaust we also know that spiritual resistance is not enough. Jews are commanded not only to realize an ideal but to survive. Once thrown into ghettoes better choices could not have been made: the underground in Warsaw practiced on the one gun it had in its possession.[15] Under these circumstances, how ludicrous to ask why they did not behave differently! Given their circumstance, they scratched holy reliefs on the walls of hell.

But we, coming after, have no excuse. We know how easily humanity descends into evil; and we had better be prepared. This time we must fight with all the power available; this time we better not be caught unaware.

We are constantly faced with having to confront terrible decisions to enable our survival, and our attempts at a life of holiness constantly present us with moral conflicts. We cannot create a separate reality in which the life of the spirit will be achieved and the rest of the world be cut off. The Jews of Eastern Europe tried that to their painful disillusionment. The destructive forces in the world will invade any realm. We must learn to engage fully in the battle if we are to preserve that which is most holy to us.

We live this side of Paradise caught in a terrible paradox that to preserve the good we sometimes must use the instrumentalities of evil. If life is a battle then we must go to war, and we must martial resources equal to those of the enemy. Martyrdom can be no ideal for us, rather we exalt the will to live—and the exaltation of the sacred amidst the labor of life.

That battle, once won, is never over. We must be constantly engaged, for there is no final line demarcating good from evil: in this world they are constantly intertwined. There is no endtime when we can rest on our laurels.

When we thought of salvation as a retreat from the world—in the life of Torah study, piety, and prayer—we could indeed dream of eternal surcease from pain, a lasting peace. But if salvation is to be present where chaos and darkness are as much at home as grace and light, then what is achievable is always tenuous, victory always fleeting. Chaos and darkness will always surge back and seek to prevail.

Modernity has provided more than enough reason to give up believing in holiness, still we have learned that to give up the struggle to achieve it means that we become less than human. As we leave the twentieth century, we discover new reasons to return to old faith. We rediscover an urgent need to defend the sacred, even as our understanding differs from our ancestors. We choose not to retreat from the world, but to struggle within it, to stain ourselves with sin even as we seek to establish the good.

14 GOD

The Holocaust causes us to revise our religious beliefs: to adopt a conception of God who does not exercise power in history and of a religious life that sees its primary drama as occurring in this world.

Suffering, true suffering, eludes memory and words. Suffering, true suffering, is watching death—dark, cunning death—drawing close to children too weak to cry. Children you love. Your own. With a piece of bread, a spoonful of soup, a bit of warmth you could chase it away, but your hands are empty, you have nothing left to offer. And you want to howl, to shout at the top of your lungs, to tear out your hair and your eyes. But you do nothing. You don't even feel guilty. Just sad. Terribly sad. And stupidly useless. You feel idle and empty—empty of faith. Forlorn. Abandoned even by imagination. A dull, heavy animal. Deaf and blind. And alone. Terribly alone.

—Elie Wiesel[16]

We sit among the ruins, amidst our ash heap—alone. We listen for a response to our suffering, but there is only silence. Our world is in ruins, and we lack understanding to comprehend it, we hear no speech.

Faith after the Holocaust does not come easily. Surely we can no longer believe in a Lord of history who will make everything right in the end, just as we cannot believe in the basic goodness of humans who will be directed by conscience and simple decency. We are conscious of the silence of God and humanity.

As we seek understanding, as we wish to approach once again the realm of the religious, we realize how changed we are. When we try to acknowledge God's presence in the world we realize that the old theological formulas do not work for us, rather they make a mockery of our condition.

We certainly cannot accept a Biblical view that God is a God of history, that good will be rewarded and evil punished, that righteousness will issue in blessing and the wages of sin will be the death of the evildoer. There are those of us who had already been affected by contemporary scientific attitudes and by philosophic criticism and found accepting any notion of God's intervention in history difficult, but even those of us who had retained a sense of God's working in the world are overwhelmed by the totality of God's absence in the events of the Holocaust.

Good and evil, scholar and simpleton, pickpocket and pietist, men, women, and children all went up in smoke and no distinction was made among them. The fate of the good was and is the same as the fate of the bad. Those who died in the ghettoes and camps and gas chambers were not differentiated in any way. Biblical theology of reward and punishment is irrelevant and absurd in this circumstance.

Nor is the appeal to an otherworldly reward helpful. Many of us had already been affected by the Enlightenment and its aftermath and had given up believing in an afterlife. Even for those who retained this belief, the rabbinic solution that the reward for good is to be found in the next world is an unsatisfactory response to the mass death experienced in the Holocaust. Can the thought that "now all who are dead are with their maker" really comfort us? Can an afterlife really make up for the terrible loss? Have all the dead, sinners and saints alike, now been given a dispensation?

While in the past romantic notions could attach themselves to the martyr's death, to speak of the witnessing of the righteous in this context seems wholly inappropriate. So many of those who died in the Holocaust desperately wanted to live, so many were killed who could ascribe no content to the word "Jew" for which they now suffered, and those who experienced malnutrition and typhus had no thought of the "Sanctification of the Name." These were not consciously chosen martyrs' deaths, and reward in the afterlife can not make up for their loss. Are all six million, believers and unbelievers, secularists and faithful, pietists and rascals, deniers of their Judaism, converts to Christianity and the defenders of the faith now to be considered martyrs? Are all those who longed to live rather than die, who did not want the afterlife but wanted the here and now, to be rewarded in the world to come? Are they now to be judged, their lives weighed and their rewards and punishments meted out? Can we imagine that such accounting would mitigate the horror of what they experienced? Appeals to an afterlife hardly seem appropriate in this circumstance.

Nor can these events be justified as a part of any Divine plan, some mysterious unfolding that will only be revealed to us in its entirety in the end of days. Given the enormity of what has occurred that seems too facile a solution, too easy a bypassing of the terror we have experienced.[17] No end could justify these means.[18]

Some have argued that we cannot question God's power but that God has handed over the realm of history to the human, whatever the consequence.[19] There is even the contention that classical Judaism never took seriously the formulation "because of our sins were we exiled"—a curious rereading of the tradition. If more is meant by the relationship with God than a simple Deistic one,[20] based on the notion that God once having set the world in motion then stepped away from that creation, then it must be realized that in the tradition God's presence was to be realized in the afterlife, an idea that provided a sense of ultimate judgment and justice.[21] But if one loses faith in a settling of accounts, then of what use is a God who once was active but is no longer? In what sense can we say God is present if the world is given over to the human? Why concern ourselves with God?

Even as they seek to justify God, these theologians agree that the pain we have suffered prevents us from believing literally and simplistically in a beneficent creator God who miraculously redeems us. The rent in the universe is too deep, the tragedy of existence too overwhelming for the goodness of God ever again to be clearly manifest to us. The destruction wrought without any Divine intervention speaks of God's absence from the stage of human action. The Holocaust is not the judgment of the God of history. We can only believe that any goodness that will intervene on our behalf will flow from the work of our own hands. Then why not cease praying for what cannot be achieved? We are past waiting for intervention from outside, for a glorious endtime that will transform existence. Our disappointment will no longer bear such a leap of faith. If the God we wanted so much did not appear when our need was so desperate, what use would that God be to us now?

To speak of God is to speak of hope. To talk of the Divine is to talk of salvation, of an era whose arrival God assures in which the longings of the righteous for a society that embodies justice and the desire for peace and contentment will be fulfilled. God was always seen as the guarantor of that vision, and it is what Jews minimally dreamed of when they spoke of the coming of the Messiah. This promise of redemption in the end of days could override the pain of existence currently experienced.

But the Holocaust is a black hole swallowing up all hope. We no longer dream of an idealized world, only one that never again will demonstrate this extent of evil. Would that we could have the simple world of the everyday—the garden variety of pain, the workaday experience of thorns and thistles. We can no longer wait for the "end of days," the time of contentment and peace; such an epoch is beyond the possibility of historical possibility. It is true that modern philosophical criticism may have questioned all teleological views of history, but it is the Holocaust that clearly puts an end to that thinking. After all, this century began with the dream of the "war to end all wars," of international institutions that would create a common global peace, in short a vision of the progress inherent in history. Genocide cannot be seen as a part of a process of development leading to some greater end. We have not progressed, only created instruments of greater terror: we are the same human beings we always were, capable of good and evil, save that we have created more sophisticated instruments of destruction.

And so even as we attempt to move on, to create a life after, a shadow follows our path, the sight of ugliness always tugging at the back of our minds. We are left with a vision of life forever threatened by chaos, a consciousness of the depth of depravity flowing within us.

Chaos overwhelms tranquility, forces of destruction are not controllable, they may break through and decimate all in their wake.

The ills we see in the world are not to be explained as some ultimate functioning of God's plan, not finally to be understood in
the unfolding of history. The evil we experienced has no meaning,
it is simply there, always there. It is a fact, a reality. Evil is a power,
a power that may rule over us, just as it ruled over an entire western nation and gathered in its wake a quarter of the civilized world.

Evil is not some apotheotized Satan, not a fallen angel, ultimately answerable to the Maker. Evil is a domain, that can well in us
all. The world is not a unity flowing from the goodness of God, not
a mysterious whole whose glory will be revealed to us in an endtime. Evil will not be redeemed in the fullness of days. The world
contains a primal chaos whose destructive power rises up again
and again in history and in the life of each person; it is a realm that
cannot be subsumed under the Divine.

Simple optimism, a theology that sees evil merely as a necessary
contingent of God's plan, as well as a faith in civilization that
speaks only of hope and not terror, becomes a cruel mockery of
our experience. Truly we know the power of evil and the demonic
more deeply than any previous generation. Not only do we know
the evil that humanity is capable of, but we have experienced the
peculiar destructiveness of the modernist mentality. To face the
world honestly is to acknowledge humanity's inherent power of
destructiveness. What we can never say after the Holocaust is that
God is the all powerful One who controls good and evil, or that
history reflects the eventual triumph of the good. Our loss
diminishes hope and lessens our sense of divine power.[22]

In a revisioning of the Messianic ideal, the twentieth-century
Catholic theologian, Teilhard de Chardin, spoke of an Omega
point—a time of evolutionary apex—toward which the world was
being pulled. To us this seems like a romantic vision. Is it possible
for us living after the Holocaust to believe that in the fullness of
time evil will be conquered?

No divine intervention will come from the outside to make history right again, just as there was no resounding miracle to save
millions of innocent people from death, nor an individual accounting of righteousness. The death camps did not end in
theophany. Traditional theologies that find an ultimate meaning
displayed by history make no sense in light of the gas chambers

and the rod of Dr. Mengele choosing who shall live and who shall die. The Messiah was buried at Auschwitz.

We live, then, with a horrible new revelation that has over-turned all that went before. We now know that to hold onto our old conceptions of God leads to madness and nothingness. That is the only resolution possible if one affirms both the classical Jewish understanding of God and history and the image of cruelty and the silence of God at Auschwitz.

Instinctively, we grasp at an alternative vision to madness and nothingness. We feel we must, if we are to go on living; if we are to re-enter the world of creating and recreating. George Steiner once responded respectfully to Elie Wiesel, "Perhaps no Jew should bear a child after Auschwitz; this is an absolute position which is unassailable. But we do come after...."[23] We seek an alternative understanding, some measure of rationality, something affirmative.

We now realize that when theologians of earlier generations spoke of God's will and power, when we imagined God watching over creation and playing the games of history, our theological language said too much. Our understanding of God's relationship to history was false. We conceived of God as too much of a person when God is really spirit. Our images of God were idolatrous and are now shattered by the events we have witnessed.

But our knowledge of the terrible evil that is at the heart of the human does not mean that there is no reality to the spiritual life, that in giving up belief in a theophany, in a final and ultimate revelation, we must give up the idea of the importance of the life of the spirit. Auschwitz does not mark the end of a meaningful religiosity.

To see only the world of chaos is to deny another reality of the Holocaust. For the story the survivor tells is not only one of horror, of tragedy, but also of how men and women sustained a way of life that was opposed to everything Nazism stood for. A holy presence even in Auschwitz. There was a miracle of life even amidst the walking dead. If you lived, it was through some act, and the memory of that act became the centerpiece of your life: someone saved me, therefore I am here. This is the story every survivor tells. The person who helped another stand upright in line so that person would not be chosen for the gas did not think of herself as heroic—she felt she was doing what she had to, yet life was given in that act. When asked why they allowed Jews to hide out in their cellars and barns at the risk of their own lives, the gentiles who hid Jews during the war usually replied simply that they felt it was the right thing to do, that it was what God taught was right. When praised or publicly thanked for their heroism, they seem embarrassed that so much fuss should be made over what was a natural act. The woman who, in Auschwitz, brought her friend a half-rotten raspberry for her birthday gave that person her life. The world of survival was built out of people reaching out to others in ways they thought were quite ordinary, but that proved to be extraordinary. Life is granted, spirit is sustained, through daily acts cultivating that realm.

We can no longer believe in a divine intervention that will come from the outside, but we must learn that we can let holiness enter, that we can make a space for the divine, that which is most deeply nourishing, that which sparks the soul of each of us. When we listen to the silent calling of God, impelling us to reach out and shatter the hard reality constructed by evil, to affirm the humanity of our neighbor—that is divine intervention.

Martin Buber reports a tale in the name of the Hasidic master, Rebi Menahem Mendel of Kotzk:

> "Where is the dwelling of God?"
> This was the question with which the Rabbi of Kotzk surprised a number of learned men who happened to be visiting him.
> They laughed at him: "What a thing to ask! Is not the whole world full of His glory?"
> Then he answered his own question:
> "God dwells wherever man lets Him in."[24]

We have relinquished the God sitting "up there," the all-powerful one guaranteeing a redemption in an unknown endtime. But we have not forsaken the process of redemption altogether.

We do not await a God who parts the seas or brings down plagues on our enemies, but we can still seek moments of holiness: a Judah approaching his brother filled with regret, the midwife who in Exodus refuses to destroy new life (celebrated in the tradition as the mother of Moses), a prophet who risks death by accusing a king of terrible misconduct, our resting on the seventh day, the washing of hands before we eat. The holy that can be encountered everywhere is as much at the heart of the universe as the darkness in which it is found. After the Holocaust we continue to testify that there is a sacred aspect to life, that the world is not simply the dwelling place of evil. Biblical religion understood that there was a fundamental distinction between God and what was life sustaining on the one hand, and death and impurity on the other. They were opposites, and if one entered the realm of death then one could not be a part of the world of the holy. The Biblical emphasis on ritual purity was a way of physically expressing the separation between life and death. (Thus the need to ritually purify oneself after contact with a corpse, a differentiation preserved even today in the ritual handwashing upon leaving a cemetery.)

We also believe in two distinct realms, but East of Eden they are terribly mixed together. After the Holocaust we realize that the Divine does not stand transcendently triumphant, overseeing the events below, but that God is found in the midst of the muck of this world and that the workings of the Divine are fragile creations. The chaos surrounding us always has the ability to overwhelm the life that manifests spirituality. The sacred must be continuously sustained, must always be protected; neglected, it has no chance of being. Sacred acts are vulnerable and hidden ones, easily lost. But the reality of holiness is as true as our knowledge of evil.

God is at the center of life, at the very heart of existence. The encounter with God has the power to create a place where evil no longer has dominion. In the anticipation and memory of ordinary acts of nurture that are woven together in time, we create the carpet for the entry of God. The redemption of evil occurs through deeds that are the very stuff of everyday existence. According to rabbinic legend, Elijah is to be found waiting outside the gates of Rome, wrapping bandages around the wounded poor. We imitate Elijah's messianic calling by offering our seat on the bus for a bent gentleman, helping a woman move a stroller up the stairs, sending a foreign visitor off in the right direction, running after someone to return a purse left behind at the cash register, listening to the sound of the bird when the rain stops, petitioning for the release of a political prisoner, talking to a homeless person, helping a family victimized by war to resettle, responding to the pain of a woman whose husband is jailed, noticing the first pale green buds of spring.

The modern mystic of Zion, Harav Kook, understood this path to redemption.

> Amidst everything you do you encounter
> sparks filled with light and life which
> yearn to rise up to the highest heavens;
> you help them to do so, and they help you.[25]

We know the divine in a new way, yet we know so little. Our entry into the mystery is through the force of will that reaches deep within us and there finds a mournful tune shattering the emptiness, the silence around us.

With this meager instrument, for one moment the veil is removed and light flashes on the other side.

> For your words are a candle for me
> a light for my way. (Psalm 119:105)

We believe not in a God of strength but in a fragile light of the spirit that is always threatened by the power of night and that must always be fought for. A place can be made to let that spirit in, human beings can act in a way that affirms another world than that of the Nazis; it is for us to choose that world we want to enter. We believe not in an omnipotent God who will transform the reality closing in around us, which is the given of our lives, but in a God who in a delicate voice calls us from within that reality to break through its hardness and create a resting place for the Divine Presence.

The good constituted in that experience of God does not necessarily overwhelm or conquer the evil in the world. In fact, many times evil will triumph. But the moment when we experience the Divine ought not to be negated should evil in the end overwhelm it. The extraordinary power of the breath of diaphanous holiness is as real as the boot of the armies of Gog and Magog. To negate the reality of either is to belie the truth of existence.

There are times when we will experience the dominion of one or the other. The night will appear so deep that everything will be pulled into the swirling abyss. Yet even in that night we can hear a faint refrain that calls us back to life. And we can experience a religious dimension so overwhelming that all existence seems suffused by it, only to find that the dream bursts when some sharp reality scrapes across us. The reality we most often meet does not usually present us with either pole, but a confusing mixture of the holy and the profane.

In Auschwitz, an SS guard took a baby born in the camp, tore him from his mother's arms and tossed him over the barbed wire into no man's land. An SS captain who had noticed the woman before and had developed a liking for her opened the gate, picked up the baby and handed him back. What is that baby, now grown into manhood, to think of his universe? Had evil triumphed, he would not be here. He almost died as an infant by the merest whim of a Nazi soldier, but because a trace of humanity, of love and grace remained in the heart of an SS officer, he is alive today. Both are true—the one who threw him away, the one who brought him back. To deny either dimension is to falsify, to fail to include either side in our understanding of reality is to commit a most grievous sin of omission.

East of Eden the world that greets us contains mixtures of good and evil. Martin Buber interprets the eating of the fruit of good and evil as marking our entrance into the world where good and evil are admixtures, that we are not presented with clear choices between the two.[26] To defend the good we may have to use violence, to remain alive we may have to act in ways that will provoke guilt so long as we exist. Those who survived the camps did so because they engaged in acts of selfishness, but no one who survived did so on their own. They were helped by others. They held on to a vision of another reality even as they had to play by the rules of this one.

A daughter of a survivor reports that her mother was able to get adequate rations because she was chosen as a nurse to care for the victims of the medical experiments performed by the hated Dr.

Mengele. To watch the sadistic horror of Mengele's ugly craft, she had to be tough. She worked in the laboratory so that she could get the extra rations available there. If the cost was to witness depravity, that was the terrible choice life had presented to her. She was able to get enough food, not only for herself but for many others as well. She survived the war, but her husband, confronted by the inhumanity of the camp, refused to eat the food his wife smuggled to him in the men's camp and died within a month of arrival.

Even when the possibility of life was given, it had yet to be willed into existence. The assertion of selfhood, the insistence on survival, was the first act of spiritual resistance. In the midst of the worst suffering of the Warsaw ghetto, a Hasidic rabbi understood this when he taught the distinction between two types of crying. You can weep over your suffering until you despair, or you can feel in your weeping that God weeps along with you: that the goodness of the world is suffering. In the latter, one does not despair but continues to hold on to something: asserting one's own dignity—a reaffirmation of the Biblical sense of being created in the image of God even at this moment. The rabbi taught that in joining God in one's suffering, one began the moment of redemption.[27] Turning one's own pain into a source of sympathy— being able to feel the cosmic pain of the universe—that was the lesson of the moment even as all other teaching made no sense. Insisting on one's own worth while the enemy tried to blot it out,[28] battling for the preservation of a friend or a neighbor or a fellow inmate in the face of the overwhelming power of death that surrounded you everywhere, was the beginning of the assertion of a world opposed to Nazism.

The survivor had to reach out to the other: the nurse not only worked in Mengele's laboratory so that she might get extra food and live, but she also helped the sick in the hospital and others interned in the camp to survive.[29]

Survivors learn to take care of themselves, but also to go beyond themselves, to assert a world beyond the camps, to balance, amidst the extreme conditions of being reduced to something less than human, both the demands of the self and the care of the other, the need to preserve a moral life: "ethical survivalism." We are preservers of the holy, within us and within the world, even in a moral wilderness.

After the Holocaust we understand life as a battle. That battle must begin with the recognition of the worthwhileness of our own individual existence, with a measure of self-concern and even selfishness, but it cannot end there. We must go beyond ourselves.

We cannot suffer those who remain above that battle, preserving their own solitary piety, for they will be carried away by the wind. Only those who fight to sustain a world that holds back the evil always waiting at the door will be a part of the stream of the life and the sacred.

There is no assurance that good will win. In fact there are many moments when evil will triumph. And in defending the good we may have to paradoxically use the instrumentalities of evil. Life is a battle we fight to defend the holy, even as we become unholy in doing it.

What is so terrifying is that good and evil live side by side. In this world the indwelling of God and the constancy of evil are found next to each other. Survival may be a necessary task, and we may have to begin with the self in order to create the possibility of ethical activity, but it is all too easy for the concern with one's own needs to become self-centered. How do we balance the demands of the self with the demands of the other? In living life in the everyday, we become conscious of how easily what is good becomes obscured, how even while we begin by pursuing worthwhile ends, we become so caught in reality's mazes that we ourselves become instruments of harm. In this world, good and evil manifest themselves as admixtures. That is why it is so important to sustain a community of argument that constantly attempts to clarify not what is an absolute right, but a justice that though imperfect can reflect the realities of this world on the way to holiness. The perspectives others provide allow us to reach beyond ourselves to see what we do in a different light. But community by itself is not an automatic safety valve defending us from error. In our own time we have seen how the instrumentalities of mass society can corrupt society and silence dissenting voices. Rather it is only an ongoing society based on a tradition of the sacredness of the human and one that constantly questions and clarifies itself that can be trusted. The sacred is such a fragile attainment that without such a community it cannot be sustained, but will easily be perverted.[30]

There is no end to history, no messianic fulfillment of time, rather there is a sustained altercation between the chaos and the sacred that constitutes our core. Life is a pilgrimage, and we are always on the way. There are oases—stopping points of the spirit—where we can be refreshed, but we ought to realize that we need move on, or the water will run out.

The awareness of the eternity of the battle between the sacred and the chaos that always seeks to overwhelm it is the story the Jew now tells. It is a Jewish story and a human story: Jewish history is once again paradigmatic of the human condition.

We are changed. Theology is transformed. We close the book on a certain kind of thinking. We open a new one that contains a humbled concept of God and of humanity. And the Jew is a teller of this new tale.

15 THIS PEOPLE ISRAEL: The Spirit of Renewal

After the Holocaust the Jewish people have returned to the exercise of national power, and now must face the question of how to sustain the ethical and holy in a violent and tragic world.

1945. Jews in deportation camps.

Limpid white skin falls in folds over calcified bones. Skeletal bodies with bald skulls shuffle about. Gaunt eyes, now darting anxiously, now staring, survey the wasteland.

To look into those eyes impels a search to discover the secrets of what they had seen. One understands that they had witnessed acts, that they had some knowledge that we outside can learn of only at great personal cost.

Those haunted, hollow eyes seem to be looking for something in the distance, looking at once outside and inside, but seeing only images of the wreckage at hand.

This was the remnant of European Jewry. They faced the world numbly. Their mothers, daughters, and brothers had died, yet the skeletons lived, suspended between death and life. They survived in part through chance, the workings of fate and circumstance, and in part because they had willed their survival, come what may.

Now they were to reconstruct their lives amidst the stench of death. The wasteland extended around them. Not infrequently survivors tried to return to their homes in Poland, Czechoslovakia, or Holland, only to discover more wasteland. Where homes had been there was emptiness. Houses were destroyed or boarded up or occupied now by non-Jews. "We thought you were dead, why have you come back?" they were asked. Returning to their homes in Poland, Jews were sometimes killed by neighboring non-Jews.

The thousand-year-old story of European Jewish life had ended. Their biographies had been excised. The haunted faces of Margaret Bourke-White's photograph were homeless, suspended ghost-like over Europe. But they were not ghosts; they had come alive. "There was a rustling sound and the bones fitted themselves together" (Ezekiel 37:7).

The skeletons began to move; life was renewed. A new time issued in a new understanding. The course of Jewish history once again turned, and a different speech animated it. The survivors had to start fresh, to reconstruct a second life. Now they were joined by Jewry around the world who took up their burden. The decision to begin again, to start a new story, was not only personal, but a collective one. Just as the former lives of the survivors had ended, and for most there was no going back, so too, a certain kind of Jewish past was gone. A new life, a new Jewish life, would be framed by understandings forged in the furnaces of Europe. There could be no simple picking up of pieces, no natural continuation of what had been left off. Everything was different. New alternatives had to be pursued.

Choosing Palestine was a hope born of desperation. Told by the British that there would be no state, threatened by neighbors promising another annihilation, the survivors boarded rusty unseaworthy ships, some sinking on the way, some turned back by the British Navy, only a few making it. Others trekked across Europe over the mountains of Turkey, sneaking overland into Palestine from the north. It was a new children's crusade.

There is a proximity between the Holocaust and the establishment of the State of Israel that is far from accidental. Before the war, Zionism was one of many competing Jewish ideologies. At the end of the war it became a dominant mode of Jewish self-perception. Other possibilities such as Yiddish Socialism that had often, in the past, overwhelmed Zionism, now seemed obviously dated. In fact only during the war years did Zionism clarify its own goals: before, even among Zionists themselves, there had not been a consensus as to what the object of Zionist struggle was, and it was only with the Biltmore Convention of 1943 that the establishment of a state was made the central goal of the Zionist movement.

In the 1920s, permanent visas for Jewish settlement in Palestine had gone begging. In many of the years before Hitler's rise to power, more Jews left Palestine than came in. Were it not for the force of events, the settlement in Palestine would have proved a romantic unrealistic dream, overwhelmed in the end by Arab nationalism. Now Zionism meant something different; now it represented an act of collective self-renewal.

Something akin to this had happened at the time of the destruction of the second Temple. Then, too, Judaism had been subject to competing ideologies and dominated by rival factions: Sadducees, Essenes, Pharisees, and a variety of Messianic and Apocalyptic sects. The Pharisees were said to be an elitist sect numbering a mere two thousand, and yet after the Destruction they represented the only party that could reconstruct a viable Jewish life for the future. All contemporary Jewish religious life traces its ideological lineage to the Pharisees; the other options were discarded in the wake of the destruction of the Temple. The same was now true of Zionism.

For many of the survivors from the wreckage of Europe, moving to Israel became the only acceptable alternative after liberation. To be sure, large numbers went to Australia, or Latin America, or to North America, anywhere that would let them in. But there were hundreds of thousands who, even having an alternative, chose Israel. It was clear to them, as it was to much of world Jewry, that to start over they would have to change the direction of Jewish history and tell a radically new story.

Similarly, although before the war Jewry throughout the diaspora had been divided as to the viability and rightfulness of Zionism, now to all but a small minority the establishment of a Jewish State was an obvious necessity. Religious reformers who had sought to define Judaism as simply a religious faith and integrate Jews into the nation states where they resided, now returned to the liturgy the prayers for the restoration of Zion and

Jerusalem that they had deleted. Whereas before, support for the settlements in Palestine had been meager, now the generosity of the diaspora made the survival of the Yishuv possible.

The world at large, too, could see the necessity of a Jewish nation state. The establishment of Israel was enacted by the United Nations, its very existence owing to a consensus among the world community. Amidst the Cold War that developed between the superpowers, the establishment of the State of Israel represented one of the few major resolutions both sides voted for. What was it that now had become clear?

The liberated skeletons needed a body. Jewish existence as *luftmenschen* suspended in spiritual animation had proved too dangerous. To survive, Jews would need a state of their own with all the instrumentalities of power that other peoples had. Jews could not depend on the good faith of others, they needed to at least have a first line of defense of their own. For Jews this was not only a matter of practical politics but the expression of a spiritual understanding as well. Jews, the most ethereal of people, Jews who had had their bodies finally turned into smoke, Jews who had been made to float above the earth, now had to reenter their bodies, now had to anchor themselves on earth, now had to have a proper space in order to live. Jews demanded the right to sheer physical existence.

Immediately, with the birth of the State of Israel, it became clear that a new drama was being enacted. When Arabs attacked from all sides, this community too seemed as if it also might be snuffed out. But Jews finally had the chance to defend themselves. The fate of Jews surrounded by armies on all sides was different from the fate of the Jews of Europe who had had no means of self-defense: a new Jewish drama was unfolding.

Physicality. At our peril we had given it up. An etherealized people had been turned into black smoke curling upward and disappearing into the heavens. Now we returned to the ground, to the soil, to the earth into which spirit had first breathed.

Rootedness, an anchor, a people in its land. What was being reenacted here was what had been learned on the brink of death, in the existence in the camps. One was faced first of all with a decision to live or die. Every concentration camp had their "Muslims," the walking dead who would no longer battle for existence. Choosing to live, inmates had discovered that survival depended on a series of daily acts of physical care, that washing oneself, driving in a nail on which to hang one's possessions, was a daily reenactment of the will to be. The first concern was physical survival and the caring for one's self, the most elemental part of existence and the one the Jew had been least prepared to deal with. Now, looking back, Jews decided that they would never again be bodiless, going up in smoke. The etherealized people whose community existed in no space, who overcame the world's tragedy by seizing a world within, would now again materialize, reappearing on the world's historical stage. The life of inwardness that had preserved the Jew through a history of persecution had proved all but fatal in the Holocaust. Only amidst the greatest threat we had confronted had we begun to learn the art of physical survival. Reconstructing life after the Holocaust, Jewry realized that a central aspect of this people's story needed to be the cultivation of material existence, symbolized by a rootedness that had not been known before.

> Then he said to me, "Son of man, these bones are the whole house of Israel. Behold they say 'Our bones are dried up, and our hope is lost; we are clean cut off.' Therefore prophesy and say to them, 'Thus says the Lord God: "Behold I will open your graves and raise you from your graves, O my people; and I will bring you home into the land of Israel. And you shall know that I am the Lord, when I open your graves, and raise you up from your graves, O my people. And I will put my Spirit within you, and you shall live, and I will place you in your own land..."(Ezekiel. 37:11-14)

Landless we had turned to the subjective life and had glorified a world beyond, giving it greater weight than this world. Now we returned to the land that first nurtured us to again heal our wounded bodies.

Even as Jews may give lip service to the old rhetoric of scholastic piety or nostalgically cultivate the study of texts and values of another time, yet the demands of the hour constantly return us to the reconstruction of the physical life of the people. The return to history, the return to existence in a land, and the demands they make constitute the ground of our new reality. Not the distant vision at history's endtime, nor eternal transcendence removed from history, but here and now in the day-to-day decisions of present living is the crucial work to be found.

What was understood at this hour by the Jewish people was an almost unarticulated theology. The God beyond history, the other-worldly God had failed. The spiritualized ideals attached to that theology, the life of study and inward piety, had proved equally disastrous in the face of modern anti-Semitism. What was needed now was a new way of Jewish living that involved first of all a return to the body, and an understanding that resistance to the enemy had to begin with physical protest. Next time we would master all the instrumentalities the enemy had used against us: we would acquire a sufficient competence in using the weapons of this world so that we would adequately defend ourselves.

Contemporary Jewry no longer makes the scholar into the Jewish prototypical hero; in fact, the popular ethos has a highly ambivalent attitude toward the scholar, the rabbi, the piously learned.[31] Instead hero worship is afforded to the one rooted in the land, defending the land. Ben Gurion, the first prime minister of the nation, wrapped himself in this new mythic consciousness and even upon retirement felt the need to join Kibbutz Sde Boker, to carve an agricultural life out of the harsh rocky sands of the desert. Since Ben Gurion's retirement and death, Jews accorded hero worship to a Moshe Dayan, a mythic soldier-farmer digging in the earth to substantiate his existence and discover his past, defending his space; or as some have glorified an Ariel Sharon, cultivating an image of the tough soldiering general who knows how to fight with an iron fist. The contemplative life is not extolled any longer as the single ideal for the Jew. And just as the learned pietist is no longer the central model, the mass of Jewry has given up as well on the God who would respond by transforming history. No answer to the Jewish situation would come through Divine intervention. Salvation would emerge from a new Jewish self-understanding, from an exertion of Jewish energy and will.

After the enslavement of the Holocaust, what was demanded was a measure of autonomy,[32] the sense that rather than be a victim of military might, Jews would now themselves control war-making instruments. No longer was it sufficient to have influence, it was necessary to have the independent ability to engage in the full range of physical resistance and defense available to governments and states as well.[33]

So Jews returned to the exercise of power. The most ethereal of peoples now raised up an army, and soldiers became the new heroes of the nation, replacing scholar-saints. More, soldiering became the daily life of the people. Israel's army is, after all, a citizen's army in that almost everyone serves. While soldiering may have a romantic appeal in the myths of national identity, the average Israeli experiences military service as a terrible disruption to his life,[34] yet each is willing to accept that if one is going to live, he or she can only do so by physically defending the land.

If you are going to lay claim to a piece of earth, if you are going to insist on your right to exist, then you must be prepared to defend your life and your land. When Israeli high school students demonstrate outside Haredi Yeshivot to protest the exemption of youngsters who engage in traditional Torah study from army service, the clash of the values of two different worlds is made visible and evident.[35] For the Haredi, the world still stands on the pillar of Torah study; for the non-Haredi Israeli, existence depends on the commitment and ability to handle arms, to place one's own life and the lives of one's children in jeopardy in defense of Israel and its people.

Perhaps it was an accident of history that placed the Arabs at war with the new nation, but for the Jew, this war-making was also crucial for the forging of a new self-image, developed not only out of historical necessity but also out of ideological longing. Each march into the Sinai, each spectacular rescue, created an image that countered and dimmed the picture of Jews as victims. Each new story was a means to overcome the painful mourning for a tragic past. To be a heroic actor on the stage of history assured the Jew that he or she was still alive. There was a certain pride in having raised tough children whose romanticized image was not intellectual or dialectic subtlety, but rather straightforward and unadorned speech; who were typically silent, but who could display the courage and skill to defend the nation. In a situation where one has always to be prepared for battle, cunning in reading a page of Talmud was less an ideal than the ability to decipher topographical maps, to know intimately the lay of the land, and to lead troops effectively.

Constant war with Arab neighbors ensured that the feeling of embattlement carried over from Europe would form a significant aspect of the psyche of the new nation. Certainly, having an enemy who always threatened to throw you into the sea meant that images of total destruction were repeatedly reinvoked. While prime minister, the diminutive Levi Eshkol (barely five feet) visited President Lyndon Johnson and, in reviewing the honor guard, walked between the over six-foot Texan and the American soldiers who are especially chosen for state events because of their physical strength and impressive height. Eshkol remarked that he felt that he was once again facing the Cossacks of his youth who at any minute might kill him. Memory forms the Jew, and Israel is especially conscious of the historic images of the Jew as victim. Every state visitor is taken to Yad Vashem, the Holocaust memorial, for without confronting it, you do not understand one of the springs of Israel's tension.

To have lived for the first twenty years of its life, from its inception to the Six-Day War, with constantly repeated threats of destruction broadcast by its neighbors only served to reinforce the power of memory. Israelis realized that this circumstance was different only because they were armed as a nation-state, otherwise, they would have been destroyed as were their brethren in Europe.

There was a demonstrable need for toughness—an image that gained its metaphoric power from the desert. The young Israeli was called a Sabra, a desert cactus: ideally soft on the inside, while decidedly tough on the outside. This toughness was an aspect of the necessary use of force and violence. Terrorists did not suffer abstruse moral arguments as to proper means of warfare. One had to sully one's hands in order to survive. To create the State amidst conditions of war, villages had to be moved, populations expelled, real and potential threats extirpated.

The strength of these formative images is demonstrated by their persistence under changed circumstances. After the Six-Day War, Israel became an occupying power but continued to see itself as victim. Even as the Jewish state operates one of the strongest armies in the world, Israel continues to feel that it may become victim at any moment.

The resumption of power, including the violence and threat that states can manipulate, raises new issues for the Jew who now can take on the characteristics of the oppressor. Power can be used not only for self-defense but also as a means of domination. Our own liberation creates for us the same opportunity and danger to which all humanity is subject. Reentering history, returning to the land that first gave us nurture, we face the same problematic that survivors in the camps did: how to balance the elemental needs of our own existence, to care for ourselves, and yet see beyond ourselves, to remember the gift of life that is in our power to give in recognizing another. In our life in the land, in our struggles with power, we are called to live out what constitutes the moral life in the twentieth century, the need to assure our own survival, while yet acknowledging that there is a beckoning beyond ourselves. This century has been blessed with freedom and liberation movements and the winning of that battle has been a significant aspect of our era. But these movements can easily turn into xenophobic nationalism and racism, and that too has been the story of humanity in this century—the ugly aspect of our history.

The lesson of the Holocaust cannot be singleminded; it cannot simply be that we as Jews must assure our own survival. Were we to do only that, then we would miss an important element of what allowed people in the Holocaust to survive: only through reaching out to the other, and by being helped by others did survivors make it through that hell. Even if all that remained to connect one to the human family was a fragile frayed thread, one needed at least that to stay alive. To be sure, one learned new arts of survival. If you did not look out for yourself, you were swept away by the cruelty of the camps, but if at some moments you did not override your own self-interest and give even of your own nourishment to another then you too did not survive. In some deep human way, which represents the image of God within us, the turning to the other is the sustenance we need to keep ourselves alive. Without that assurance of the worthwhileness of life, we become the walking dead.

In a sense we are called to affirm in our new life in the land both aspects of what the Nazis sought to destroy: a living Jewish community and a life of caring.[36] To achieve this, to remain on the high wire without falling, would be an accomplishment at which the world would rightfully stare. To be able to balance the need for survival in a hostile world with the courage to recognize the conflicting claims and rights of others would be to enunciate a new moral order of which the world is sorely in need. The Jew, therefore, is tested in a new way: can we create a state where not only survival is made possible, but where respect for the other also forms the basic values of the nation? Can we assure the legitimate needs of the security of the Jewish people once again re-constituting itself while recognizing the basic rights of the Arabs who also live in this land, affirming their national aspirations? Fac-ing this task, Jews become a model of the moral order to be forged in our time. This century has been characterized by the worst racism and genocide in the history of humanity, and the question facing the Jew is not only whether he or she can survive this evil but whether Jews can create a society that points to a world beyond. This is the meaning of being a light unto the nations in our time.

The Jewish story now involves a constant argument of where and how to draw the line: what instrumentalities are needed for survival? What moral demands must we respond to? This is the discussion that we are now pulled into and that we need to center our moral and spiritual life on. When Jews fight between left and right, between those who advocate the transfer of all Arabs who live in Israel, those who would not permit any Palestinian state to exist, and those who insist on its establishment, they are fighting over the power and interpretation of memory: What does it mean to be a Jew? What is the lesson of our past, both that of antiquity and that of this century? How much can we be called upon to give to the other, and how much do we need for our own survival?

However dangerous this new decision making may be, we prefer it to the world we came from. Now we must deal with the tough questions that the exercise of power thrusts upon us, to face ourselves even as we may become an oppressor, to deal with the destructive consequences of the armaments we possess. We choose this over the retreat into a spiritual realm outside history that was the path of other generations. Our spiritual life is to be had only by facing these terrible questions.

After the Holocaust, the Jewish people understood they must behave differently, and to articulate the motives was not even necessary: in light of the events that had occurred Jewish behavior could be easily understood. The establishment of the State of Israel, the transformation of Jewish life after massive destruction, constitutes the triumph of a new set of Jewish instincts, the attachment to new self-understandings. But the working out of this new path has been largely instinctual and reactive.

As time moves on, and as power is exercised on broader fronts, there is a danger in depending on instinctual behavior. Survivalism can spill over into hatred of the other; Jewish self-interest can take on the visage of racism. With the passage of time, as memory becomes myth, there is a danger that memory will distort the perception of reality and that Jews will act inappropriately. The Jewish people initially coalesced out of the transformation of Israel's own experience into moral demand: remember the oppressed, for you yourselves were once like them, and know what that condition feels like from the inside. But there was no inner necessity in this leap. Jews could have acted with the same resentment that any other recently liberated people exhibits. There is no inner logic that compels the assumption of moral superiority on the part of the victim. The Jewish understanding that a moral command, an obligation to others, issued from their own history of oppression was a unique moment in the history of peoples.

To save ourselves in our time from the danger of becoming oppressors and victimizers, we must be clear about our own motives and spell out the limits to which we will go. While defending ourselves, it is important that we engage in earnest and open debate that provokes self-analysis, so that we do not lose sight of our moral obligations, if our character as a holy people, a people compelled by an ideal, a people striving to maintain a sense of the sacred as central to its self-conscious definition as a community, is to be preserved.

People stumble; knowing where to draw the line that justice demands is not always possible. Frequently that kind of demarcation can only be found by trial and error. But there is a marked difference between a society that makes the values of caring for the other explicit and one in which consideration of the other retreats into a "not knowing" or worse, reduction of the other into someone who does not share one's own basic humanity. The specific decisions the nation makes may prove right or wrong; to be human is to hit the mark only sometimes and to miss it many times. But if there is no intentionality regarding the need for excellence, then marksmanship will never be achieved. The question of how to behave ethically under conditions of embattlement has to be addressed.

In entering that discussion we would do well to be tempered by the texts of our heritage. These are the texts we pored over for generations, seeking a Divine truthfulness that at its heart must be moral. In this generation, with the stakes raised to precipitous heights, the questions have become ever more serious—to shoot or not to shoot; rubber bullets or real ones; negotiation or deportation; tear gas or counter terror—and are all too often asked in a vacuum, a vacuum sealed off by fear and momentary instinct. If our moral decision making is an argument about setting priorities, about where to place limits, limits on ourselves and limits on others, then we need to be drawn back into the texts that formed us. While study should not become an end in itself, an idealized Jewish spiritual form for meeting the Divine, we do recognize that the texts that fashioned us are characterized by the struggle with ethical decision making. Biblical prophecy grows out of a spiritual confrontation with the power of the state; the Talmud is quintessentially a book containing arguments over limits: where to set boundaries, how to create a legal system reflective of religious principle. A normative Talmudic discussion involves questions of where to put up fences, how much privacy need the law protect, what are the bounds of the self the law must guarantee, what are the communal obligations that it ought to require,[37] and equally, as can be seen from the following, questions of life and death.

> If two people were travelling in the desert, and one of them was carrying a canteen that had sufficient water so that if one drank he would be able to reach a settlement, but if both drank they would both die, Ben Petura taught that it is better for both to die than for one to see the death of the other, but R. Akiva came and taught, "And your brother shall live with you" (Leviticus 25), your life precedes that of your neighbor.[38]

For a thousand years after this comment was written, there was little interpretative discussion of this text. Finally in Eastern Europe the argument was expanded: what if three people are walking and there is enough water for only two, what if the future is more cloudy and the people have no idea of how much distance they yet have to traverse? Whom does one save? How is the choice made of whom to save? This discussion tested the borders of the moral claim being made, and these texts formed the basis of religious decision making in the ghettoes of Eastern Europe under Nazi occupation.[39] What matters less is the specific outcome— sages have always disagreed with one another—but what marks us is that we are a culture that engages in this discussion, whose texts are resources for debating these issues.

What is striking about the passage quoted is that while future generations assumed the law followed Rabbi Akiva (it is hard to imagine any society that could decide otherwise), the opinion of Bar Petura continued to be taught and was included in the official rescension of the Mishna. The rabbinic authors may be trying to say that even as we engage in acts of selfishness, we must remember that there is an absolute value of human worth that we are laying aside, that even as we make difficult ethical decisions, whatever the outcome, we need to hold onto the tension animating the decision making, for if we lose the memory of one of the poles, we will forget the demands of either the self or the other. Circumstances may necessitate tough decisions, ones that require consideration of the self over the other, but even under these conditions the knowledge that the person I face makes a demand of me cannot be forgotten.

Rabbinic texts that deal with how a victim is to behave abound; fewer texts emerge from a history of the exercise of state power, for during these two thousand years that has hardly been our fate. The conditions of contemporary Jewish life constitute a fundamental break with the perspectives and circumstances that animated those traditional texts, and the rise of the State of Israel creates a set of conditions different from those the rabbis of the Talmud had to face. The Talmud does not, for instance, discuss the issue of warmaking in a way that can be meaningfully used by a modern state. Yet even when our circumstances change and the perspective is no longer that of victim, the values enunciated in the textual discussions we inherit still have the power to instruct us. What they teach in a significant way is how to conduct our own moral discussion, even though the specific content may change with new circumstances.

We face then a terrible rupture. Moral dilemmas in the present force us to look for guidance within a tradition that has been formative of who we are, but our present circumstance is quite different from the situation that formed the basic texts of the tradition. Being Jewish today and wanting to place oneself within the tradition is therefore an act of reaching across an abyss, of translating what has been into a new context. To be Jewish is to place oneself within an ongoing community and tradition of argument. That discussion takes place from our new perspectives: our memories of recent history and the new situation we find ourselves in.

This is a demanding task from which many would flee, either by leaving off the Jewish world and entering into the seemingly simpler circumstance of Western life, or by retreating into an other worldly spirituality, whether Buddhist or Haredi. But the story our situation calls upon us to write is a different one: we have given up discovering the sacred by withdrawing from life in the world. For us, the holy will now be manifest only amidst physical existence, amidst day-to-day life. We recognize that chaos and evil are at the heart of humanity and that to survive we cannot afford to evolve a morality for the end of days, a life of messianic dreaming, a life that withdraws from the demands of history. But we are also called to recognize that there is a possibility of creating a holy way in the here and now. The piety we are now called upon to develop is not one in which God is found in the life of inwardness, but rather we search for the sacred in the celebration of life, in the mediation of self and other, in the establishment of the conditions of our own existence and in our nurturing the life of our neighbor. In the daily decision making, defining, and discovering self and dealing with otherness, in balancing selfishness and selflessness, we walk on the way that contains within it the possibility of allowing the spirit to enter the world and sustain it.

If in light of the Holocaust we have made certain choices and adopted decided attitudes, we now face yet another choice: do we intend, through the life we create here in the land, to uncover the holy, or have we given up on all religious possibility? Is the sacred forever buried in Auschwitz? Did we emerge from there with no larger set of obligations than our own survival, or did we learn something else—how not to become Nazis, how to make way for the holy by reaching beyond ourselves, even as we will our own survival?

God's response to Job in the whirlwind is that Job is unaware of the primal battle of existence, that Job has wanted a pure justice, simple reward and punishment. He is told that in this world that is not a given. Good and evil are mixed together and the stuff of everyday life does not allow for a singleminded Divine response. Job was wrong to think that the good will always win out.

If the rabbis felt closer to the response to tragedy offered by Isaiah and essentially rejected the way of Job, we now feel closer to the story of the one who did not make peace with suffering than to the glorification of the suffering servant.

Job learns that there are limits to what he can expect of God, that the justice we demand of the universe is unreasonable. We, too, have discovered that left to its own devices there can be a terrible cruelty at the heart of humanity, that the possibilities of the victory of evil are real and that there is no guarantee of a Messianic future, a happy ending to our story. Since that is the case, we must first of all insure our own defense, our own survival. But we can continue struggling with the sacred, continue to make way for God's manifestation.

Even as Job discovers that there is a deeper meaning to existence, that good and evil, the power God exercises in the world are different from what he thought, yet he is precious to God for never having broken off the discussion. We are the people who continue to argue about the meaning of the sacred in our lives.

16 HISTORY TODAY

Even as we push forward in time and enter a new era history reverberates within us. The arguments of Job and Isaiah, the clashings of Talmudic discussion and the ethical debate which Jewish texts engaged in continue to speak to our generation, but in new ways.

We have come full circle.

Once again we take up the telling of the tale. Once again the Jewish people, as they contemplate their own history, must find a message within. And once again, amidst a hostile world, we listen to hear the call to witness the possibility of meaning and holiness.

Even as we move toward places we have never been, our roots search down to find nourishment in our past. Our post-modern consciousness discovers a connectedness with other generations. All Jewish theology is a conversation across time, each generation adding its own voice to the discourse. The questions that are the concern of our generation—the understanding of suffering, the meaning of redemption—are the eternal questions of Jewish history.

As we seek to find our own voice, voices of other Jewish times reverberate within us. To understand the present, we turn to the ancient past. There is a commonality that echoes across the abyss of time. Repeatedly, at each new articulation of Jewish history, the same questions are raised. Each generation shatters its past with its questing; each new questing needs to articulate the divine speech in its own voice. Yet even as the meaning we find cloaks itself in contemporary language, we recognize the inherited frame that it enfolds. All of Jewish thought seems to be an encircling around a pole that forms its center. The circles widen, the radii enlarge, but the center always remains the same. Each generation needs to find its own responses, but the quest ultimately remains the same: to recover a vision of the sacred amidst a tragic reality.

The initial responses to the quest achieve their first formulation in the biblical canon, and anyone who wishes to understand these questions must turn to those scrolls for a pristine vision that no subsequent generation can achieve. The biblical response is forever uniquely fresh like all first times. Yet anyone who studies the course of Jewish thought knows that the responses that Jews enunciate are not limited to the biblical answers. Instead, they are ever again renewed elaborations, exegetically—midrashically—expanding the range of Jewish thought into a new time, into a new language. For the past, whispering in faded voice may yet signal the coordinates for locating ourselves amidst our own uncharted time.

In the revival of Hebrew and the return to the land of our forebears, we rediscover our biblical roots where the call of God challenged those who would exercise power to act on the most primal truths of religious understanding. That grappling with history and existence in the world so characteristic of the Bible was, in part, camouflaged by the rabbis after Bar Kochba and by the Jewish experience in the Middle Ages. The Holocaust and the return to the land uncovers the primal confrontation between God's call and the world. So, we awaken in ourselves that first exploration of religious quest even as we reach toward a time that has never been known before. As we move forward in time and discover new understandings, different ways of viewing God, humanity, and Israel, yet we also find that we continue the vocabulary and the argument that has been at the center of our existence.

Torah will not be an end for us; it will not constitute the experience of time out of history, but it can keep alive in us the sensitivities found in the resources of our past. Torah represents one of the few ways we have of assuring the weighing of values necessary in these new and dangerous times.

We will not look to the tradition for law, for an absolute guidance, for our circumstances and theology are conditioned by new events and understandings, but we can be sustained by the vocabulary that the tradition offers us for self-knowledge.

We will not receive singleminded direction from our study of the tradition, but in engaging in open-ended argument regarding what we must do, we will be bounded by the values of survival and otherness, of the knowledge of evil and the will to do good, of the needs of the self and the need to reach out to the other. We will go out to create a new life, one that will reveal through its existence the divine calling. As much as the return to the land is an expression of a new Jewish story, it is equally an expression of continuity, of a determination to continue Jewish life as a witnessing, as a message aimed equally at the inner life of Jews and all humanity. In an unredeemed world, our task is to be a blessing to ourselves and to others.

Once this people was called to witness, to give its message to humanity and now yet again. This new calling has within it, for all its innovation, a deep connectedness with that earlier one. The quest for holiness amid a violent and tragic world is still our task.

We have traveled far, only to continue walking on the way.

As Martin Buber taught in a series of lectures delivered after the war:

> Creation is incomplete because discord still reigns within it, and peace can only emerge from the created. That is why, in Jewish tradition, he who brings about peace is called the companion of God in the work of creation.[40]

The word is spoken, the silence becomes articulate, but the mystery is not dispelled; it only beckons us to move on.

> Adam lay with his wife again. She bore a son and named him Seth [the one who is placed before us] "for," she said, "God has granted me another son in the place of Abel because Cain killed him." Seth too had a son whom he called Enosh [humanity]. At this time people began to invoke the Lord [YHVH] by name. (Genesis 4:25-26)

We stir toward each other. We reach out. In the darkness, we see only a profile. Having borne rage, having known violence, having witnessed fratricide, we have no expectations for what will come. What will be is a gift. We shall treat it as a mysterious treasure. Perhaps that is the secret of our humanity. Perhaps that is what is meant by the sacred...Such thoughts can only last a moment... And then the terror, the emptiness will be upon us again... I touch the face of the one beside me...

NOTES

Part One

1. Our current numbering system of Biblical chapters originated with the early Christians long after the completion of the Hebrew Bible. It is clear, though, that the first seven days constitute one literary unit, that the story of the Garden is a second independent literary unit, and that the story of the seventh day should be included in chapter one, not two.

2. George Steiner in *After Babel* writes, "Unlike the animal species we are out of balance with and in the world. Speech is the consequence and maintainer of this disequilibrium."

3. Jeremiah 7:4, 22. Unless indicated otherwise, Biblical quotations in this chapter are from the Jewish Publication Society translation, hereafter cited as JPS.

4. JPS translation.

5. This is the insightful reading of the book that Alan Mintz gives in his *Hurban: Responses to Catastrophe in Hebrew Literature*, ch. 1, pp. 17ff.

6. Martin Buber, *The Prophetic Faith*, p. 189.

7. Translations of the Book of Job are from Robert Gordis, *The Book of God and Man*.

8. See George Steiner in footnote 2.

9. *New English Bible* translation; hereafter cited as NEB.

10. "The implication seems to be that there are some corners of the world where God's sway is less than total, so that a few forms of wickedness escape his punishment." Robert Gordis, *God and Man*, p. 301.

11. "Most of what has been written on the Book of Job has been done out of an only partial understanding of even the literal meaning of the book, since more than 100 words have not been properly defined..." Tur-Sinai in the *Biblical Encyclopedia* (Hebrew), "Job," vol. I, p. 301. Tur-Sinai is pointing to the fact that much of the vocabulary of The Book of Job is unique and therefore irretrievable to us. Tur-Sinai further complicates the matter by arguing that the book as we have it is a translation from an Aramaic original. I believe he is wrong, but what the argument points to is the overwhelming feeling of distance that a contemporary reader feels from the language of this book.

12. "It is scarcely possible to speak of the author of any Biblical book in the modern sense of the word, for virtually all Biblical books are composite in some degree, as were most literary productions in the ancient Near East." Marvin Pope, *Job*, p. xxxvii. It is generally agreed that the first two chapters and the ending of the Book of Job have been reworked from an older narrative. Some think that the Elihu

speeches are an intrusion. In addition, Job's final speeches in the midsection of the book are general wisdom statements that even undercut Job's argument and so are clearly a separate body of material.

13. Buber, *Prophetic Faith*.

14. Translations of Isaiah are taken from the NEB.

Part Two

1. NEB translation.

2. *The Jewish Wars*, VII, pp. 332-33.

3. *Sifre*, Nitzavim, Piska 305, Finkelstein ed., p. 325. See *ad loc.* for parallels. This midrashic sermon is quoted by Salo Baron along with a number of other legends which speak from the same perspective, see his *A Social and Religious History of the Jews*, vol II, pp. 113-14.

4. T.B. Gittin 55b-56a. The Talmudic presentation of this tale adds another level of theological subtlety. It begins: "The destruction of Jerusalem came through a Kamza and a Bar Kamza; the destruction of Tur Malka came through a cock and a hen; the destruction of Betar came through a shaft of leather." This reduction of crucial historical events to seeming trivialities represents by its ironic tone a subtle theological questioning and an argument against any meaning to be found in history. But the Talmud itself is a post-Akibean composition—see the following chapters in this part for an elaboration of that argument.

5. Mishna Sotah 1:7-8. See also Mishna Shabbat 2:6. For the notion of balance in Rabbinic theology see G. F. Moore, *Judaism*, part VI, ch. iv, "Chastisement," pp. 248 ff.; and E. Urbach, *Hazal*, pp. 389ff.

6. Mishna Avot 5:11-14. Similar enumerations, with differences in detail, appear in Avot of Rabbi Nathan, version I, ch. 38, and version II, ch. 41, Schechter ed., p. 113; and in T.B. Sabbath 32b-33a.

7. Mishna Kidushin 1:10.

8. JPS translation. Although only the introductory phrase is quoted in the text itself, there is no doubt that the allusion is to the extended thought.

9. Mechilta of R. Ishmael, Mishpatim ch. 18, Horovitz-Rabin ed., p. 313. See also E. Urbach, *Hazal*, p. 398; English edition, p. 492.

10. *I and II Esdras*, translation by Jacob B. Myers (1974).

11. NEB translation.

12. What, of course, the Maccabeans do not emphasize in their own telling of the story is that their final victory was assured only through their calling on Rome to

intervene in their behalf. Although Rome did not find it necessary to send troops, their siding with Israel led to the agreement by the Syrians not to push further.

13. Menahem Stern in his entry in *The Encyclopedia Judaica* romantically describes the events: "...for the first time in the history of mankind, an epic chapter of martyrdom on a large scale [occurred] to bequeath in the resistance of the martyrs and Hasideans during the religious persecutions, a symbol and an example throughout all succeeding generations to both Jews and non-Jews" (vol 8, p. 629).

14. II Maccabees tr. by Jonathan Goldstein, p. 289. Whether or not these stories are historical or legendary makes little difference for the argument being developed here since there is no doubt that in either case this work represents the development of a new mentality in the second century B.C.E.

15. This theme of vicarious atonement receives even greater emphasis in the later retelling of the story of Elazar and Hannah and the seven brothers in IV Maccabees: "But when the fire already reached to his bones and he was about to give up the ghost, he lifted up his eyes to God and said 'Thou, O God, knowest that though I might save myself I am dying by fiery torments for they Law. Be merciful unto thy people, and let our punishment be a satisfaction in their behalf. Make my blood their purification, and take my soul to ransom their souls'" (6:27-29). *Pseudopigrapha*, Charles, ed., p. 674.

16. See p. 34 herein.

17. For the historical aspects of the Bar Kochba revolt, I have depended on S. Yeivan, *Milhemet Bar Kochba*; Michael Avi Yona, Bimei Roma U'byzantium, now available in English as *The Jews of Palestine*; and also on Gedaliah Alon, *Toldot Hayehudim*. All of them base their account on the third-century Roman historican Dio Cassius, whose work achieves confirmation and supplementation through modern archaeological evidence. For that archaeological history see Yigael Yadin, *Bar Kochba*.

18. Dio Cassius, LXIX, 12.

19. Some coins were struck with Bar Kochba on one side, and an Elazar, the priest, otherwise unknown, but perhaps the designated High Priest, on the other, indicating the religious motivation of the restoration of the Temple as a central concern of the revolt. Many coins featured Jerusalem prominently and are dated as of the "Freedom of Jerusalem." It is Yigael Yadin's archaeological work that finally succeeded in unravelling the mystery of Bar Kochba's name, see his *Bar Kochba*, where he also has an extensive discussion of the design of the coins of this period.

20. Salo Baron, *A Social and Religious History of the Jews*, vol. II, p. 101.

21. Dio Cassius, LXIX, 13, pp. 449-51. One is of course naturally skeptical of the huge numbers, yet the modern historian Avi Yona confirms this impression of depopulation: "...we arrive at an estimate of the total Jewish population of Palestine before the war of Bar Kochba as 1,300,000. After the fall of Betar there were left only between seven and eight hundred thousand, of which three and four hundred thousand were concentrated in Galilee," *Bimei Roma U'byzantium*, p. 19.

22. *Ibid*.

23. T.B. Kidushin 39b. The passage is paralleled in T. J. Hagiga 2:1 where it is Judah ha-Nahtom whose tongue is played with by a dog.

24. The line that follows here in the printed text and that forms the prelude to R. Akiva's response, "May he go to hell," is clearly an interpolation since (a) R. Akiva

would hardly have introduced his comments with this remark, which undercuts the next statement, and (b) the switch to third person from second removes it from direct speech.

25. Translated according to Jastrow (1971) who reads Ahat.

26. T.J. Sotah 5:5. The same story is found in T.J. Berachot 9:5 and in a slightly different version in T.B. Berachot 61b, which adds the ending: "The angels asked God, 'This Torah, and this is its reward?' ...God's echo, responded, 'Blessed are you Akiva, who are summoned to a future world.'"

27. This goes well beyond the Christian Testament's view of Jesus' death that in one account Jesus himself can not understand and which in Pauline theology becomes an atonement for original sin. See Urbach, *Hazal*, note, p. 391.

28. To the disappointment of the leadership, only the Jews of the Land of Israel joined in the revolt, and it was only there that the practice and teaching of Judaism was interdicted.

29. Mechilta, Jethro, Masechta D'bahodesh, ch. 6, Rabin-Horowitz ed., p. 227. The last line is a pun on the alliterative *av* and *ahov*. A similar midrash is reported in the name of R. Nehemiah in Leviticus Rabbah 32:1, Margoliot ed., p. 735.

30. This Mishnaic teaching is part of a sequence of teachings which all begin, "On that day...." Nowhere in the sequence is there any indication as to what the referent is. The Babylonian Talmud (Berachot 28a) offers that it was the day when the Joshua faction seized control of the rabbinic assembly, deposing its head and installing R. Elazar b. Azariah. However, it is unclear whether the Babylonian Talmud is right in its assumption. Albeck in his notes on this Mishna, pp. 384-85, argues that "On that day" refers to the day on which R. Joshua praised the interpretations of his student, Akiba, which is the subject of the previous three Mishnayot, and that Akiba having taught before his teacher another student of R. Joshua's—R. Joshua ben Hyrcanus—also taught and was praised.

R. Joshua b. Hyrcanus is mentioned nowhere else in rabbinic literature. It is hard to believe that he is the brother of Eleazar b. Hyrcanus, the well-known rabbinic teacher whom we discuss below; since the latter was a student of R. Yochanan b. Zakkai and thus a contemporary of the R. Joshua who praises R. Joshua b. Hyrcanus, it makes little sense that he would have had a younger brother who would have studied with R. Joshua. It may be that a descendant of the Hyrcanus family studied with Joshua and that Hyrcanus here is a family name rather than specifically a patronymic. If so it is hard to believe that Joshua is a direct descendant of Eleazar since the latter was frequently at odds with the R. Joshua who is here represented as the teacher and was finally excommunicated by him and his colleagues.

The Tosefta offers a variation in which a similar teaching is given in the name of R. Judah the Prince, the editor of the Mishna: "Rebi taught: Abraham is called 'one who fears God' and so too Job—just as Abraham worshipped God out of love, so too Job. All of Job's shouting and imprecations flung at heaven are only literary devices used to impress on us how much Job suffered." Some manuscripts ascribe this teaching to R. Meir, the student of R. Akiba. Either way, the tradition the Tosefta represents is that this reinterpretation of the figure of Job is the work of the generation or two following Bar Kochba (Tosefta Sotah 6:1, Lieberman ed. pp. 182-322). In any case, clearly this reinterpretation of the figure of Job is the work of Akiba and his school.

31. Mishna Sotah 5:5.

32. R. Meir is following a common legendary interpretation that Isaac was a willing partner in his own sacrifice. The underlying assumption is that Abraham would never have slain Isaac without his permission. The Jerusalem Targum (Gen. 22:8, 10) even incorporates this interpretation in its translation.

33. *Sifre Va'ethanan*, ch. 6, Piska 32, Finkelstein ed., pp. 58-59. The Hebrew is a pun on the similarly sounding meod—might, and modeh—acquiescence and acceptance. The editor of this chapter of Sifre has brought together a variety of differing doctrines regarding suffering, see beginning p. 56 and ff.

34. For R. Simeon, the world to come is the real life and is therefore what is alluded to in this verse. The text is from *Sifre*, ch. 32.

35. *Sifre*, ch. 32. The verb used here for suffering, *ysr*, is the same as that used in the previous citation. In both cases the double meaning of *ysr* as instruction and as chastening is played on. The play is probably etymologically correct, instruction being conceived of as the whipping the teacher gave to discipline his students.

36. Genesis Rabbah 9:10.

37. T. B. Berachot 61b.

38. T.B. Kidushin 39b.

39. The Babylonian Talmud concisely summarizes R. Jacob's message: "There is no reward in this world for the performance of commandments."

40. Gen. Rab. 9:5.

41. On the life of Simeon b. Yohai see A. Marmorstein, and also Shmuel Safrai, pp. 31-32.

42. The legend exists in many versions; the one here appears in T.B. Sabbath 33b. The last phrase has the sense that it is suffering that enabled R. Simeon to become a great master of Torah, so the Talmudic elaboration ad loc. The last part of the tale is clearly an addition—the character of R. Eliezer disappears entirely—and indicates the way this story is built up out of disparate legendary materials. The historical core is irrecoverable.

43. Mishna Avot 3:11. Some manuscripts read R. Jacob as the author of this dictum. See Taylor, ad loc., (Hebrew section). R. Jacob was a younger contemporary of R. Simeon and is otherwise close to the former's theological position.

44. T.J. Berachot 1:2.

45. Mishna Kidushin 4:14.

46. Mechilta Beshalach, Masechta d'vayisa, ch. 2. Rabin-Horowitz ed. p. 161; see also commentary *ad loc.*

47. B.T. Sanhedrin 99b.

48. *Ibid.* R. Meir continues that the profitability of an enterprise is not based on skill, but on fate, thus separating business success from any notion of merit. R. Meir's position is a practical one. Rabbi Noharai's opinion in preceding paragraph is from Mishna Kidushin 4:14; R. Judah Ilai's is from Tosefta Kidushin 4:14; Lieberman, pp. 279–80.

49. Mishna Avot IV:8.

50. Avot of R. Nathan, Version I, ch. 28. Schechter ed., p. 86. It is clear that the continuation of this midrash is a conflate with another probably Jewish gnostic midrash, a point already made by Bacher

51. Avot 6:4.

52. S. Abramsky, *Bar Kochba,* p. 135, maintains that in 136-137, just a year after the revolt had been fully suppressed, Jerusalem was a fully rebuilt city with theaters and circuses.

53. Alon, *Toldot Hayehudim,* vol. II, pp. 43–45. Abramsky, *op. cit.,* p. 135. Most of the Talmudic source material on which this observation is based is quoted in the chapter herein.

54. Tosefta Eruvin 5:24, Lieberman, p. 117.

55. See p. 43 herein.

56. As a legal saying in Mishna Berachot 9:5, and as here and T.J. Berachot. See also T.B. Berachot 63a.

    That this position remained controversial is shown by its exclusion from some manuscripts of the Mishna and of the removal of the word "because" so that the Hebrew more clearly agrees with the plain meaning of the original verse, to wit, that the time for acting is when the Torah is violated. Margoliot argues that the statement of R. Nathan is a beraita tacked on later to a Mishna. While this would explain its absence from some manuscripts, it does not question the authenticity of the saying. See his Encyclopedia of the Masters of the Talmud, vol. II, p. 680. As to the various versions see Dikdukei Soferim, *ad loc.* The more radical version accepted here which is also the standard printed text and one known to Rashi and Maimonides—though the latter interprets it in an entirely different manner, seeing it as a Messianic teaching—has the most authentic voice and is consistent with the other statement of R. Nathan quoted next. (See commentaries of Rashi and Maimonides, *ad loc.*) It should be noted that the version found in the printed text of the Mishna by including R. Nathan's statement as a coda to the very first Tractate whose subject matter is the quintessential rabbinical innovation-prayer makes R. Nathan's dictum into a kind of slogan describing the essential creed of the Mishna.

    Misinterpretations have arisen because of a lack of understanding of the Yerushalmi; see Albeck in his edition of the Mishna and the P'nai Moshe, *ad loc.,* last section of the Yerushalmi Berachot. The statement quoted there in the name of Simeon b. Yohai refers to a time later than the one discussed here. It is a voice that speaks to the depressed time after the defeat: if you see people who have given up all hope and washed their hands of Torah, redouble your own efforts on its behalf, for you will receive the reward of them all. When do we know this, is from the verse "they violate your Torah, therefore it is the time to serve the Lord." Thus is a biblical verse politicized for the sake of heaven.

57. Mechilta, Ki Tisa, Masechta D'Shabata 1:3, Rabin-Horowitz ed., p. 341.

58. The related verses to which R. Akiva undoubtedly also alludes are illuminating for the ironic interpretation R. Akiva is now giving them: "I have put before you life and death, blessing and curse. Choose life—if you and your off-spring would live—by loving the Lord your God, heeding His commands, and holding fast to Him, for thereby you shall have life and shall long endure upon the soil..." (JPS translation).

59. T.B. Berachot 61b.

60. Jeremiah 29.

61. See Jacob Neusner's life of Yochanan b. Zakkai, *Development of a Legend.* Similarly, in his *First Century Judaism in Crisis,* p. 192: "He chose a middle way. He prayed for

the rebuilding of the Temple, but he took full account of the needs of the generation which had to live without it. He did not expect that centuries would pass without the restoration of a permanent Temple in Jerusalem."

62. Salo Baron, *A Social and Religious History of the Jews*, vol. II, p. 117.

63. This point is masterfully developed by Robert Goldenberg in his "The Broken Axis: Rabbinic Judaism and the Fall of Jerusalem."

64. For a complete listing and analysis, see Neusner's Development of a Legend. For a summary, see his *First Century Judaism*, p. 191.

65. Goldenberg, *op. cit.*, makes a similar point from other materials, p. 876.

66. *Sifre*, Ekeve, ch. 11, Finkelstein ed., p. 85. Mechilta D'Rashbi 1:17, Epstein-Melamed eds., p. 19, and numerous parallels; see e.g., the listing in Finkelstein, *ad loc*. Almost all modern Jewish historians of the period have discussed this passage and have seen it as a strategic political discussion in connection with the Bar Kochba revolt. The most notable exception is Gedaliah Alon, who argues that R. Tarfon was too old to have lived through the Bar Kochba revolt and that R. Jose, the Galilean who is mentioned in the continuation of this passage, is not mentioned at all in connection with Bar Kochba and was not among the martyred. See Alon, *Toldot*, vol. I, p. 134. Neusner seeks to remedy these objections by dating the meeting at 120-130, that is, as a kind of planning meeting before the revolt began. However, Neusner's suggestion, though a clever compromise, is unlikely since it does not take into account the genesis of the revolt as a reaction to the visit of Hadrian; secondly, no one could have really expected the subsequent ferocity of Roman persecution since it was unusual by Roman standards and duplicated nowhere else in the empire. See Neusner, *History and Torah*, pp. 97-98. Our own time has seen aged leaders playing pivotal roles, and there is no reason to believe that in this respect we are unique. By everyone's consensus R. Tarfon lived a long time, having seen the Temple, studied with Yochanan b. Zakkai and presided over the court when Akiva was in his prime.

The placing of the meeting at Lydda and the importance of the figure of R. Tarfon dates this text as later than 116, for before then R. Tarfon did not stand at the head of the court and an official meeting would not have met in his own hometown (see Neusner, *op. cit.*). The parallel version in the Palestinian Talmud which uses the language "Gamarnu" conveys the sense of a formal halachic decision having been taken. Moreover, it makes sense that in order to make a formal decision of this quasi-Jewish government that the elders would travel to the home of their "presiding officer," especially if he were old and unable to travel.

Interestingly, the decision regarding martyrdom (see above) also takes place in Lydda, and the Babylonian version even places it as having taken place in the same house as our story! (B.T. Kidushin 40b).

One might think of a series of decisions on the part of the rabbinic leadership, perhaps moving from one secret hiding place to another (meeting in the upper chamber) in the home city of the aged head of the court, R. Tarfon. The most fitting time for such discussion to have taken place would be at the beginning of the persecutions, which can either be dated with the occupation of Galilee, which occurred almost at the outset of the revolt, or with its final quashing in 135. R. Tarfon, already in his eighties or nineties, probably died before he, too, could be caught and martyred.

If this reading is correct, what was decided was that although laymen need not risk martyrdom except in the most adverse of circumstances, the rabbis themselves would insist on the transmission and teaching of Torah, even while risking martyrdom.

67. I have translated the Hebrew *yoshev*—"to sit"—as a technical term, i.e., "to hold court."

68. T.B. Avoda Zarah 18a, tr. by A. Mishcon (London: Soncino Press, 1935). See also Tractate Semachot, ch. 8: "But, if it is for the Torah Scroll that you are weeping, lo, the Torah is fire, and fire cannot consume fire. Behold the letters are flying in the air, and only the parchment itself is burning." The Tractate on Mourning, tr. by Dov Zlotnik. The martyrdom of Hanina b. Teradyon is also attested to in the Tannaitic source *Sifre Deuteronomy*, Ha'azinu ch. 32, Piska 307, Finkelstein ed., p. 346. There it is similarly mentioned that he died with a Sefer Torah although the accompanying legend is lacking.

69. Mishna Avot 3:3.

70. Mishna Avot 3:5-6. Ezekiel is clearly referring to the reconstructed Temple. See also Marmorstein, "Maalat Talmud Torah," p. 170.

71. Avot of R. Nathan, Version I, ch. 4, Schechter ed., p. 18. English tr. by Judah Goldin, p. 32. See also Version II, ch. 8, Schechter, p. 22. In both cases the editor has arranged the text so that the importance of benevolent deeds—Gemilut Hasadim—with which the text is concerned is undercut. Thus, there is a kind of editorial comment that Torah and not Gemilut Hasadim should be the new source of atonement.

72. And not, as Urbach claims an older student of R. Akiva; see his "Asceticism and Suffering in the Teaching of the Sages," p. 61. Note Mishna Yevamot 16:7, where Akiva reports a teaching in the name of Judah b. Babba—hardly a master-disciple relationship.

73. T.B.Sanhedrin 14a.

74. T.J. Berachot 1:2.

75. T.B. Yoma 79b. The Talmud construes this report to mean that snacks may be eaten outside of the Succah, but this interpretation negates the force of R. Judah's report, "When we would learn Torah with R. Elazar b. Shammua..." Clearly it is the context of study which permitted the infraction.

76. Avot of Rabbi Nathan, Version A, ch. 4, Schechter ed., p. 18.

77. Avot of Rabbi Nathan, Version A, ch. 4, Schechter ed., pp. 18-19. The translation is by Judah Goldin, pp. 32-33. The teachings attributed to Judah IIai in T.B. Ketubot 17a and Megillah 29a are derived from here. However, the teaching attributed to him in T.J. Hagiga 1:7 that action precedes study, is more correctly attributed to Judah the Prince as it is in T.P. Pesahim. See Marmorstein, p. 168.

78. Mishna Peah 1:1. (Should we here apply the dictum that an anonymous Mishna is authored by R. Meir in the manner of R. Akiva?)

79. I have already argued that rabbis occupying official positions had necessarily to be more concerned with action. The statement in Avot 1:17 that action, not study, is essential is the same as the statement quoted here, and is said either by Judah's father or great-grandfather. It thus can be viewed as a tradition of the Patriarchate.

   Judah does reflect the theology of his teachers in relationship to other issues. Thus, for instance: "Anyone who enjoys the pleasure of this world is denied the pleasure of the world to come" (Avot of R. Nathan, Version I, c. 28). This supports the argument I have made here that action was exalted by rabbis in official positions more out of reasons of practical necessity than out of theological motive. R. Judah, the Patriarch, like his teachers, does not see this world as the primary stage in meeting the divine.

80. T.J. Pesahim 3:7 and not R. Judah Ilai as in T.J. Hagiga 1:7.

81. T.B. Sabbath 11a. The Palestinian version understands R. Yochanan to be talking about R. Simeon's statement in regard to the recitation of the Shema. See T.J. Berachot 1:2, and T.J. Sabbath 1:2. There R. Yochanan is the one who reports the statement of R. Simeon, which makes his disagreement even more pointed, although the phraseology is slightly different from in the Babylonian version: "But we who do not occupy ourselves with Torah...." R. Judah the Prince seems to have taken a position somewhere in the middle of this question, seemingly saying that one should stop only to say the first verse of the Shema. See Kesef Mishna on Maimonides, Hilchot Kriyat Shema, 2:5.

82. T.B. Avoda Zarah 17b., tr. by A. Mishcon (London: Soncino Press, 1935). Interestingly, the Talmud itself, ad loc., is astounded that such a story could be told of Hanina b. Teradyon, who was the treasurer of a welfare fund and known for his acts of piety. It points to the need of the anonymous reporter to defame the ideology we have presented here no matter what the distortions.

83. Our collection of Sifre incorporates some materials from the school of Ishmael. Similarly, our version of the Mechilta is from the school of Ishmael, although a Mechilta of R. Simeon has been reconstructed. Excepting these, it is correct to say that the Tanaitic materials we have are primarily of the school of Akiva. The process of writing and collecting the "Torah Sheba'al Peh" was a long and arduous task which is quite simplified in our presentation here. There is no doubt though that something crucially different takes place in the generation under discussion and that the material of the tradition is arranged in a new way for publication. For the best summary of this process of compilation see N.H. Epstein.

84. Sanhedrin 86a, and numerous parallels.

85. R. Meir, R. Judah, R. Simeon, and the other rabbis we have cited here are the rabbis most frequently named in the Mishna and their concerns form the basis of the structuring of the text. For instance Jacob Neusner has shown how the Mishna on the Law of Purities is centered on the ritual reconstruction which this generation adopted: recovering a sense of ritual purity even while the means of purification practiced in the Temple were no longer available. In other words, the primary non-biblical texts which Jews studied were the work of the generation after Bar Kochba and reflected its concerns.

86. *European Jewry and the First Crusade*, p. 230.

87. *Ibid.*, p. 236. And certainly they could believe that the Crusaders' defeat was a result of God's retribution.

88. *Ibid.*, p. 237.

89. I, 1, Pines ed. p. 23.

90. *Ibid.*, III, 54, p. 635.

91. *Ibid.*, III, 51, p. 627-28

92. Research into Jewish mysticism is only in its early stages, and so I do not feel comfortable incorporating that phenomenon, which in its own right forms such a rich response to Jewish tragedy, into this book. I have nothing to add to the works

of Gershom Scholem and his students, who have done the pioneering work in this field. I adduce the material cited here to show how the issue of continuity and discontinuity of ideas in Jewish mysticism remains a complex question.

93. Moshe Idel's recent work, *Kabbalah*, is an important corrective to the Scholem's central theses. Yet even though Idel is quite right to point up the importance of Abulafia and his school, and so emphasize the more active elements in mystical speculation, I believe the Abulafian school did not achieve acceptance as a major normative movement until the generation following the expulsion from Spain and the revolution of the Lurianic school. In the fourth section, I will pick up on the themes of Tikkun—active participation in salvation—that is then introduced. It is correct to say, though, that for none of these medieval movements is history a significant religious category.

94. R. Yaakov Yosef of Polnoye, Toldot Yaakov Yosef, Parashat Vayetze. I am grateful to the fellows of the Shalom Hartman Institute for sharing this passage.

95. Enos, *Hayyim Nahman Bialik*.

Part Three

1. Holocaust is the word the King James Bible uses to refer to the whole burnt sacrificial offering in the Temple. Hebrew has similarly departed from previous nomenclature and uses the word *Shoah*, meaning "terrible devastation" and carrying a hint of return to nothingness, a word used by the prophets to indicate destruction: "But what shall you do at that certain time, when devastation/*Shoah* comes from afar? —to whom shall you run for help...?" (Isaiah 10:3).

   The Yiddish term *Hurban* revives a name that has not been used for two thousand years, a name used only for the destruction of the Temple and therefore a term of overwhelming cataclysm. Thus, all three languages have instinctively seen the necessity of evolving a new vocabulary for this devastation. (My thanks to Rabbi Max Ticktin, who first brought these issues of nomenclature to my attention.)

2. Trunk, *Judenrat*, p. 398.

3. *Ibid.*

4. Recently controversy has once again erupted regarding this point with the publication in Israel of a portion of Nathan Alterman's journals, *Between Two Roads*. Alterman argued that of the "two ways" —resistance and revolt, or cooperation—that the latter made more sense since it bought time, that the Jewish councils represented people who were acting rationally to try to save what they could, and that to think of resistance was merely a flight of imagination and not a realistic option.

   While this controversy essentially concerns what was the proper policy to follow once the ghettoes had been set up, I am arguing that the ghettoes themselves could never have been set up if not for the playing on older motifs.

5. Testimony of SS Judge Dr. Konrad Morgen, in Naumann, *Auschwitz*, p. 105.

6. Testimony of Dr. Ella Lingens, *ibid.*, p. 94.

7. Testimony of Jenny Schaner, *ibid.*, p. 129.

8. *Ibid.*

9. *Ibid.*, p. 151.

10. Richard Rubenstein, *After Auschwitz*, p. 39.

11. *Ibid.*, p. 33.

12. Bruno Bettleheim, *The Informed Heart*, pp. 119-27.

13. Donat, *op. cit.*, p. 10.

14. Sala Pawlowicz with Kevin Klein, *I Will Survive*, p. 104.

15. Lucy Dawidowicz, *The War Against the Jews, 1933-1945*, p. 201.

16. Terrence des Pres, *The Survivor*, p. 63, quoting Donat, *The Holocaust Kingdom*, p. 178.

17. des Pres, p. 58, quoting Giscell Perl.

18. *Ibid.*

19. Yankel Wiernick, "Uprising in Treblinka," in Leo Schwarz, *The Root and the Bough*, p. 116.

20. Testimony of Josef Kral in *Auschwitz, op. cit.*, p. 146.

21. Elie Wiesel, *Gates of the Forest*, p. 203.

22. Alexander Donat, *The Holocaust Kingdom*, p. 8.

23. Wiesel, *Legends of our Time*, p. 52.

24. Richard Rubenstein, *After Auschwitz*, p. 80.

25. *Auschwitz*, the testimony of Dunia Wasserstrom, p. 132.

26. Wiesel, *Legends*, p. 36.

27. Accusations by the Satmar Hasidim and others that God brought the Holocaust as a punishment for Zionism are simply ugly. Who would want to worship a God who acted in this way?

    Similarly there are others who argue that the Holocaust was God's response to assimilation and reform, offering that that is why it started in Germany. Such an explanation fails to take into account why the most pious Jewish community—Poland—was almost totally devastated while half of German Jewry was saved. But even having to respond to such accusations causes one to descend into a kind of accounting that violates the memory of the dead. The victims were human beings, certainly not more sinful than most. To say they deserved their cruel fate is to violate our sense of humanity.

28. See Joshua Trachtenberg, *The Devil and the Jews*.

29. See, ch. 8 herein for a record of the martyrdoms during the Crusades.

30. Emil Fackenheim develops this point. See his *God's Presence in History*, p. 70.

31. Leib Garfunkel, responding to Mark Dworzicki in *Jewish Resistance During the*

Holocaust, op. cit., p. 184.

32. Estimates are that from 5 to 25 percent of the population of the ghettoes of Eastern Europe died of disease, see Lucy Dawidowicz, *The War Against the Jews, 1933-1945,* p. 214. Of course, in the camps dysentery and disease was the common lot.

33. Terrence des Pres, *The Survivor,* quoting Donat, *op. cit.,* p. 269.

34. Wiesel, *Legends,* p. 162.

35. *Ibid.*

36. This is essentially Richard Rubenstein's point in the second essay in *After Auschwitz.*

37. Jacob Glatstein, *Poems,* selected and translated by Etta Blum, pp. 43-47. Glatstein's poem first appeared in a collection, *Radiant Jews* (1946), which contains some of the best poetry on the Holocaust by a Jewish writer.

38. Martin Buber, *On Judaism,* p. 223. Emil Fackenheim follows this line developed by Buber.

39. Buber, *ibid.,* p. 224.

40. *Ibid.*

41. *Ibid.,* p. 225

42. Wiesel, *The Accident,* p. 42.

43. Rubenstein, *After Auschwitz,* pp. 128-29.

44. Article in weekend edition of *Maariv.* I am grateful to Rabbi Max Ticktin for sharing this piece with me.

45. "Today I think that if for no other reason than that an Auschwitz existed, no one in our age should speak of Providence. But without doubt in that hour the memory of Biblical salvations in times of extreme adversity passed like a wind through all our minds." Primo Levi, *Survival in Auschwitz.*

46. *Ibid.,* p. 36.

47. *Ibid.,* p. 50.

48. Leo Baeck, "A People Stands Before its God," in *We Survived,* ed. by Eric Boehm. Heinrich Liebrecht, also interned in Theresienstadt, writes of the devastating effect of a dysentery epidemic. "A dysentery epidemic broke out, and many of the older people were affected. The water came from wells, and few of the houses had modern hygienic plumbing. There were only two or three toilets for a hundred inmates, and people had to wait in line, writhing in pain and terribly ashamed if they could not get up, and literally died in their own excrement"; "Therefore Will I Deliver Him," in the same volume.

49. des Pres, *op. cit.,* p. 70, quoting Donat, *The Holocaust Kingdom.*

50. *Ibid.,* p. 71, quoting Primo Levi, *Survival in Auschwitz.*

51. As reported by Nathan Eck, *Hatoim Bedarchei Hamavet,* p. 37; also quoted in Mordechai Eliav, *Ani Maamin,* p. 12 and Jacob Shalhev, "The Sanctification of Life during the Holocaust," p. 19. R. Nissenbaum was transported from the Warsaw ghetto in September 1943, as reported in a note in the diary of Yitzchak Katznelson. See Rabbi Nissenbaum's biography, *Rabbi Isaac Nissenbaum,* by Israel Schapiro, pp. 64-65.

52. Eck, *Hatoim Bedarchei Hamavet*, p. 244.

53. des Pres, *op. cit.*, p. 115.

54. Primo Levi, *op. cit.*, p. 84.

55. "Apologia of a Physician" in Schwarz, *op. cit.*

56. *Ibid.*, pp. 146-47, quoting Donat, *The Holocaust Kingdom*, p. 237.

57. Primo Levi, *op. cit.*, p. 111.

58. des Pres, *op. cit.*, p. 161, quoting Gerda Klein.

59. *Ibid.*, pp. 104-5, quoting Leon Szelet.

60. Eliezer Berkovitz, *Faith After the Holocaust*, pp. 76, 84.

61. Eck, *op. cit.*, p. 244.

62. Leo Baeck, *This People Israel*.

Part Four

1.   For instance, William Sloan Coffin, the minister and political activist, reports that he became a pacifist after viewing the results of the Nazi Holocaust.

2.   See des Pres *op. cit.*, ch ii, "The Will to Bear Witness," pp. 27ff.

3.   Arendt was referring to Eichmann who used this plea in his defense. I disagree with her assessment of Eichmann, who I believe was an active anti-Semite, but her point is well taken regarding the participation of others; see her *Eichmann in Jerusalem*.

4.   Arendt sums up and quotes the court psychiatrist who examined Eichmann and found that "his attitude toward his wife and children, mother, and father, brothers, sisters and friends, was 'not only normal but most desirable,'" *Eichman* p. 22. Recently Robert Jay Lifton has shown how the medical profession typified the process being described here, in *The Nazi Doctors*.

5.   Arendt argues that, "the new type of criminal... commits his crimes under circumstances that make it well-nigh impossible for him to know or to feel that he is doing wrong." *Eichmann*, p. 253.

6.   The first chapter of Richard Rubenstein's *After Auschwitz* constitutes the best analysis of how the Jew was turned into a non person.

7.   E.g., Albert Speer in his autobiography.

8.   Arendt, *Eichmann*.

9. To be sure Nazism also appealed to a romantic nostalgia of a great German past, and volkisch elements were significant in Nazi ideology. Modern political movements are able to simultaneously engage in appeals to the past and play on nationalist fervor criticizing modernity, while yet also using those elements of modern thought that it finds useful. Holding on to contradictory positions was in fact critical to Nazi thought; e.g., Jews were said to be both capitalists and communists.

10. Genesis, ch. 1.

11. Philosophically this faith receives expression at the dawn of the Enlightenment, with Descartes lying in bed arguing that he will believe no truth that he can not create out of his own imagining.

12. This is effectively Arthur Cohen's position in *The Tremendum*. By theologically arguing that the Holocaust is outside of understanding, he places it outside of history and so deprives it of having any logical consequence.

13. Arendt, *Eichmann*, p. 212.

14. des Pres, *op. cit.*, p. 5.

15. Guttman, *The Warsaw Ghetto*. See also Alterman's justified criticism of those who would judge the behavior of the ghetto leadership negatively, *Between Two Worlds*.

16. *Legends of Our Time*, p. 36.

17. For example, arguments given by Zvi Yehudah Kook and his students that the Holocaust was the necessary operation God performed on the Jewish people in order to end the psychology of exilic existence. See Shlomo Hayim Hacohen Aviner, "Faith and Redemption," in *Faith During the Holocaust: A Critique of the Meaning of Religious Judaism During the Holocaust*.

18. These arguments have all been elaborated in the preceding part of this study.

19. The Orthodox theologians Eliezer Berkovitz and David Hartman both seem to be arguing this position, the former explicitly so regarding the Holocaust, the latter implicitly.

20. God as a first cause, but not a God who has an ongoing relationship in the sustenance of the world.

21. This connection was demonstrated in part two herein. The crucial classic exception may be Maimonides. Contemporary scholars debate how to read Maimonides on this question. If the radical reading of Maimonides is correct: that he did not believe in miracles, or in God's acting in history, nor did he believe in an afterlife, then he may be seen as having adumbrated the essential line being argued here, though his solution to the problem, that salvation lies in the philosophic contemplation of God, hardly seems tenable.

22. After the war, Buber saw the necessity of rethinking the question of evil and spoke of "radical evil" that can blot out the ability to turn toward God by basing its view of existence on the 'lie'," *Good and Evil*. As we have seen above, Buber then went on to talk about the hiding God, a corollary of this revision of his thinking. See the analysis in part three.

23. "Jewish values in the Post-Holocaust Future: A Symposium," p. 289.

24. *Hasidism and Modern Man*, p. 175-76.

25. Orot Hakodesh II, 343.

26. *Good and Evil.*

27. Pesach Shindler, "Hasidic Reactions to the Holocaust," in *Faith During the Holocaust*, p. 74.

28. "In an anti-society geared to torture and death, mere living is not 'mere.' When law defines existence itself as a crime... when a system makes surrender to death the norm, survival becomes a heroic act of resistance. When every effort is made to reduce dying to a banality, life does not need to be sanctified. It already is holy." Emil Fackenheim, *The Jewish Return to History*, p. 249.

29. Robert Jay Lifton found that there was an enormous difference in behavior and sensitivity to moral dilemmas between the SS doctors in the camps and the prisoner doctors there. See his *The Nazi Doctors.*

30. Religious perspectives that do not subject themselves to a process of self-scrutiny and self-questioning and that disparage pluralism can be as dangerous as societies that negate the sacredness of the human.

31. We can speculate to what degree the post-Holocaust Jewish psyche has ingested the poisonous disdain anti-Semites have felt for this 2,000-year-old symbol of the Jews.

32. That emotion-laden value is often stated as the need not to be dependent on others, even though that has never been true of Israel's situation and is not descriptive of the human condition.

33. What is significant about these almost mythological elements of Zionist self-understanding is not so much their facticity but their hold on popular imagination, e.g., Israel is in fact deeply dependent on the international community but that element is not allowed to become a conscious fact of national identity.

34. Not only do Israeli citizens serve in the standing army from the ages of 18 to 21, they are also called up for reserve duty for one to two months a year all through middle age. The havoc this wreaks on one's business, one's professional life, and the strain it places on the citizen's family are enormous.

35. Such an incident, for instance, occurred in January 1990.

36. Emil Fackenheim has argued that after the Holocaust there is a 614th command to live as Jews, and to ensure the ongoing quality of Jewish life. Fackenheim, while conscious of the conflict that sometimes attends the needs of Jewish survival and the life of caring for the other, does not essentially take this dilemma into account, but largely emphasizes the single pole of the continued existence of the Jewish people.

37. *Viz.* the first chapter of T.B. Baba Bathra.

38. T.B. Metzia, 62a. Seemingly, R. Akiva is interpreting the verse to mean that you are only responsible for allowing your neighbor to live with you, but the condition for this happening is that you yourself are living. Several commentators interpret Ben Petura's position as being based on the alternative verse from Leviticus, "You shall love your neighbor as yourself" (19), i e , that you can not give precedence to your own life over that of your neighbor's.

39. See for instance the response of Ephraim Oshry, *Sheelot Uteshuvot Mimaamakim.*

40. Buber, *At the Turning,* p. 39.

GLOSSARY

Agada   Non-legal rabbinic sayings including legends and folkloric material.

Bund   The association of Yiddishist Socialists organized in the late nineteenth century in Eastern Europe. They were a Marxist workers' movement that promoted a distinct Jewish culture whose center was the Yiddish language.

Halacha   The formal exposition of Jewish law.

Haredi   The right wing of the Orthodox movement. The outward characteristics are that males usually wear black hats, and women, headcoverings and long dresses or skirts.

Maskilim   Nineteenth- and twentieth-century Eastern European and Central European Jews who joined the movement toward Enlightenment.

Midrash   Rabbinic commentaries on Biblical passages. There are formal collections of midrashim while other commentaries are strewn throughout rabbinic literature.

Mishna   The collection of Jewish law arranged topically and edited by R. Judah the Prince around the year 200 C.E. It was the normative collection of law for rabbinic Judaism. Mishna Avot, otherwise known as the Ethics of the Fathers, is a slightly later work which was attached to the Mishna and forms a kind of philosophical epilogue to it.

Musar   A pietist movement that developed in Eastern Europe in the nineteenth century which emphasized the negation of ego and the importance of personal ethics.

Shema   The first word of Deuteronomy 6:4-9. "Hear O Israel, the Lord our God, the Lord is One...." These verses constitute one of the two central moments of Jewish liturgy.

Talmud   The commentary on the Mishna existing in two versions—the Palestinian, edited about 450, and the Babylonian, edited some one-hundred years later. The Talmud includes both halachic and agadic materials. Since the Talmud closely follows the Mishna, and the two are published together, popular parlance sometimes conflates the two and the word "Talmud" is used to refer to both the Mishna and the Talmudic commentary.

Torah   The five books of Moses which are written as a single scroll, read liturgically in the synagogue and are considered to have an even more normative status than the rest of the Bible. The rabbis understood that their commentary constituted a legitimate extension of the five books. They therefore referred to the written Torah and the oral Torah. When they refer to the study of Torah they mean the study of both.

Tosefta   Teachings of the Rabbis who wrote the Mishna, yet for some reason these sayings were not included in the latter but collected separately. They therefore have less normative status.

Yeshiva   The central institution of traditional Jewish study, the curriculum of which is usually Talmud study.

Yishuv   The pre-statist Zionist settlement in Palestine.

BIBLIOGRAPHY

CLASSICAL SOURCES:

Bible:

Job. Introduction, Translation and Commentary by Marvin Pope. Anchor Bible Series, Doubleday and Co., 1965.

The New English Bible with the Apocrypha. Oxford, 1971.

Tanakh: A New Translation. Jewish Publication Society.

Apocrypha, Greek and Roman Historians:

Apocrypha and Pseudopigrapha. Ed. by R.C. Charles. Oxford, 1965.

Dio Cassius. *Dio's Roman History.* Trans. by E. Cary. Loeb Classical Series, 1925.

I and II Esdras. Introduction, Translation and Commentary by Jacob M. Myers. The Anchor Bible Series, Doubleday and Co., 1974.

Josephus. *The Jewish Wars.* Trans. and ed. by H. St. J. Thackery. Loeb Classical Series, Harvard University Press, 1928.

II Maccabees. A New Translation with Introduction and Commentary by Jonathan A. Goldstein. Anchor Bible Series, Doubleday & Co., 1983.

Critical Editions of Rabbinic Literature:

Avot of Rabbi Nathan. Ed. by Solomon Schechter. Feldheim, 1967.

Avot of Rabbi Nathan. Trans. by Judah Goldin. Yale University Press, 1955.

Mechilta D'Rebi Ishmael. Ed. with a commentary by Saul Horowitz and Israel Rabin. Wahrman, 1970.

Sayings of the Jewish Fathers: Pirqe Avot. Trans. by Charles Taylor. Ktav, 1969.

Sifre on the Book of Deuteronomy. Ed. with a commentary by Louis Finkelstein. The Jewish Theological Seminary of America, 1969.

The Six Orders of Mishna. Ed. with a commentary by Hanoch Albeck. Dvir, 1959.

The Tosefta. Ed. with a commentary by Saul Lieberman. The Jewish Theological Seminary of America, 1955–1988.

The Tractate on Mourning, Ed. by Dov Zlotnick. Yale Judaic Series, 1966.

MODERN WORKS:

Abramsky, S. *Bar Kochba*. Masada, 1961.*

Alon, Gedaliah. *Toldot Hayehudim*. Hameuchad, 1967.*

Alterman, Nathan. *Between Two Roads: Selections From a Diary*. Ed., annotated and afterword by Dan Laor. Tel Aviv, 1989.*

Arendt, Hannah. *Eichmann in Jerusalem*. Penguin Books, 1964.

Avi Yona, Michael. *Bimei Roma U'byzantium*. Mosad Bialik, 1962.* Issued in English as *The Jews of Palestine*. Schocken 1976.

Baeck, Leo. *This People Israel*. Trans. by Albert Friedlander. Holt, Rinehart, 1964.

Baron, Salo. *A Social and Religious History of the Jews*. Vol II. Columbia University Press, 1952.

Beer, Moshe. "Talmud Torah and Derekh Eretz." *Bar Ilan Annual* 2 (1964).

Berkovitz, Eliezer. *Faith After the Holocaust*. Ktav, 1973.

Bettleheim, Bruno. *The Informed Heart*. Avon, 1971.

Bialik, Hayyim Nahman. *Complete Poetic Works*. Trans. by Israel Efros. Histadruth Ivrith, 1948).

Boehm, Eric, ed. *We Survived*. Clio Press, 1966.

Buber, Martin. *At the Turning: Three Addresses on Judaism*. Farrar, Strauss and Young. 1952.

———. *Good and Evil*. Scribner, 1953.

———. *Hasidism and Modern Man*. ed. and trans. by Maurice Friedman. Harper, 1958.

———. *On Judaism*. Ed. by Nahum Glatzer. Schocken, 1967.

———. *The Prophetic Faith*. Trans. by Carlyle Witton-Davies. Macmillan, 1949.

Chazan, Robert. *European Jewry and the First Crusade*. University of California Press, 1987.

Cohen, Arthur. *The Tremendum: A Theological Interpretation of the Holocaust*. Crossroad, 1981.

Dawidowicz, Lucy. *The War Against the Jews, 1933-1945*. Holt, Rinehart and Winston, 1975.

des Pres, Terrence *The Survivor*. Pocket Books, 1977.

Donat, Alexander. *The Holocaust Kingdom*. Holt, Rinehart and Winston. 1965.

Dworzicki, Meir. "The-Day-to-Day Stand of the Jews." In *Jewish Resistance During the Holocaust: Proceedings of the Conference on Manifestations of Jewish Resistance*. Yad Vashem, 1971.

Eck, Nathan. *Hatoim Bedarchei Hamavet*. Yad Vashem, 1960.*

Eliav, Mordechai. *Ani Maamin*. Mosad Harav Kook, 1965.*

The Encyclopedia Judaica. Keter Publishing House, 1972.

Encyclopedia Mikrait. Mosad Bialik, 1965-82.

Epstein, N.H. *Introduction to Tanaitic Literature: Mishna Tosefta and Halachic Midrashim*. Ed. by E. Z. Melamed. Magnes-Dvir, 1957.*

Fackenheim, Emil. *God's Presence in History*. Harper, 1970.

———. *The Jewish Return into History*. Shocken,1978.

Faith During the Holocaust: Analysis of the Jewish Religious Significance of the Holocaust. Government of Israel, Ministry of Education and Culture, Religious-Cultural Division, 1980.*

Glatstein, Jacob. *Poems*. Selected and trans. by Etta Blum. Peretz Publishing, 1970.

Goldenberg, Robert. "The Broken Axis: Rabbinic Judaism and the Fall of Jerusalem." *Journal of the American Academy of Religion*. Vol. 45, no. 3, supplement, pp. 870-79.

Gordis, Robert. *The Book of God and Man*. University of Chicago Press, 1966.

Gutman, Israel. *The Jews of Warsaw, 1939-1943: Ghetto, Underground, Revolt*. Trans. by Ina Friedman. Indiana University Press, 1982.

Hartman, David. *A Living Covenant: The Innovative Spirit in Traditional Judaism*. The Free Press, Macmillan, 1985.

Idel, Moshe. *Kabbalah: New Perspectives*. Yale University Press, 1988.

"Jewish Values in the Post-Holocaust Future: A Symposium." *Judaism* 16, no. 3 (Summer, 1967).

Kook, Abraham Isaac. *Orot Hakodesh*. Mosad Harav Kook 1969.*

Levi, Primo. *Survival in Auschwitz*. Trans. by Stuart Woolf. Collier Books, 1973.

Lifton, Robert Jay. *The Nazi Doctors: Medical Killing and the Psychology of Genocide*. Basic Books, 1986.

Oshry, Ephraim. *Sheelot Uteshuvot Mimaamakim*. N.p., 1959.*

Maimonides, Moses. *The Guide of the Perplexed*. Trans. by Shlomo Pines. The University of Chicago Press, 1969.

Marmorstein, A. "Maalat Talmud Torah—B'maamare Rebi Shimon B. Yohai." *B. M. Levin Festschrift*. Pp. 161-170.*

Mintz, Alan. *Hurban: Responses to Catastrophe in Hebrew Literature.* Columbia University Press, 1984.

Moore, G.F. *Judaism.* Harvard University Press, 1927.

Naumann, Bernd. *Auschwitz.* Trans. by Jean Steinberg. Praeger,1966.

Neusner, Jacob. *Development of a Legend.* Brill, 1970.

————. *First Century Judaism in Crisis.* Abington Press, 1975.

————. *History and Torah.* Valentine Mitchell, 1965.

————. *A Life of Rabban Johanan b. Zakkai.* Brill, 1962.

Pawlowicz, Sala, with Kevin Klein. *I Will Survive.* Norton, 1962.

Rubenstein, Richard. *After Auschwitz.* Bobbs Merrill, 1966.

Safrai, Shmuel. *R. Akiva b. Yosef: His Life and Teaching.* Mosad Bialik, 1970.*

Schapiro, Israel. *Rabbi Isaac Nissenbaum.* The Jewish Agency, 1950.*

Schwarz, Leo. *The Root and the Bough.*

Shalhev, Jacob. "The Sanctification of Life During the Holocaust." *Deot,* vol. 19.*

Speer, Albert. *Inside the Third Reich.* Trans. by Richard and Clara Winston. Avon, 1971.

Steiner, George. *After Babel.* Oxford University Press, 1975.

Trachtenberg, Joshua. *The Devil and the Jews.* Harper, 1943.

Trunk, Isiah. *Judenrat: The Jewish Councils in Eastern Europe under Nazi Occupation.* Macmillan, 1972.

Urbach, E. E. *Hazal: Pirkei Emunot V'deot (The Sages: Their Concepts and Beliefs).* Magnes, 1969.

————. "Asceticism and Suffering in the Teaching of the Sages." *Yitscahak Baer Jubilee Volume.* Israel Historical Society, 1960.*

Wiesel, Elie. *The Accident.* Trans. by Anne Borchardt. Hill and Wang, 1962.

————. *Gates of the Forest.* Avon, 1966.

————. *Legends of Our Time.* Avon, 1970.

Yadin, Yigael. *Bar Kochba.* Random House, 1971.

Yeivan, S. *Milhememt Bar Kochba.* Mosad Bialik, 1957.*

*indicates works in Hebrew.

INDEX

ABOUT THE AUTHOR

Edward Feld is currently rabbi-in-residence at The Jewish Theological Seminary, where he mentors a new generation of student rabbis. He has served as a college chaplain at Princeton University, Smith and Amherst Colleges, and the University of Illinois. He has also served as rabbi to New York's Society for the Advancement of Judaism. He is currently chair of the new High Holiday Prayerbook Commission of the Rabbinical Assembly and a member of the steering committee of Rabbis for Human Rights, North America. Active as a teacher of spirituality to university students, scholars, and rabbis, he has also worked with Catholic and Protestant spiritual leaders. He was a senior fellow at the Shalom Hartman Institute in Jerusalem, and the organizer of its theology seminar.

Sharing his unique and moving message with people around the world, Rabbi Feld has lectured at many institutions of learning, including: The Jewish Theological Seminary; Mt. Saviour Monastery; The Reconstructionist Rabbinical College; the University of California; and the University of Chicago.

Children's Books

Because Nothing Looks Like God
By Lawrence and Karen Kushner

What is God like? The first collaborative work by husband-and-wife team Lawrence and Karen Kushner introduces children to the possibilities of spiritual life. Real-life examples of happiness and sadness invite us to explore, together with our children, the questions we all have about God, no matter what our age.

11 x 8½, 32 pp, Full-color illus., Hardcover, ISBN 1-58023-092-X **$16.95** *For ages 4 & up*

Also Available: **Because Nothing Looks Like God Teacher's Guide**
8½ x 11, 22 pp, PB, ISBN 1-58023-140-3 **$6.95** *For ages 5–8*

Board Book Companions to *Because Nothing Looks Like God*
5 x 5, 24 pp, Full-color illus., SkyLight Paths Board Books, **$7.95** each *For ages 0–4*

What Does God Look Like? ISBN 1-893361-23-3

How Does God Make Things Happen? ISBN 1-893361-24-1

Where Is God? ISBN 1-893361-17-9

The 11th Commandment: Wisdom from Our Children
by The Children of America

"If there were an Eleventh Commandment, what would it be?" Children of many religious denominations across America answer this question—in their own drawings and words.

8 x 10, 48 pp, Full-color illus., Hardcover, ISBN 1-879045-46-X **$16.95** *For all ages*

Jerusalem of Gold: Jewish Stories of the Enchanted City
Retold by Howard Schwartz. Full-color illus. by Neil Waldman.

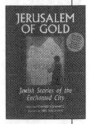

A beautiful and engaging collection of historical and legendary stories for children. Each celebrates the magical city that has served as a beacon for the Jewish imagination for three thousand years. Draws on Talmud, midrash, Jewish folklore, and mystical and Hasidic sources.

8 x 10, 64 pp, Full-color illus., Hardcover, ISBN 1-58023-149-7 **$18.95** *For ages 7 & up*

The Book of Miracles: A Young Person's Guide to Jewish Spiritual Awareness
By Lawrence Kushner. All-new illustrations by the author.
6 x 9, 96 pp, 2 color illus., Hardcover, ISBN 1-879045-78-8 **$16.95** *For ages 9–13*

In Our Image: God's First Creatures
By Nancy Sohn Swartz

9 x 12, 32 pp, Full-color illus., Hardcover, ISBN 1-879045-99-0 **$16.95** *For ages 4 & up*

From SKYLIGHT PATHS PUBLISHING

Becoming Me: A Story of Creation
By Martin Boroson. Full-color illus. by Christopher Gilvan-Cartwright.

Told in the personal "voice" of the Creator, a story about creation and relationship that is about each one of us. In simple words and with radiant illustrations, the Creator tells an intimate story about love, about friendship and playing, about our world—and about ourselves.

8 x 10, 32 pp, Full-color illus., Hardcover, ISBN 1-893361-11-X **$16.95** *For ages 4 & up*

Ten Amazing People: And How They Changed the World
By Maura D. Shaw. Foreword by Dr. Robert Coles. Full-color illus. by Stephen Marchesi.

Black Elk • Dorothy Day • Malcolm X • Mahatma Gandhi • Martin Luther King, Jr. • Mother Teresa • Janusz Korczak • Desmond Tutu • Thich Nhat Hanh • Albert Schweitzer • This vivid, inspirational, and authoritative book will open new possibilities for children by telling the stories of how ten of the past century's greatest leaders changed the world in important ways.

8½ x 11, 48 pp, Full-color illus., Hardcover, ISBN 1-893361-47-0 **$17.95** *For ages 7 & up*

Where Does God Live? *By August Gold and Matthew J. Perlman*
Using simple, everyday examples that children can relate to, this colorful book helps young readers develop a personal understanding of God.

10 x 8½ , 32 pp, Full-color photo illus., Quality PB, ISBN 1-893361-39-X **$8.95** *For ages 3–6*

Children's Books
by Sandy Eisenberg Sasso

Adam & Eve's First Sunset: God's New Day
Engaging new story explores fear and hope, faith and gratitude in ways that will delight kids and adults—inspiring us to bless each of God's days and nights.
9 x 12, 32 pp, Full-color illus., Hardcover, ISBN 1-58023-177-2 **$17.95** *For ages 4 & up*

But God Remembered
Stories of Women from Creation to the Promised Land
Four different stories of women—Lillith, Serach, Bityah, and the Daughters of Z—teach us important values through their faith and actions.
9 x 12, 32 pp, Full-color illus., Hardcover, ISBN 1-879045-43-5 **$16.95** *For ages 8 & up*

Cain & Abel: Finding the Fruits of Peace
Shows children that we have the power to deal with anger in positive ways. Provides questions for kids and adults to explore together.
9 x 12, 32 pp, Full-color illus., Hardcover, ISBN 1-58023-123-3 **$16.95** *For ages 5 & up*

God in Between
If you wanted to find God, where would you look? This magical, mythical tale teaches that God can be found where we are: within all of us and the relationships between us.
9 x 12, 32 pp, Full-color illus., Hardcover, ISBN 1-879045-86-9 **$16.95** *For ages 4 & up*

God's Paintbrush: Special 10th Anniversary Edition
Wonderfully interactive, invites children of all faiths and backgrounds to encounter God through moments in their own lives. Provides questions adult and child can explore together.
11 x 8½, 32 pp, Full-color illus., Hardcover, ISBN 1-58023-195-0 **$17.95** *For ages 4 & up*

Also Available: **God's Paintbrush, 1st Edition** ISBN 1-879045-22-2 **$17.95**

Also Available: **God's Paintbrush Teacher's Guide**
8½ x 11, 32 pp, PB, ISBN 1-879045-57-5 **$8.95**

God's Paintbrush Celebration Kit
A Spiritual Activity Kit for Teachers and Students of All Faiths, All Backgrounds
Additional activity sheets available:
8-Student Activity Sheet Pack (40 sheets/5 sessions), ISBN 1-58023-058-X **$19.95**
Single-Student Activity Sheet Pack (5 sessions), ISBN 1-58023-059-8 **$3.95**

In God's Name
Like an ancient myth in its poetic text and vibrant illustrations, this award-winning modern fable about the search for God's name celebrates the diversity and, at the same time, the unity of all people.
9 x 12, 32 pp, Full-color illus., Hardcover, ISBN 1-879045-26-5 **$16.95** *For ages 4 & up*

Also Available as a Board Book: **What Is God's Name?**
5 x 5, 24 pp, Board, Full-color illus., ISBN 1-893361-10-1 **$7.99** *For ages 0–4 (A SkyLight Paths book)*

Also Available: **In God's Name video and study guide**
Computer animation, original music, and children's voices. 18 min. **$29.99**

Also Available in Spanish: **El nombre de Dios**
9 x 12, 32 pp, Full-color illus., Hardcover, ISBN 1-893361-63-2 **$16.95** *(A SkyLight Paths book)*

Noah's Wife: The Story of Naamah
When God tells Noah to bring the animals of the world onto the ark, God also calls on Naamah, Noah's wife, to save each plant on Earth. Based on an ancient text.
9 x 12, 32 pp, Full-color illus., Hardcover, ISBN 1-58023-134-9 **$16.95** *For ages 4 & up*

Also Available as a Board Book: **Naamah, Noah's Wife**
5 x 5, 24 pp, Full-color illus., Board, ISBN 1-893361-56-X **$7.95** *For ages 0–4 (A SkyLight Paths book)*

For Heaven's Sake: Finding God in Unexpected Places
9 x 12, 32 pp, Full-color illus., Hardcover, ISBN 1-58023-054-7 **$16.95** *For ages 4 & up*

God Said Amen: Finding the Answers to Our Prayers
9 x 12, 32 pp, Full-color illus., Hardcover, ISBN 1-58023-080-6 **$16.95** *For ages 4 & up*

Current Events/History

The Story of the Jews: A 4,000-Year Adventure—A Graphic History Book
Written & illustrated by Stan Mack
Through witty, illustrated narrative, we visit all the major happenings from biblical times to the twenty-first century. Celebrates the major characters and events that have shaped the Jewish people and culture.
6 x 9, 288 pp., illus., Quality PB, ISBN 1-58023-155-1 **$16.95**

The Jewish Prophet: Visionary Words from Moses and Miriam to Henrietta Szold and A. J. Heschel   *By Rabbi Michael J. Shire* 6½ x 8½, 128 pp, 123 full-color illus., Hardcover, ISBN 1-58023-168-3 **$25.00**

Shared Dreams: Martin Luther King, Jr. & the Jewish Community
By Rabbi Marc Schneier. Preface by Martin Luther King III.
6 x 9, 240 pp, Hardcover, ISBN 1-58023-062-8 **$24.95**

"Who Is a Jew?": Conversations, Not Conclusions   *By Meryl Hyman*
6 x 9, 272 pp, Quality PB, ISBN 1-58023-052-0 **$16.95**

Ecology

Ecology & the Jewish Spirit: Where Nature & the Sacred Meet
Edited by Ellen Bernstein 6 x 9, 288 pp, Quality PB, ISBN 1-58023-082-2 **$16.95**

Torah of the Earth: Exploring 4,000 Years of Ecology in Jewish Thought
Vol. 1: Biblical Israel: One Land, One People; Rabbinic Judaism: One People, Many Lands
Vol. 2: Zionism: One Land, Two Peoples; Eco-Judaism: One Earth, Many Peoples
Edited by Rabbi Arthur Waskow
Vol. 1: 6 x 9, 272 pp, Quality PB, ISBN 1-58023-086-5 **$19.95**
Vol. 2: 6 x 9, 336 pp, Quality PB, ISBN 1-58023-087-3 **$19.95**

Grief/Healing

Against the Dying of the Light: A Parent's Story of Love, Loss and Hope
By Leonard Fein
In this unusual exploration of heartbreak and healing, Leonard Fein chronicles the sudden death of his 30-year-old daughter and shares the hard-earned wisdom that emerges in the face of loss and grief.
5½ x 8½, 176 pp, Hardcover, ISBN 1-58023-110-1 **$19.95**

Grief in Our Seasons: A Mourner's Kaddish Companion *By Rabbi Kerry M. Olitzky*
4½ x 6½, 448 pp, Quality PB, ISBN 1-879045-55-9 **$15.95**

Healing of Soul, Healing of Body: Spiritual Leaders Unfold the Strength & Solace in Psalms *Edited by Rabbi Simkha Y. Weintraub, C.S.W.*
6 x 9, 128 pp, 2-color illus. text, Quality PB, ISBN 1-879045-31-1 **$14.95**

Jewish Paths toward Healing and Wholeness: A Personal Guide to Dealing with Suffering *By Rabbi Kerry M. Olitzky. Foreword by Debbie Friedman.*
6 x 9, 192 pp, Quality PB, ISBN 1-58023-068-7 **$15.95**

Mourning & Mitzvah, 2nd Edition: A Guided Journal for Walking the Mourner's Path through Grief to Healing *By Anne Brener, L.C.S.W.*
7½ x 9, 304 pp, Quality PB, ISBN 1-58023-113-6 **$19.95**

The Perfect Stranger's Guide to Funerals and Grieving Practices
A Guide to Etiquette in Other People's Religious Ceremonies *Edited by Stuart M. Matlins*
6 x 9, 240 pp, Quality PB, ISBN 1-893361-20-9 **$16.95** *(A SkyLight Paths book)*

Tears of Sorrow, Seeds of Hope: A Jewish Spiritual Companion for Infertility and Pregnancy Loss *By Rabbi Nina Beth Cardin*
6 x 9, 192 pp, Hardcover, ISBN 1-58023-017-2 **$19.95**

A Time to Mourn, A Time to Comfort: A Guide to Jewish Bereavement and Comfort *By Dr. Ron Wolfson* 7 x 9, 336 pp, Quality PB, ISBN 1-879045-96-6 **$18.95**

When a Grandparent Dies: A Kid's Own Remembering Workbook for Dealing with Shiva and the Year Beyond *By Nechama Liss-Levinson, Ph.D.*
8 x 10, 48 pp, 2-color text, Hardcover, ISBN 1-879045-44-3 **$15.95** *For ages 7–13*

Abraham Joshua Heschel

The Earth Is the Lord's: The Inner World of the Jew in Eastern Europe
5½ x 8, 128 pp, Quality PB, ISBN 1-879045-42-7 **$14.95**

Israel: An Echo of Eternity *New Introduction by Susannah Heschel*
5½ x 8, 272 pp, Quality PB, ISBN 1-879045-70-2 **$19.95**

A Passion for Truth: Despair and Hope in Hasidism
5½ x 8, 352 pp, Quality PB, ISBN 1-879045-41-9 **$18.99**

Holidays/Holy Days

7th Heaven: Celebrating Shabbat with Rebbe Nachman of Breslov
By Moshe Mykoff with the Breslov Research Institute
Based on the teachings of Rebbe Nachman of Breslov. Explores the art of consciously observing Shabbat and understanding in-depth many of the day's traditional spiritual practices.
5⅛ x 8¼, 224 pp, Deluxe PB w/flaps, ISBN 1-58023-175-6 **$18.95**

The Women's Passover Companion
Women's Reflections on the Festival of Freedom
Edited by Rabbi Sharon Cohen Anisfeld, Tara Mohr, and Catherine Spector
A groundbreaking collection that captures the voices of Jewish women who engage in a provocative conversation about women's relationships to Passover as well as the roots and meanings of women's seders.
6 x 9, 352 pp, Hardcover, ISBN 1-58023-128-4 **$24.95**

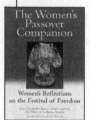

The Women's Seder Sourcebook
Rituals & Readings for Use at the Passover Seder
Edited by Rabbi Sharon Cohen Anisfeld, Tara Mohr, and Catherine Spector
This practical guide gathers the voices of more than one hundred women in readings, personal and creative reflections, commentaries, blessings, and ritual suggestions that can be incorporated into your Passover celebration as supplements to or substitutes for traditional passages of the haggadah.
6 x 9, 384 pp, Hardcover, ISBN 1-58023-136-5 **$24.95**

Creating Lively Passover Seders: A Sourcebook of Engaging Tales, Texts & Activities
By David Arnow, Ph.D.
7 x 9, 416 pp, Quality PB, ISBN 1-58023-184-5 **$24.99**

Hanukkah, 2nd Edition: The Family Guide to Spiritual Celebration
By Dr. Ron Wolfson. Edited by Joel Lurie Grishaver.
7 x 9, 240 pp, illus., Quality PB, ISBN 1-58023-122-5 **$18.95**

The Jewish Family Fun Book: Holiday Projects, Everyday Activities, and Travel Ideas with Jewish Themes *By Danielle Dardashti and Roni Sarig. Illus. by Avi Katz.*
6 x 9, 288 pp, 70+ b/w illus. & diagrams, Quality PB, ISBN 1-58023-171-3 **$18.95**

The Jewish Gardening Cookbook: Growing Plants & Cooking for Holidays & Festivals *By Michael Brown*
6 x 9, 224 pp, 30+ illus., Quality PB, ISBN 1-58023-116-0 **$16.95**;
Hardcover, ISBN 1-58023-004-0 **$21.95**

Passover, 2nd Edition: The Family Guide to Spiritual Celebration
By Dr. Ron Wolfson with Joel Lurie Grishaver
7 x 9, 352 pp, Quality PB, ISBN 1-58023-174-8 **$19.95**

Shabbat, 2nd Edition: The Family Guide to Preparing for and Celebrating the Sabbath
By Dr. Ron Wolfson 7 x 9, 320 pp, illus., Quality PB, ISBN 1-58023-164-0 **$19.95**

Sharing Blessings: Children's Stories for Exploring the Spirit of the Jewish Holidays
By Rahel Musleah and Michael Klayman
8½ x 11, 64 pp, Full-color illus., Hardcover, ISBN 1-879045-71-0 **$18.95** *For ages 6 & up*

Inspiration

God in All Moments
Mystical & Practical Spiritual Wisdom from Hasidic Masters
Edited and translated by Or N. Rose with Ebn D. Leader
Hasidic teachings on how to be mindful in religious practice and how to cultivate everyday ethical behavior—*hanhagot*.
5½ x 8½, 192 pp, Quality PB, ISBN 1-58023-186-1 **$16.95**

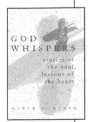

The Dance of the Dolphin: Finding Prayer, Perspective and Meaning in the Stories of Our Lives *By Karyn D. Kedar* 6 x 9, 176 pp, Hardcover, ISBN 1-58023-154-3 **$19.95**

The Empty Chair: Finding Hope and Joy—Timeless Wisdom from a Hasidic Master, Rebbe Nachman of Breslov *Adapted by Moshe Mykoff and the Breslov Research Institute*
4 x 6, 128 pp, 2-color text, Deluxe PB w/flaps, ISBN 1-879045-67-2 **$9.95**

The Gentle Weapon: Prayers for Everyday and Not-So-Everyday Moments—Timeless Wisdom from the Teachings of the Hasidic Master, Rebbe Nachman of Breslov *Adapted by Moshe Mykoff and S. C. Mizrahi, together with the Breslov Research Institute*
4 x 6, 144 pp, 2-color text, Deluxe PB w/flaps, ISBN 1-58023-022-9 **$9.95**

God Whispers: Stories of the Soul, Lessons of the Heart *By Karyn D. Kedar*
6 x 9, 176 pp, Quality PB, ISBN 1-58023-088-1 **$15.95**

An Orphan in History: One Man's Triumphant Search for His Jewish Roots
By Paul Cowan. Afterword by Rachel Cowan. 6 x 9, 288 pp, Quality PB, ISBN 1-58023-135-7 **$16.95**

Restful Reflections: Nighttime Inspiration to Calm the Soul, Based on Jewish Wisdom
By Rabbi Kerry M. Olitzky & Rabbi Lori Forman
4½ x 6¼, 448 pp, Quality PB, ISBN 1-58023-091-1 **$15.95**

Sacred Intentions: Daily Inspiration to Strengthen the Spirit, Based on Jewish Wisdom
By Rabbi Kerry M. Olitzky and Rabbi Lori Forman
4½ x 6¼, 448 pp, Quality PB, ISBN 1-58023-061-X **$15.95**

Kabbalah/Mysticism/Enneagram

Seek My Face: A Jewish Mystical Theology
By Dr. Arthur Green
This classic work of contemporary Jewish theology, revised and updated, is a profound, deeply personal statement of the lasting truths of Jewish mysticism and the basic faith claims of Judaism. A tool for anyone seeking the elusive presence of God in the world. 6 x 9, 304 pp, Quality PB, ISBN 1-58023-130-6 **$19.95**

Zohar: Annotated & Explained
Translation and annotation by Dr. Daniel C. Matt. Foreword by Andrew Harvey, SkyLight Illuminations series editor.
Offers insightful yet unobtrusive commentary to the masterpiece of Jewish mysticism that explains references and mystical symbols, shares wisdom of spiritual masters, and clarifies the *Zohar*'s bold claim: We have always been taught that we need God, but in order to manifest in the world, God needs us.
5½ x 8½, 160 pp, Quality PB, ISBN 1-893361-51-9 **$15.99** *(A SkyLight Paths book)*

Cast in God's Image: Discover Your Personality Type Using the Enneagram and Kabbalah
By Rabbi Howard A. Addison
7 x 9, 176 pp, Quality PB, Layflat binding, 20+ journaling exercises, ISBN 1-58023-124-1 **$16.95**

Ehyeh: A Kabbalah for Tomorrow *By Dr. Arthur Green*
6 x 9, 224 pp, Hardcover, ISBN 1-58023-125-X **$21.99**

The Enneagram and Kabbalah: Reading Your Soul *By Rabbi Howard A. Addison*
6 x 9, 176 pp, Quality PB, ISBN 1-58023-001-6 **$15.95**

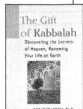

Finding Joy: A Practical Spiritual Guide to Happiness *By Dannel I. Schwartz with Mark Hass*
6 x 9, 192 pp, Quality PB, ISBN 1-58023-009-1 **$14.95**; Hardcover, ISBN 1-879045-53-2 **$19.95**

The Gift of Kabbalah: Discovering the Secrets of Heaven, Renewing Your Life on Earth
By Tamar Frankiel, Ph.D.
6 x 9, 256 pp, Quality PB, ISBN 1-58023-141-1 **$16.95**; Hardcover, ISBN 1-58023-108-X **$21.95**

The Way Into Jewish Mystical Tradition *By Lawrence Kushner*
6 x 9, 224 pp, Quality PB, ISBN 1-58023-200-0 **$18.99**; Hardcover, ISBN 1-58023-029-6 **$21.95**

Life Cycle

Parenting

The New Jewish Baby Album: Creating and Celebrating the Beginning of a Spiritual Life—A Jewish Lights Companion
By the Editors at Jewish Lights. Foreword by Anita Diamant. Preface by Sandy Eisenberg Sasso.
A spiritual keepsake that will be treasured for generations. More than just a memory book, *shows you how—and why it's important*—to create a Jewish home and a Jewish life. Includes sections to describe naming ceremony, space to write encouragements, and pages for writing original blessings, prayers, and meaningful quotes throughout.
8 x 10, 64 pp, Deluxe Padded Hardcover, Full-color illus., ISBN 1-58023-138-1 **$19.95**

The Jewish Pregnancy Book: A Resource for the Soul, Body & Mind during Pregnancy, Birth & the First Three Months
By Sandy Falk, M.D., and Rabbi Daniel Judson, with Steven A. Rapp
Includes medical information on fetal development, pre-natal testing and more, from a liberal Jewish perspective; prenatal *Aleph-Bet* yoga; and ancient and modern prayers and rituals for each stage of pregnancy.
7 x 10, 208 pp, Quality PB, b/w illus., ISBN 1-58023-178-0 **$16.95**

Celebrating Your New Jewish Daughter: Creating Jewish Ways to Welcome Baby Girls into the Covenant—New and Traditional Ceremonies
By Debra Nussbaum Cohen 6 x 9, 272 pp, Quality PB, ISBN 1-58023-090-3 **$18.95**

The New Jewish Baby Book: Names, Ceremonies & Customs—A Guide for Today's Families *By Anita Diamant* 6 x 9, 336 pp, Quality PB, ISBN 1-879045-28-1 **$18.95**

Parenting As a Spiritual Journey: Deepening Ordinary and Extraordinary Events into Sacred Occasions *By Rabbi Nancy Fuchs-Kreimer*
6 x 9, 224 pp, Quality PB, ISBN 1-58023-016-4 **$16.95**

Embracing the Covenant: Converts to Judaism Talk About Why & How
Edited and with introductions by Rabbi Allan Berkowitz and Patti Moskovitz
6 x 9, 192 pp, Quality PB, ISBN 1-879045-50-8 **$16.95**

The Guide to Jewish Interfaith Family Life: An InterfaithFamily.com Handbook
Edited by Ronnie Friedland and Edmund Case 6 x 9, 384 pp, Quality PB, ISBN 1-58023-153-5 **$18.95**

Making a Successful Jewish Interfaith Marriage: The Jewish Outreach Institute Guide to Opportunities, Challenges and Resources
By Rabbi Kerry Olitzky with Joan Peterson Littman 6 x 9, 176 pp, Quality PB, ISBN 1-58023-170-5 **$16.95**

The Perfect Stranger's Guide to Wedding Ceremonies
A Guide to Etiquette in Other People's Religious Ceremonies *Edited by Stuart M. Matlins*
6 x 9, 208 pp, Quality PB, ISBN 1-893361-19-5 **$16.95** *(A SkyLight Paths book)*

How to Be a Perfect Stranger, 3rd Edition

The Essential Religious Etiquette Handbook
Edited by Stuart M. Matlins and Arthur J. Magida
The indispensable guidebook to help the well-meaning guest when visiting other people's religious ceremonies.
A straightforward guide to the rituals and celebrations of the major religions and denominations in the United States and Canada from the perspective of an interested guest of any other faith, based on information obtained from authorities of each religion. Belongs in every living room, library, and office.
6 x 9, 432 pp, Quality PB, ISBN 1-893361-67-5 **$19.95** *(A SkyLight Paths book)*

Divorce Is a Mitzvah: A Practical Guide to Finding Wholeness and Holiness When Your Marriage Dies *By Rabbi Perry Netter. Afterword by Rabbi Laura Geller.*
6 x 9, 224 pp, Quality PB, ISBN 1-58023-172-1 **$16.95**

A Heart of Wisdom: Making the Jewish Journey from Midlife through the Elder Years
Edited by Susan Berrin. Foreword by Harold Kushner. 6 x 9, 384 pp, Quality PB, ISBN 1-58023-051-2 **$18.95**

So That Your Values Live On: Ethical Wills and How to Prepare Them
Edited by Jack Riemer and Nathaniel Stampfer 6 x 9, 272 pp, Quality PB, ISBN 1-879045-34-6 **$18.95**

Meditation

The Handbook of Jewish Meditation Practices
A Guide for Enriching the Sabbath and Other Days of Your Life
By Rabbi David A. Cooper
Easy-to-learn meditation techniques for use on the Sabbath and every day, to help us return to the roots of traditional Jewish spirituality where Shabbat is a state of mind and soul. 6 x 9, 208 pp, Quality PB, ISBN 1-58023-102-0 **$16.95**

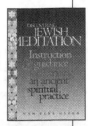

Discovering Jewish Meditation: Instruction & Guidance for Learning an Ancient Spiritual Practice *By Nan Fink Gefen, Ph.D.* 6 x 9, 208 pp, Quality PB, ISBN 1-58023-067-9 **$16.95**

A Heart of Stillness: A Complete Guide to Learning the Art of Meditation
By Rabbi David A. Cooper
5½ x 8½, 272 pp, Quality PB, ISBN 1-893361-03-9 **$16.95** *(A SkyLight Paths book)*

Meditation from the Heart of Judaism: Today's Teachers Share Their Practices, Techniques, and Faith *Edited by Avram Davis*
6 x 9, 256 pp, Quality PB, ISBN 1-58023-049-0 **$16.95**

Silence, Simplicity & Solitude: A Complete Guide to Spiritual Retreat at Home
By Rabbi David A. Cooper
5½ x 8½, 336 pp, Quality PB, ISBN 1-893361-04-7 **$16.95** *(A SkyLight Paths book)*

Three Gates to Meditation Practice: A Personal Journey into Sufism, Buddhism, and Judaism *By Rabbi David A. Cooper*
5½ x 8½, 240 pp, Quality PB, ISBN 1-893361-22-5 **$16.95** *(A SkyLight Paths book)*

The Way of Flame: A Guide to the Forgotten Mystical Tradition of Jewish Meditation
By Avram Davis 4½ x 8, 176 pp, Quality PB, ISBN 1-58023-060-1 **$15.95**

Ritual/Sacred Practice

The Jewish Dream Book
The Key to Opening the Inner Meaning of Your Dreams
By Vanessa L. Ochs with Elizabeth Ochs; Full-color Illus. by Kristina Swarner
Vibrant illustrations, instructions for how modern people can perform ancient Jewish dream practices, and dream interpretations drawn from the Jewish wisdom tradition help make this guide the ideal bedside companion for anyone who wants to further their understanding of their dreams—and themselves.
8 x 8, 120 pp, Full-color illus., Deluxe PB w/flaps, ISBN 1-58023-132-2 **$16.95**

The Rituals & Practices of a Jewish Life: A Handbook for Personal Spiritual Renewal *Edited by Rabbi Kerry M. Olitzky and Rabbi Daniel Judson*
6 x 9, 272 pp, illus., Quality PB, ISBN 1-58023-169-1 **$18.95**

The Book of Jewish Sacred Practices: CLAL's Guide to Everyday & Holiday Rituals & Blessings *Edited by Rabbi Irwin Kula and Vanessa L. Ochs, Ph.D.*
6 x 9, 368 pp, Quality PB, ISBN 1-58023-152-7 **$18.95**

Science Fiction/ Mystery & Detective Fiction

Mystery Midrash: An Anthology of Jewish Mystery & Detective Fiction
Edited by Lawrence W. Raphael. Preface by Joel Siegel.
6 x 9, 304 pp, Quality PB, ISBN 1-58023-055-5 **$16.95**

Criminal Kabbalah: An Intriguing Anthology of Jewish Mystery & Detective Fiction
Edited by Lawrence W. Raphael. Foreword by Laurie R. King.
6 x 9, 256 pp, Quality PB, ISBN 1-58023-109-8 **$16.95**

More Wandering Stars: An Anthology of Outstanding Stories of Jewish Fantasy and Science Fiction *Edited by Jack Dann. Introduction by Isaac Asimov.*
6 x 9, 192 pp, Quality PB, ISBN 1-58023-063-6 **$16.95**

Wandering Stars: An Anthology of Jewish Fantasy & Science Fiction
Edited by Jack Dann. Introduction by Isaac Asimov.
6 x 9, 272 pp, Quality PB, ISBN 1-58023-005-9 **$16.95**

Spirituality

The Alphabet of Paradise: An A–Z of Spirituality for Everyday Life
By Rabbi Howard Cooper
In twenty-six engaging chapters, Cooper spiritually illuminates the subjects of our daily lives—A to Z—examining these sources by using an ancient Jewish mystical method of interpretation that reveals both the literal and more allusive meanings of each. 5 x 7¼, 224 pp, Quality PB, ISBN 1-893361-80-2 **$16.95** *(A SkyLight Paths book)*

Does the Soul Survive?: A Jewish Journey to Belief in Afterlife, Past Lives & Living with Purpose   *By Rabbi Elie Kaplan Spitz. Foreword by Brian L. Weiss, M.D.*
Spitz relates his own experiences and those shared with him by people he has worked with as a rabbi, and shows us that belief in afterlife and past lives, so often approached with reluctance, is in fact true to Jewish tradition.
6 x 9, 288 pp, Quality PB, ISBN 1-58023-165-9 **$16.95**; Hardcover, ISBN 1-58023-094-6 **$21.95**

First Steps to a New Jewish Spirit: Reb Zalman's Guide to Recapturing the Intimacy & Ecstasy in Your Relationship with God
By Rabbi Zalman M. Schachter-Shalomi with Donald Gropman
An extraordinary spiritual handbook that restores psychic and physical vigor by introducing us to new models and alternative ways of practicing Judaism. Offers meditation and contemplation exercises for enriching the most important aspects of everyday life. 6 x 9, 144 pp, Quality PB, ISBN 1-58023-182-9 **$16.95**

God in Our Relationships: Spirituality between People from the Teachings of Martin Buber   *By Rabbi Dennis S. Ross*
On the eightieth anniversary of Buber's classic work, we can discover new answers to critical issues in our lives. Inspiring examples from Ross's own life—as congregational rabbi, father, hospital chaplain, social worker, and husband—illustrate Buber's difficult-to-understand ideas about how we encounter God and each other. 5½ x 8½, 160 pp, Quality PB, ISBN 1-58023-147-0 **$16.95**

The Jewish Lights Spirituality Handbook: A Guide to Understanding, Exploring & Living a Spiritual Life   *Edited by Stuart M. Matlins*
What exactly is "Jewish" about spirituality? How do I make it a part of my life? Fifty of today's foremost spiritual leaders share their ideas and experience with us.
6 x 9, 456 pp, Quality PB, ISBN 1-58023-093-8 **$19.99**; Hardcover, ISBN 1-58023-100-4 **$24.95**

Bringing the Psalms to Life: How to Understand and Use the Book of Psalms
By Dr. Daniel F. Polish
6 x 9, 208 pp, Quality PB, ISBN 1-58023-157-8 **$16.95**; Hardcover, ISBN 1-58023-077-6 **$21.95**

God & the Big Bang: Discovering Harmony between Science & Spirituality
By Dr. Daniel C. Matt 6 x 9, 216 pp, Quality PB, ISBN 1-879045-89-3 **$16.95**

Godwrestling—Round 2: Ancient Wisdom, Future Paths
By Rabbi Arthur Waskow 6 x 9, 352 pp, Quality PB, ISBN 1-879045-72-9 **$18.95**

One God Clapping: The Spiritual Path of a Zen Rabbi   *By Rabbi Alan Lew with Sherril Jaffe*
5½ x 8½, 336 pp, Quality PB, ISBN 1-58023-115-2 **$16.95**

The Path of Blessing: Experiencing the Energy and Abundance of the Divine
By Rabbi Marcia Prager 5½ x 8½, 240 pp., Quality PB, ISBN 1-58023-148-9 **$16.95**

Six Jewish Spiritual Paths: A Rationalist Looks at Spirituality   *By Rabbi Rifat Sonsino*
6 x 9, 208 pp, Quality PB, ISBN 1-58023-167-5 **$16.95**; Hardcover, ISBN 1-58023-095-4 **$21.95**

Soul Judaism: Dancing with God into a New Era
By Rabbi Wayne Dosick 5½ x 8½, 304 pp, Quality PB, ISBN 1-58023-053-9 **$16.95**

Stepping Stones to Jewish Spiritual Living: Walking the Path Morning, Noon, and Night   *By Rabbi James L. Mirel and Karen Bonnell Werth*
6 x 9, 240 pp, Quality PB, ISBN 1-58023-074-1 **$16.95**; Hardcover, ISBN 1-58023-003-2 **$21.95**

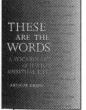

There Is No Messiah... and You're It: The Stunning Transformation of Judaism's Most Provocative Idea   *By Rabbi Robert N. Levine, D.D.*
6 x 9, 192 pp, Hardcover, ISBN 1-58023-173-X **$21.95**

These Are the Words: A Vocabulary of Jewish Spiritual Life   *By Dr. Arthur Green*
6 x 9, 304 pp, Quality PB, ISBN 1-58023-107-1 **$18.95**

Spirituality/Lawrence Kushner

The Book of Letters: A Mystical Hebrew Alphabet
Popular Hardcover Edition, 6 x 9, 80 pp, 2-color text, ISBN 1-879045-00-1 **$24.95**
Deluxe Gift Edition with slipcase, 9 x 12, 80 pp, 4-color text, Hardcover, ISBN 1-879045-01-X **$79.95**
Collector's Limited Edition, 9 x 12, 80 pp, gold foil embossed pages, w/limited edition silkscreened print, ISBN 1-879045-04-4 **$349.00**

The Book of Miracles: A Young Person's Guide to Jewish Spiritual Awareness
All-new illustrations by the author
6 x 9, 96 pp, 2-color illus., Hardcover, ISBN 1-879045-78-8 **$16.95** *For ages 9–13*

The Book of Words: Talking Spiritual Life, Living Spiritual Talk
6 x 9, 160 pp, Quality PB, ISBN 1-58023-020-2 **$16.95**

Eyes Remade for Wonder: A Lawrence Kushner Reader
Introduction by Thomas Moore
6 x 9, 240 pp, Quality PB, ISBN 1-58023-042-3 **$18.95;** Hardcover, ISBN 1-58023-014-8 **$23.95**

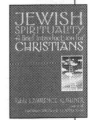

God Was in This Place & I, i Did Not Know
Finding Self, Spirituality and Ultimate Meaning
6 x 9, 192 pp, Quality PB, ISBN 1-879045-33-8 **$16.95**

Honey from the Rock: An Introduction to Jewish Mysticism
6 x 9, 176 pp, Quality PB, ISBN 1-58023-073-3 **$16.95**

Invisible Lines of Connection: Sacred Stories of the Ordinary
5½ x 8½, 160 pp, Quality PB, ISBN 1-879045-98-2 **$15.95**

Jewish Spirituality—A Brief Introduction for Christians
5½ x 8½, 112 pp, Quality PB Original, ISBN 1-58023-150-0 **$12.95**

The River of Light: Jewish Mystical Awareness
6 x 9, 192 pp, Quality PB, ISBN 1-58023-096-2 **$16.95**

The Way Into Jewish Mystical Tradition
6 x 9, 224 pp, Quality PB, ISBN 1-58023-200-0 **$18.99;** Hardcover, ISBN 1-58023-029-6 **$21.95**

Spirituality/Prayer

Pray Tell: A Hadassah Guide to Jewish Prayer
By Rabbi Jules Harlow, with contributions from Tamara Cohen, Rochelle Furstenberg, Rabbi Daniel Gordis, Leora Tanenbaum, and many others
A guide to traditional Jewish prayer enriched with insight and wisdom from a broad variety of viewpoints—from Orthodox, Conservative, Reform, and Reconstructionist Judaism to New Age and feminist. Offers fresh and modern slants on what it means to pray as a Jew, and how women and men might actually pray. 8½ x 11, 400 pp, Quality PB, ISBN 1-58023-163-2 **$29.95**

My People's Prayer Book Series
Traditional Prayers, Modern Commentaries
Edited by Rabbi Lawrence A. Hoffman
Provides diverse and exciting commentary to the traditional liturgy, helping modern men and women find new wisdom in Jewish prayer, and bring liturgy into their lives. Each book includes Hebrew text, modern translation, and commentaries from all perspectives of the Jewish world.

Vol. 1—The *Sh'ma* and Its Blessings
7 x 10, 168 pp, Hardcover, ISBN 1-879045-79-6 **$23.95**
Vol. 2—The *Amidah*
7 x 10, 240 pp, Hardcover, ISBN 1-879045-80-X **$24.95**
Vol. 3—*P'sukei D'zimrah* (Morning Psalms)
7 x 10, 240 pp, Hardcover, ISBN 1-879045-81-8 **$24.95**
Vol. 4—*Seder K'riat Hatorah* (The Torah Service)
7 x 10, 264 pp, Hardcover, ISBN 1-879045-82-6 **$23.95**
Vol. 5—*Birkhot Hashachar* (Morning Blessings)
7 x 10, 240 pp, Hardcover, ISBN 1-879045-83-4 **$24.95**
Vol. 6—*Tachanun* and Concluding Prayers
7 x 10, 240 pp, Hardcover, ISBN 1-879045-84-2 **$24.95**
Vol. 7—Shabbat at Home
7 x 10, 240 pp, Hardcover, ISBN 1-879045-85-0 **$24.95**

Spirituality/The Way Into... Series

The Way Into... Series offers an accessible and highly usable "guided tour" of the Jewish faith, people, history and beliefs—in total, an introduction to Judaism that will enable you to understand and interact with the sacred texts of the Jewish tradition. Each volume is written by a leading contemporary scholar and teacher, and explores one key aspect of Judaism. *The Way Into...* enables all readers to achieve a real sense of Jewish cultural literacy through guided study.

The Way Into Encountering God in Judaism   *By Neil Gillman*
6 x 9, 240 pp, Quality PB, ISBN 1-58023-199-3 **$18.99**; Hardcover, ISBN 1-58023-025-3 **$21.95**

Also Available: **The Jewish Approach to God: A Brief Introduction for Christians**
By Neil Gillman 5½ x 8½, 192 pp, Quality PB, ISBN 1-58023-190-X **$16.95**

The Way Into Jewish Mystical Tradition   *By Lawrence Kushner*
6 x 9, 224 pp, Quality PB, ISBN 1-58023-200-0 **$18.99**; Hardcover, ISBN 1-58023-029-6 **$21.95**

The Way Into Jewish Prayer   *By Lawrence A. Hoffman*
6 x 9, 224 pp, Quality PB, ISBN 1-58023-201-9 **$16.99**; Hardcover, ISBN 1-58023-027-X **$21.95**

The Way Into Torah   *By Norman J. Cohen*
6 x 9, 176 pp, Quality PB, ISBN 1-58023-198-5 **$16.99**; Hardcover, ISBN 1-58023-028-8 **$21.95**

Spirituality in the Workplace

Being God's Partner
How to Find the Hidden Link Between Spirituality and Your Work
By Rabbi Jeffrey K. Salkin. Introduction by Norman Lear.
6 x 9, 192 pp, Quality PB, ISBN 1-879045-65-6 **$17.95**

The Business Bible: 10 New Commandments for Bringing Spirituality & Ethical Values into the Workplace   By Rabbi Wayne Dosick
5½ x 8½, 208 pp, Quality PB, ISBN 1-58023-101-2 **$14.95**

Spirituality and Wellness

Aleph-Bet Yoga
Embodying the Hebrew Letters for Physical and Spiritual Well-Being
By Steven A. Rapp. Foreword by Tamar Frankiel, Ph.D., and Judy Greenfeld. Preface by Hart Lazer
7 x 10, 128 pp, b/w photos, Quality PB, Layflat binding, ISBN 1-58023-162-4 **$16.95**

Entering the Temple of Dreams
Jewish Prayers, Movements, and Meditations for the End of the Day
By Tamar Frankiel, Ph.D., and Judy Greenfeld
7 x 10, 192 pp, illus., Quality PB, ISBN 1-58023-079-2 **$16.95**

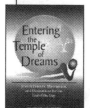

Minding the Temple of the Soul
Balancing Body, Mind, and Spirit through Traditional Jewish Prayer, Movement, and Meditation   By Tamar Frankiel, Ph.D., and Judy Greenfeld
7 x 10, 184 pp, illus., Quality PB, ISBN 1-879045-64-8 **$16.95**
Audiotape of the Blessings and Meditations: 60 min. **$9.95**
Videotape of the Movements and Meditations: 46 min. **$20.00**

Spirituality/Women's Interest

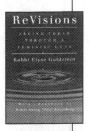

Lifecycles, Vol. 1: Jewish Women on Life Passages & Personal Milestones
Edited and with introductions by Rabbi Debra Orenstein
6 x 9, 480 pp, Quality PB, ISBN 1-58023-018-0 **$19.95**

Lifecycles, Vol. 2: Jewish Women on Biblical Themes in Contemporary Life
Edited and with introductions by Rabbi Debra Orenstein and Rabbi Jane Rachel Litman
6 x 9, 464 pp, Quality PB, ISBN 1-58023-019-9 **$19.95**

Moonbeams: A Hadassah Rosh Hodesh Guide *Edited by Carol Diament, Ph.D.*
8½ x 11, 240 pp, Quality PB, ISBN 1-58023-099-7 **$20.00**

ReVisions: Seeing Torah through a Feminist Lens *By Rabbi Elyse Goldstein*
5½ x 8½, 224 pp, Quality PB, ISBN 1-58023-117-9 **$16.95**

White Fire: A Portrait of Women Spiritual Leaders in America
By Rabbi Malka Drucker. Photographs by Gay Block.
7 x 10, 320 pp, 30+ b/w photos, Hardcover, ISBN 1-893361-64-0 **$24.95** *(A SkyLight Paths book)*

Women of the Wall: Claiming Sacred Ground at Judaism's Holy Site
Edited by Phyllis Chesler and Rivka Haut
6 x 9, 496 pp, b/w photos, Hardcover, ISBN 1-58023-161-6 **$34.95**

The Women's Haftarah Commentary: New Insights from Women Rabbis on the
54 Weekly Haftarah Portions, the 5 Megillot & Special Shabbatot
Edited by Rabbi Elyse Goldstein 6 x 9, 560 pp, Hardcover, ISBN 1-58023-133-0 **$39.99**

The Women's Torah Commentary: New Insights from Women Rabbis on the 54
Weekly Torah Portions *Edited by Rabbi Elyse Goldstein*
6 x 9, 496 pp, Hardcover, ISBN 1-58023-076-8 **$34.95**

The Year Mom Got Religion: One Woman's Midlife Journey into Judaism
By Lee Meyerhoff Hendler
6 x 9, 208 pp, Quality PB, ISBN 1-58023-070-9 **$15.95**; Hardcover, ISBN 1-58023-000-8 **$19.95**

See Holidays for *The Women's Passover Companion: Women's Reflections on
the Festival of Freedom* and *The Women's Seder Sourcebook: Rituals &
Readings for Use at the Passover Seder.*

Travel

Israel—A Spiritual Travel Guide: A Companion for the Modern Jewish Pilgrim
By Rabbi Lawrence A. Hoffman 4¼ x 10, 256 pp, Quality PB, illus., ISBN 1-879045-56-7 **$18.95**
Also Available: **The Israel Mission Leader's Guide** ISBN 1-58023-085-7 **$4.95**

12 Steps

100 Blessings Every Day
Daily Twelve Step Recovery Affirmations, Exercises for Personal Growth &
Renewal Reflecting Seasons of the Jewish Year
By Rabbi Kerry M. Olitzky. Foreword by Rabbi Neil Gillman.
Using a one-day-at-a-time monthly format, this guide reflects on the rhythm of the
Jewish calendar to help bring insight to recovery from addictions and compulsive
behaviors of all kinds. Its exercises help us move from *thinking* to *doing.*
4½ x 6½, 432 pp, Quality PB, ISBN 1-879045-30-3 **$14.99**

Recovery from Codependence: A Jewish Twelve Steps Guide to Healing Your Soul
By Rabbi Kerry M. Olitzky 6 x 9, 160 pp, Quality PB, ISBN 1-879045-32-X **$13.95**

Renewed Each Day: Daily Twelve Step Recovery Meditations Based on the Bible
By Rabbi Kerry M. Olitzky and Aaron Z.
Vol. 1—Genesis & Exodus:
6 x 9, 224 pp, Quality PB, ISBN 1-879045-12-5 **$14.95**
Vol. 2—Leviticus, Numbers & Deuteronomy:
6 x 9, 280 pp, Quality PB, ISBN 1-879045-13-3 **$14.95**

Twelve Jewish Steps to Recovery
A Personal Guide to Turning from Alcoholism & Other Addictions—Drugs, Food,
Gambling, Sex...
By Rabbi Kerry M. Olitzky and Stuart A. Copans, M.D. Preface by Abraham J. Twerski, M.D.
6 x 9, 144 pp, Quality PB, ISBN 1-879045-09-5 **$14.95**

Theology/Philosophy

Aspects of Rabbinic Theology
By Solomon Schechter. New Introduction by Dr. Neil Gillman.
6 x 9, 448 pp, Quality PB, ISBN 1-879045-24-9 **$19.95**

Broken Tablets: Restoring the Ten Commandments and Ourselves
Edited by Rachel S. Mikva. Introduction by Lawrence Kushner. Afterword by Arnold Jacob Wolf.
6 x 9, 192 pp, Quality PB, ISBN 1-58023-158-6 **$16.95**; Hardcover, ISBN 1-58023-066-0 **$21.95**

Creating an Ethical Jewish Life
A Practical Introduction to Classic Teachings on How to Be a Jew
By Dr. Byron L. Sherwin and Seymour J. Cohen
6 x 9, 336 pp, Quality PB, ISBN 1-58023-114-4 **$19.95**

The Death of Death: Resurrection and Immortality in Jewish Thought
By Dr. Neil Gillman 6 x 9, 336 pp, Quality PB, ISBN 1-58023-081-4 **$18.95**

Evolving Halakhah: A Progressive Approach to Traditional Jewish Law
By Rabbi Dr. Moshe Zemer
6 x 9, 480 pp, Quality PB, ISBN 1-58023-127-6 **$29.95**; Hardcover, ISBN 1-58023-002-4 **$40.00**

Hasidic Tales: Annotated & Explained
By Rabbi Rami Shapiro. Foreword by Andrew Harvey, SkyLight Illuminations series editor.
5½ x 8½, 240 pp, Quality PB, ISBN 1-893361-86-1 **$16.95** (A SkyLight Paths Book)

A Heart of Many Rooms: Celebrating the Many Voices within Judaism
By Dr. David Hartman
6 x 9, 352 pp, Quality PB, ISBN 1-58023-156-X **$19.95**; Hardcover, ISBN 1-58023-048-2 **$24.95**

Judaism and Modern Man: An Interpretation of Jewish Religion
By Will Herberg. New Introduction by Dr. Neil Gillman.
5½ x 8½, 336 pp, Quality PB, ISBN 1-879045-87-7 **$18.95**

Keeping Faith with the Psalms: Deepen Your Relationship with God Using the
Book of Psalms By Daniel F. Polish
6 x 9, 272 pp, Hardcover, ISBN 1-58023-179-9 **$24.95**

The Last Trial
On the Legends and Lore of the Command to Abraham to Offer Isaac as a Sacrifice
By Shalom Spiegel. New Introduction by Judah Goldin.
6 x 9, 208 pp, Quality PB, ISBN 1-879045-29-X **$18.95**

A Living Covenant: The Innovative Spirit in Traditional Judaism
By Dr. David Hartman 6 x 9, 368 pp, Quality PB, ISBN 1-58023-011-3 **$18.95**

Love and Terror in the God Encounter
The Theological Legacy of Rabbi Joseph B. Soloveitchik
By Dr. David Hartman
6 x 9, 240 pp, Quality PB, ISBN 1-58023-176-4 **$19.95**; Hardcover, ISBN 1-58023-112-8 **$25.00**

Seeking the Path to Life
Theological Meditations on God and the Nature of People, Love, Life and Death
By Rabbi Ira F. Stone 6 x 9, 160 pp, Quality PB, ISBN 1-879045-47-8 **$14.95**

The Spirit of Renewal: Finding Faith after the Holocaust
By Rabbi Edward Feld 6 x 9, 224 pp, Quality PB, ISBN 1-879045-40-0 **$16.95**

Tormented Master: The Life and Spiritual Quest of Rabbi Nahman of Bratslav
By Dr. Arthur Green 6 x 9, 416 pp, Quality PB, ISBN 1-879045-11-7 **$19.99**

Your Word Is Fire: The Hasidic Masters on Contemplative Prayer
Edited and translated by Dr. Arthur Green and Barry W. Holtz
6 x 9, 160 pp, Quality PB, ISBN 1-879045-25-7 **$15.95**

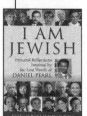

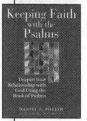

I Am Jewish
Personal Reflections Inspired by the Last Words of Daniel Pearl
Almost 150 Jews—both famous and not—from all walks of life, from all around the world, write about Identity, Heritage, Covenant/Chosenness and Faith, Humanity and Ethnicity, and *Tikkun Olam* and Justice.
Edited by Judea and Ruth Pearl
6 x 9, 304 pp, Hardcover, ISBN 1-58023-183-7 **$24.99**

About Jewish Lights

People of all faiths and backgrounds yearn for books that attract, engage, educate, and spiritually inspire.

Our principal goal is to stimulate thought and help all people learn about who the Jewish People are, where they come from, and what the future can be made to hold. While people of our diverse Jewish heritage are the primary audience, our books speak to people in the Christian world as well and will broaden their understanding of Judaism and the roots of their own faith.

We bring to you authors who are at the forefront of spiritual thought and experience. While each has something different to say, they all say it in a voice that you can hear.

Our books are designed to welcome you and then to engage, stimulate, and inspire. We judge our success not only by whether or not our books are beautiful and commercially successful, but by whether or not they make a difference in your life.

For your information and convenience, at the back of this book we have provided a list of other Jewish Lights books you might find interesting and useful. They cover all the categories of your life:

Bar/Bat Mitzvah	Life Cycle
Bible Study / Midrash	Meditation
Children's Books	Parenting
Congregation Resources	Prayer
Current Events / History	Ritual / Sacred Practice
Ecology	Spirituality
Fiction: Mystery, Science Fiction	Theology / Philosophy
Grief / Healing	Travel
Holidays / Holy Days	Twelve Steps
Inspiration	Women's Interest
Kabbalah / Mysticism / Enneagram	

Stuart M. Matlins, Publisher

Or phone, fax, mail or e-mail to: **JEWISH LIGHTS Publishing**
Sunset Farm Offices, Route 4 • P.O. Box 237 • Woodstock, Vermont 05091
Tel: (802) 457-4000 • Fax: (802) 457-4004 • www.jewishlights.com
Credit card orders: **(800) 962-4544** (8:30AM–5:30PM ET Monday–Friday)
Generous discounts on quantity orders. SATISFACTION GUARANTEED. Prices subject to change.